OXFORD MONOGRAPHS ON SOCIAL ANTHROPOLOGY

General Editors

E. E. EVANS-PRITCHARD   B. E. B. FAGG

A. MAYER   D. POCOCK

Yoruba Towns and Cities

AN ENQUIRY
INTO THE NATURE OF
URBAN SOCIAL PHENOMENA

BY

EVA KRAPF-ASKARI

CLARENDON PRESS · OXFORD

1969

Oxford University Press, Ely House, London W.1

GLASGOW NEW YORK TORONTO MELBOURNE WELLINGTON
CAPE TOWN SALISBURY IBADAN NAIROBI LUSAKA ADDIS ABABA
BOMBAY CALCUTTA MADRAS KARACHI LAHORE DACCA
KUALA LUMPUR SINGAPORE HONG KONG TOKYO

Printed in Great Britain by
Alden & Mowbray Ltd
at The Alden Press, Oxford

IN MEMORIAM

E. E. KRAPF

PREFACE

Much of the material contained in this book originally formed part of a thesis presented for the degree of Bachelor of Letters to the Faculty of Anthropology and Geography at the University of Oxford in 1964. I should like to take this opportunity of thanking the Nuffield Foundation, whose award of a Sociological Scholarship enabled me, first to write that thesis, and later to extend and deepen my knowledge of Yoruba towns by means of direct field experience: during my fieldwork (1964–1966) I was able to visit Abẹokuta, Ado Ekiti, Ibadan, Ifẹ, Ikerre, Ilẹsha, Ilọrin, Isẹyin, Kabba, Ogbomọshọ, Ondo, Oshogbo, Ọyọ and Shagamu. It is in the light of this field experience, as well as of recent publications on this and related subjects, that I have revised and re-arranged my thesis material. One important work, however, A. L. Mabogunje's study of *Urbanization in Nigeria*, has appeared since this book went to press, so that it was unfortunately too late for me to include it in my review of the literature in this field.

I have left unchanged the figures I used in my 1964 thesis, which were (except where otherwise indicated) taken from the *Population Census of the Western Region of Nigeria 1952*; I note that the same course has been adopted by Professor Mabogunje. Detailed figures from subsequent Censuses (which have in any case been the subject of much controversy) were not published at the time of writing.

I should like to thank Mr Edwin Ardener, whose comments and criticism have been invaluable at every stage of the writing; as well as Professor E. E. Evans-Pritchard, Dr R. E. Bradbury and Dr R. G. Lienhardt for much advice and encouragement.

CONTENTS

LIST OF MAPS, PLANS AND DIAGRAMS xi

LIST OF ABBREVIATIONS xii

I. The Yoruba pattern of settlement 1

II. The terminological problem 9

III. Lay-out and appearance 39

IV. Kinship, descent, residence, and neighbourhood 63

V. Interest groups and associations 82

VI. Social stratification 131

VII. Conclusions 154

SELECT BIBLIOGRAPHY 165

MAPS, PLANS AND DIAGRAMS 177

INDEX 191

LIST OF MAPS, PLANS AND DIAGRAMS
(*as pp. 177-90*)

MAP 1. Location of Main Yoruba Towns and Cities (from LLOYD: *Yoruba Land Law*)

MAP 2. Yoruba Towns and Cities by population size (from OJO: *Yoruba Culture*)

MAP 3. Distribution of *ÌLÚ ALÁDÉ* (from OJO: *Yoruba Culture*)

TOWN PLAN 1. Town plan of Ifẹ (from MABOGUNJE: *Yoruba Towns*)

TOWN PLAN 2. Town plan of Ilẹsha (from OJO: *Yoruba Culture*)

TOWN PLAN 3. Arrangement of quarters and compounds in relation to the palace in Ado Ekiti (from OJO: *Yoruba Palaces*)

TOWN PLAN 4. The Palaces of Abẹokuta (from OJO: *Yoruba Palaces*)

TOWN PLAN 5. Location of the Palace in Ọwo in relation to the town and compounds of the Inner Council Chiefs (from OJO: *Yoruba Palaces*)

TOWN PLAN 6. Town Plan of Ondo (from LLOYD: *Yoruba Land Law*)

SCHEMA 1. Pattern of distribution of Temples and Domestic Shrines in Ọyọ (from MORTON-WILLIAMS: *An Outline of the Cosmology and Cult Organization of the Oyo Yoruba*)

SCHEMA 2. Functional areas of Ibadan (from MABOGUNJE: *Yoruba Towns*)

DIAGRAM 1. Types of settlement pattern (schematic representation) (from LLOYD: *Yoruba Land Law*)

DIAGRAM 2. Ego's view backwards over time of the various ọmọ iyá of which he is a member in a cognatic descent system

DIAGRAM 3. Ego's view backwards over time of the various ọmọ iyá of which he is a member in an agnatic descent system

LIST OF ABBREVIATIONS

A.A.	*American Anthropologist.*
Am. J. Soc.	*American Journal of Sociology.*
B. J. Soc.	*British Journal of Sociology.*
C.U.P.	Cambridge University Press.
H.M.S.O.	His (Her) Majesty's Stationery Office.
I.A.I.	International African Institute.
I.F.A.N.	Institut Français de l'Afrique Noire.
I.N.C.I.D.I.	Institute of Differing Civilizations.
J.R.A.I.	*Journal of the Royal Anthropological Institute*
Man/J.R.A.I., n.s.	*Man; The Journal of the Royal Anthropological Institute.*
N.I.S.E.R.	Nigerian Institute of Social and Economic Research.
n.d.	no date.
n.s.	new series.
O.U.P.	Oxford University Press.
O.U.P./I.A.I.	Oxford University Press for the International African Institute.
P.U.F.	Presses Universitaires de France.
Soc. Rev.	*The Sociological Review.*
U.C.I.	University College of Ibadan.
U.N.E.S.C.O.	United Nations Educational, Scientific and Cultural Organization.
W.A.I.S.E.R.	West African Institute of Social and Economic Research.

I

THE YORUBA PATTERN OF SETTLEMENT

I

THE Yoruba are a West African people of between 5 and 10 million, of whom the largest section—approximately 5,046,800 in 1952—live in Nigeria, mainly in the former Western Region, though they also form a majority of the population in the new West-Central State in the north. Further groups live in Dahomey and Togo; and in smaller, ethnically and culturally homogeneous colonies, form a part of the population of several cities of the African West Coast. The slave trade[1] took many of them to the New World, where elements of their language and culture persist in recognizable form in Brazilian[2] and Caribbean[3] Negro populations; some of these dispersed Yoruba were later to return[4] and themselves affect their traditional homeland as carriers of different skills and values learned during their sojourn abroad. Here we shall be concerned purely with the Yoruba now living in Nigeria.

The Yoruba are united by language (although there are considerable dialectal variations in different parts of the area), to a large extent by culture, and also by the traditional belief that they are all descended from Odùduwà, a mythical demiurge held to have come down from Heaven and instituted both the cosmic and the political order as the Yoruba know it.[5] There is no indication, however, that they were ever united into one political whole in pre-colonial days; and their own myths present them as having been organized, ever since Odùduwà's time, into a series of tribal kingdoms of varying size and importance. These kingdoms are said to have been founded by the sons and grandsons of Odùduwà, emigrating from the sacred city of Ilé Ifẹ̀ which he himself founded; at the head of each was a sacred king or ọba, whose title

[1] Newbury, 1961; Verger, 1964. [2] Verger, 1953, 1957, and 1964.
[3] Herskovits, 1947. [4] Biobaku, 1957; Verger, 1953.
[5] Johnson, 1921; Idowu, 1962.

was validated by genealogically authenticated descent from Odùduwà. Commoner Yoruba had no need to trace their own descent from Odùduwà in this way. Relations between these tribal kingdoms seem to have been characterized by a loose and shifting system of wars and alliances, the smaller ones being by turns independent and subordinate to the more powerful Ifẹ[1] and Old Ọyọ. The administrative districts established by British colonial power tended very largely to follow the boundaries of these kingdoms as they were at the time of its inception, and the operation of Indirect Rule has tended to maintain the ọbas in office, though altering, and in some respects strengthening, their position.

Geographically, Yorubaland falls into three main zones: a low coastal area characterized by very high rainfall (70 to 100 inches), lagoons, and mangrove swamps; a fertile rain-forest belt with heavy clay soils and a rainfall varying between 50 and 70 inches, and a higher-lying savannah zone to the north, where the rainfall gradually decreases northwards and the forest becomes deciduous and by degrees sparser, being finally replaced by tall grass. Nearer the coast, the climate is hot and humid, the heavy rains falling annually from April to August, followed, after the 'little dry season', by a further spate during September and October. The many streams which cross the land, from the Niger watershed to the sea, are not navigable: swollen during the rains, they dwindle to almost nothing during the dry season.

The traditional economy of the Yoruba was based on hoe agriculture, farm-plots being cleared in the 'bush' with axe or cutlass, cultivated over a longer or shorter period, and then left to lie fallow; the fallow period being normally longer than that of cultivation. The traditional staple was and is yams, though nowadays maize, bananas, and cassava are also grown, with coco-yams, beans, pumpkins, and peppers as subsidiary crops in most areas. The farm-work was mostly done by the men, the women doing the processing and trading, and also tending the small livestock: fowls, goats, and dwarf cattle (tse-tse fly makes the forest belt unsuitable for other varieties of cattle). The diet was further supplemented by small-scale hunting and fishing, as well as by some gathering, particularly of the kernels of the wild oil-palm and by the tapping of the 'wine' both of this and of the raphia palm.

As elsewhere in colonial Africa, this subsistence pattern of

[1] i.e., Ilé Ifẹ̀.

agriculture has been substantially modified by the introduction of cash crops. The most important of these for Yorubaland is cocoa. It is not grown all over Yorubaland: the trees require a minimum rainfall of 45 inches, which excludes the drier upland country; and near the coast, where rainfall is abundant, the soils are rendered unsuitable by their high acid content. The 'cocoa belt' is thus confined to a zone within the rain-forest area, most of it being grown in the Ibadan and Ifẹ-Ilẹsha Divisions of Ọyọ Province, in Ijẹbu-Ode and in Abẹokuta Province. Even within this zone, in 1954, only 4 per cent of the total area of the principal producing provinces was under cocoa, though of course some districts grow more than others.[1] Production is most highly concentrated around Ibadan; about 25 per cent of the farmers in that area were dependent on cocoa for their living in 1954. It is not a crop requiring large production units; cocoa plots range from 1 to 50 acres, but the modal size is somewhat less than 10 acres.

Two other major commercial crops are harvested: palm oil and kernels, now from both wild and cultivated palms; and kola, in which a brisk trade is driven with Northern Nigeria, where the Hausa provide a substantial market.[2] Oil-palm products are particularly important in Ijẹbu and Ondo Provinces (where rights in harvesting them are increasingly leased to immigrant Urhobo from the south-east).[3] Elsewhere, the processing and trade of these products is still, as traditionally, largely in the hands of Yoruba women; as is the trade in kola.

Cocoa, however, has exercised an influence on the Yoruba way of life out of all proportion to the actual acreage grown. After a late and slow start, and very wide fluctuations in price during the inter-war years, it has, since the end of the Second World War, made the Yoruba one of the richest peoples in Africa.[4] Non-cocoa-growing areas too have shared, though to a lesser extent, both in the prosperity brought by cocoa and in some of its social consequences.

This prosperous agricultural economy, together with the economic activities based on it, supports a very dense population, approaching 1,000 per square mile in the most densely populated areas. But whereas the neighbouring Ibo, with an equally stable agriculture and even higher population densities, live in dispersed village groups, the Yoruba pattern of settlement characteristically

[1] Galletti *et al.*, 1956. [2] For the organization of the kola trade, cf. Cohen, 1966.
[3] P. C. Lloyd, 1962.   [4] P. C. Lloyd, 1967.

takes the form of large, dense, nucleated settlements in which an ethnically homogeneous population of farmers, artisans, and traders live cheek by jowl with one another.

Moreover, the existence of these large nucleated settlements cannot be regarded as, in itself, the result of a colonial situation. There has been little industrialization; nor has migration played any great part in the development of most of these centres of population.[1] Many of them have existed since before the beginnings of even a contact situation with Europeans; travellers and explorers have been remarking on their existence from the end of the fifteenth century onwards.[2] The antiquity of the settlement pattern must, of course, be distinguished from that of actual nucleations; but even about these, more or less continuous information has been available for over 100 years.

Various attempts have been made to explain the Yoruba pattern of nucleated settlement. The geographer G. J. A. Ojo[3] is certainly right in stressing the importance of 'permissive environmental factors'; but as the contrary instance of the Ibo shows, such factors cannot in themselves suffice. Another geographer, N. C. Mitchel,[4] has sought a partial explanation of the growth of the city of Ifẹ (which Yoruba themselves see as the cradle of their urban culture) in the expansion of the sacred power of its king, the Oni; and certainly, much may be attributed to the Yoruba political system:[5] as we shall see, in most cases the town in fact radiates out from the palace of the king or ọba.[6] However, as Ojo also points out,[7] concrete historical factors have also contributed to the growth, and in some cases led to the foundation, of the towns we know today, whereas their actual positioning has often been determined by strategic considerations.

II

Many of the cities visited by Clapperton and Lander[8] in the 1820s had ceased to exist by the time Bowen[9] arrived in mid-century; and others had arisen in the meantime. S. Johnson,[10] the Yoruba historian, gives December 1830 as the date of the destruc-

[1] Schwab, 1965.   [2] Pacheco Pereira, 1937.   [3] Ojo, 1966(a).
[4] Mitchel, 1961.   [5] Cf. Ojo, op. cit.   [6] Cf. below, Chapter III.
[7] Op. cit.   [8] Clapperton, 1829.   [9] Bowen, 1857.
[10] Johnson, 1937.

tion of 'the great Metropolis, "Eyeo or Katunga", the ancient Ọyọ', and leaves us to infer the following year for the foundation of present-day Ọyọ on the site of a former small settlement called Agọ Ọja; a modern authority, R. S. Smith,[1] gives the date as *circa* 1837.

Johnson also describes in some detail[2] how, after the devastation of the small Ẹgba towns during the same wave of tribal wars[3] that razed Old Ọyọ to the ground, the scattered remnants of their populations 'escaped to Abẹokuta then a farm village of an Itoko man, and a resting place for traders to and from the Okè Ogun districts. . . . This was about the year 1830.'[4]

Meanwhile, a mixed group of marauding armies, consisting of 'the Ifẹ, Ijẹbu, Ọyọ, and Ẹgba chiefs with their men'[5] were en-camping on the 'still habitable'[6] site of one of the ruined Ẹgba settlements. Out of their military alliance grew Ibadan:

Its position on the edge of the grassland, and the protection which it was afforded by the large expanse of lateritic outcrop in the area, made it an ideal place of refuge from the Fulani cavalry attacking from the north, and from the [other] hostile Ẹgba in the neighbourhood.

What was intended primarily as a camp, therefore, soon became a permanent settlement where these wandering soldiers from Ile Ifẹ, Ijẹbu and the Ọyọ empire made their home. The Ọyọ and the Ifẹ settled around the present Ọja Iba[7] and Mapo Hall. . . . The Ijẹbu settled at Isalẹ Ijẹbu to the south-east in the area closest to their own country, whilst the remaining Ẹgba settled at Iyẹosa.[8]

Smith[9] gives the date of the foundation of Ibadan at *circa* 1829; and B. Awe[10] adds: 'It was, however, a settlement not without growing pains. Its heterogeneous nature, as well as the insubordinate spirit bred by the wandering life of those who had been soldiers of fortune, made peaceful settlement difficult. Moreover, the leadership was not clear-cut and Ibadan therefore became the scene of frequent civil wars in the continuous struggle for leadership.'

However, the pressing military needs of the new settlement did

---

[1] Smith, in Ajayi and Smith, 1964. [2] Op. cit.
[3] A good chronological classification of these frequently confusing conflicts will be found in Smith, op. cit.
[4] This agrees with the date given by Smith, loc. cit. [5] Johnson, op. cit.
[6] Awe, 1967.
[7] The present principal market of Ibadan. Cf. below, Chapter III, Section III.
[8] Awe, loc. cit. [9] Loc. cit. [10] Loc. cit.

necessitate some sort of political organization. Commanders, both civil and military, were clearly needed, and were instituted accordingly; but there was no one on the freebooting armies qualified by descent to hold the sacred title of *ǫba*. As we shall see, Ibadan bears the marks of her origin to this day.[1]

Both Abęokuta and Ibadan, then, are new towns, less bound than certain others by the traditional pattern of Yoruba urban life; the later history of both reinforced this characteristic, though in different ways for each. In Ibadan, emancipation from tradition went so far as to dispense the town from the form of government culturally associated with large centres of population; in Abęokuta, on the other hand, the homeless refugees went to some pains to regroup themselves in accordance with their ancient structures.[2] And a modern authority[3] notes that: 'The initial settlements at the new capital were widely separated; they were described as camps (*ago*), the Ęgba still thinking of an eventual return to their former towns. Each new group of arrivals settled with people from its own town, founding a new compound. Thus the constituent units of Abęokuta are the townships, each with its well defined boundaries,' which may well account for the unusually dispersed settlement pattern peculiar to this centre. The townships did in the end coalesce sufficiently, under pressure of the threats of Dahomeyan invasion in 1851, to recognize the Alakę, the *ǫba* of one of the sectional townships, as the ruler of the whole of Abęokuta; before that, their political organization as a single unit had taken a form similar to that of Ibadan, with civil and military chiefs selected for achievement and promoted by seniority, but no *ǫba* for the whole town. The first Alakę, crowned partly at the instigation of the C.M.S. Mission, which had established itself early in Abęokuta (about 1850),[4] never quite attained the status of an ancient traditional *ǫba*: J. F. A. Ajayi[5] notes wryly that he had 'effective power largely in Ake alone'. The Ęgba war chiefs (now known as 'general titled chiefs') continued to be appointed; and *ǫba*s of the constituent townships began to make their appearance: the Owu people installed at Olowu in 1855, an Agura followed in 1870, and an Ǫşilę in 1897. A recent Alakę was recognized as the Olubara

---

[1] A still current Yoruba saying about Ibadan runs something as follows: 'We all have our faults; that of Ibadan is constant internal strife.' (Cited in Awe, loc. cit.)

[2] Johnson, op. cit.; Biobaku, 1957.   [3] P. C. Lloyd, 1962.

[4] Ibid.   [5] Ajayi, in Ajayi and Smith, op. cit.

of Ibara, an Ẹgbado town which took refuge on the outskirts of Abẹokuta. All these are sectional ọbas, representing the constituent townships. The much older town of Ado Ekiti consists of the three adjacent 'settlements' of Oke Ewi, Odo Ado, and Oke Ila, each with its own separate political structure; though the Ewi of Oke Ewi is recognized as ọba of the whole town.[1] This may well represent an evolution from similar origins over a longer period of time.

Historically, Ọyọ could also be said to be the result of the wars; but Ọyọ seems to have been established with conscious conservatism,[2] to replace the Old Ọyọ which had been destroyed, and which appears at one time to have exercised a somewhat vague and variable political suzerainty over a number of other settlements. Johnson[3] says: 'Thus Agọ . . . became the royal city of Yoruba and as such it was no longer called Agọ-Ọya but Ọyọ as the Alafin now resides there. And hence it is often styled by way of disparagement Agọ d'Ọyọ (Agọ which became Ọyọ). This is the present city of Ọyọ.' It was built up, in fact, around the Alafin (the title of the Ọyọ ọba) and Johnson tells us that 'He took forcible means to enlarge it. Several of the surrounding towns and villages were depopulated and their inhabitants transported to the new city.' But with Ibadan and Abẹokuta, which lacked such a political core, their recent origin may have made them vulnerable to change, as its geographical position did Lagos.

Thus, though the pattern of Yoruba clustered settlement is an ancient one, three of the largest cities are not themselves ancient, but were founded at approximately known dates and are the result of the large-scale population movements produced by the nineteenth-century wars. The pattern of settlement itself was strong enough for both Ibadan and Abẹokuta to conform to it with varying degrees of exactitude; but the traditional political structure was in one case by-passed, in the other re-established only late and partially, and we shall see that this is visible in the physical lay-out of both towns. We may further surmise that the newness of these towns made them less stable, more open to further change arising out of closer European contact and the colonial situation, than the settlements which pre-date the tribal wars and were only more or less marginally affected by them.

And indeed, other centres have been much more stable. The

---

[1] P. C. Lloyd, 1954. Cf. also Krapf-Askari, 1966.   [2] Cf. below.
[3] Op. cit.

myths of Ijẹbu Ode, in 1952 a compact, wealthy town of 28,000, relate that the town has never been destroyed since the reign of Obanta, the founding *ọba* or Awujalẹ; and the Awujalẹ reigning in 1921 was reputed to be the 52nd in succession to Obanta.[1] This checks with Duarte Pacheco Pereira's account[2] of 'a very large city called Geebuu' in 1505–8; 'Jubu', 'Iubu', 'Jabou', 'Jebou', or 'Jaboo' appear on various maps of Africa throughout the eighteenth century.[3] 'Eyo' appears during the same period. Ondo (population according to 1952–3 Census: 36,000) also claims great antiquity.

Ilé Ifẹ is, in Yoruba belief, the oldest of them all, since it was from there that all the others were founded; this also receives confirmation from Pacheco Pereira,[4] who mentions a monarch called the Ogane, whom modern scholarship has plausibly identified with the Oni of Ifẹ.

If this combination of evidence were accepted, it would mean that both the Yoruba pattern of urbanism and some of the actual towns existing today are over four centuries old. We shall see in the next chapter that this respectable degree of antiquity, taken in combination with some of their other characteristics, has made Yoruba towns something of a test case within the wider context of African urban sociology.

[1] Johnson, op. cit.   [2] Pacheco Pereira, 1937.
[3] Bascom, 1959.   [4] Op. cit.

II

THE TERMINOLOGICAL PROBLEM

I

SINCE the end of the Second World War, there has grown up a literature, still small but increasing, on 'African urban problems.' It consists of works varied not only in their subject-matter, which is scattered over every part of Africa, but also in scope, approach, method of collection, and presentation of facts. Yet these works and their authors, to a considerable extent, share a common background of theoretical and practical preoccupations. These are perhaps most succinctly expressed by G. Balandier[1] in the Introduction to his study of the 'black Brazzavilles', the African quarters of that city:

This study of the black Brazzavilles is one of the first attempts to describe an African city and to understand this radically new milieu—since we are here dealing with *peoples who had no urban tradition*. [This study] was a necessary part of our research devoted to the *social changes* characteristic of Gabonese and Camerounian societies; for it was impossible to attempt to understand the transformations affecting so-called traditional society without precise knowledge of what are known as 'extra-traditional' milieus[2] and of their influence. It was necessary insofar as it constituted an extraordinarily rich field for sociological research, and still more insofar as *administrations cannot now evade the grave problems posed by the African town*—and which concern an ever increasing part of the population. [Italics mine.]

Balandier, writing in 1955, is here, in fact, looking both back to the past and forward into the future of African urban studies. The first work on African urban centres to appear after the end of the Second World War had grown directly out of the concern of colonial administrations with 'the grave problems posed by the

---

[1] Balandier, 1955(a); cf. also Mitchell, 1966.

[2] '*la société dite coutumière . . . des milieux dits "extra-coutumiers"*.' The pair of opposed adjectives, *coutumier* and *extra-coutumier* have become, for all practical purposes, technical terms in French Colonial administrative language.

African town'—practical rather than academic problems. These early studies, exemplified by A. Capelle's on Leopoldville[1] and J. Guilbot's on Douala,[2] were avowedly pragmatic and limited in scope. Both these authors concern themselves mainly with 'social problems': Guilbot, an *Inspecteur du Travail* by training, deals principally with factors affecting manpower efficiency: Capelle, a former *Administrateur Territorial* of Leopoldville—itself at that time one of the largest industrial centres in Africa—has sections on administrative and political organization, demography, police and immigration controls, housing and public utilities, economic life and the food supply, the labour force, 'the social situation', social services, hygiene and diseases, taxes, schools and missions, and the legal system.

As sources of information, both books suffer from the inadequacy with which sources and methods of collection of data are indicated; as aids to sociological understanding, they make little or no attempt to elucidate the attitudes or motives of the peoples they are describing, and indeed shed more light on colonial attitudes to the African urban proletariat than on that proletariat itself: thus Capelle uses the expression 'family parasitism' to cover all types of traditional kinship obligations, which he describes as 'the plague of the African proletariat'.

In English-speaking Africa, a similar concern with practical urban problems was expressed in surveys attempting a more comprehensive treatment, beginning with K. A. Busia's Sekondi-Takoradi.[3] Here the presentation is also centred around specific problems of municipal administration; but the information collected appears to go further in depth. Busia writes:

I have tried to combine the methods of the survey with those of the social anthropologist; the compilation of social data capable of expression in numerical form, with the lengthy first-hand observation of attitudes and beliefs. In collecting our information, we have used all the five techniques most generally used in the collection of social data; direct observation of behaviour, examination of documents, 'free' interview, questionnaire, and interview by schedule.

He mentions 'sampling techniques', but these are not clearly specified; as a result, the statistical part of the report is its weakest side. The 'methods . . . of the social anthropologist', however,

---

[1] Capelle, 1947.   [2] Guilbot, 1947.   [3] Busia, 1950.

have yielded interesting though necessarily imprecise results, particularly in the discussion of the causes and effects of the breakdown of the family group, a theme which runs like a thread through most of the chapters.

The tradition of the mixed-method survey has continued in English-speaking Africa, with, in some cases, considerable refinements of technique. Busia's book stands, in a sense, at the beginning of interest in African urban life on the part of professional social scientists; though the expression of this interest was (and is) still largely channelled by the practical problems on which administrators require information. These problems are complex as well as various; a first formal attempt to pool existing knowledge on the subject was made by the Conference on the Social Implications of Industrialization and Urbanization in Africa South of the Sahara, convened by U.N.E.S.C.O. at Abidjan in 1954,[1] and which co-ordinated the work of social anthropologists, sociologists, and economists.

The title of the Conference is itself significant. Urbanization and industrialization were, in the minds of its conveners, almost inextricably intertwined as regards their practical 'social implications' in Africa; they were seen, almost implicitly, as aspects of a single process of 'change' that had to be dealt with as a pragmatic unity.

This particular problem at least has now come out into the open. The development economist, D. Lerner,[2] suggests in a recent article the use of the hyphenated term 'urbanization-industrialization'; whereas A. L. Epstein[3] pleads that urbanization be kept analytically distinct from 'industrialization, Westernization, the growth of settler communities, etc.'. But even at the time, the papers presented to the conference by Balandier, Southall, Malengreau, Mitchell and other scholars, then engaged in field studies of urban centres in different parts of Africa,[4] reflected more positive theoretical preoccupations. Thus Balandier,[5] whose Brazzaville study was at the time in progress, writes of

the great scientific interest of a survey centred around the problem of the inception of social classes (or groups of a similar nature) as a result of the introduction of colonial capitalism. But there are other and equally important phenomena. Changes in the relationship between the

[1] Forde (ed.), 1956.   [2] Lerner, 1967.   [3] Epstein, 1967.
[4] Forde (ed.), 1956, Part IV.   [5] Ibid.

sexes, in relations resulting from family ties, the importance of the relations among neighbours (the role of the 'quarter') and of those which arise for vocational reasons or owing to the development of an urban type of economy; the far-reaching changes to be noted in religious practices; the influence of what might be called 'peripheral' relationships maintained with the different home districts, etc.—all these are factors which contribute to the building up of a new type of community in the African town. It is thus a type which displays society in what might be called a positive phase, and which provides a field of research whose almost 'experimental' value should not be underestimated . . . Urban society is characterized to some extent by the scope it allows for improvisation and by the number of subordinate groups which arise in it (recreational associations, 'friendly societies', associations of people with the same name, etc.) . . . the towns, by serving as a field for wider and fuller contacts, act as a kind of 'laboratory' for the formation of new cultural patterns. . . .

Here, as in the passage quoted above from *Les Brazzavilles noires*, Balandier is presenting African urban life as an interesting field of study in its own right, a positive sociological phenomenon with characteristic features, a 'laboratory' in which hypotheses of social change can be tested. Such an attitude is radically different from that which underlay Capelle's and Guilbot's, and to a lesser extent Busia's studies: from being seen in a purely negative perspective, as 'detribalized' people suffering from either the 'plague' of 'family parasitism' or 'the breakdown of family life' (depending on the author's point of view), urban Africans have become, for Balandier, 'society in what might be called a positive phase', the creators of 'new cultural patterns'.

The emphasis, indeed, is on this newness; on 'the transformations affecting what is usually called traditional society' in the new field provided by the towns. 'Social change', still the centre of concern, is seen as 'the building up of a new type of community in the African town', in which new relationships arise through an 'improvisation' born out of 'wider and fuller contacts'. Balandier instances relationships between neighbours in the urban quarter, 'those which arise for vocational reasons or owing to the development of an urban economy', and 'subordinate groups' of a mainly sociable or recreational character. He also posits the existence of a 'problem of the inception of social classes (or groups of a similar nature) as a result of the introduction of colonial capitalism'. All these phenomena, as well as the 'changes in the relationship between the sexes, in relations resulting from family ties', are seen as rapid transformations in the lives of people who, before they came to town, lived in a rural and traditional milieu which (it is implied) was by comparison static. Balandier, indeed, criticizes 'Anglo-Saxon anthropologists' for their over-simplified model of 'culture contact' which takes no account of the special features of what he defines as 'the colonial situation.'[1] Yet his own conception of 'social change' is equally simple: 'social change' is produced by the impact of a 'colonial situation' on the lives of tribal Africans, and by their reactions to it. To Balandier, it is this type of change for which the African town, itself a product of the same colonial situation, provides a useful laboratory.

The urban milieu as the crucible of European-induced social change; the transformation of kinship relations; the emergence of associations in 'improvised' response to the new conditions of life; 'the problem of the inception of social classes'—these have remained, since the mid-1950s, the central theoretical preoccupations of African urban sociology.[2]

Along with these theoretical interests has gone a constant concern with method;[3] this also appears already in the papers presented to the 1954 U.N.E.S.C.O. Conference, as well as in the 'Survey of recent and current field studies on the social effects of economic development in inter-tropical Africa' written by M. McCulloch[4] for the 1956 report on the Conference. The central problem here is that of combining the research techniques developed by anthropology for the study of culturally unfamiliar societies with those devised by sociologists for dealing with large units and rapid change. The former techniques—direct observation and participation, the use of indivdual open-ended interviews with a small number of informants—could be fully effective only in small social units where homogeneity and a measure of stability could be assumed; the latter—random sampling, questionnaires, the formal interviewing of large numbers of people—were applicable without modification only in culturally familiar contexts. Clearly, some hybrid method was required that would combine the virtues, and neutralize the defects, of both sorts of techniques,

---

[1] Balandier, 1955(b).

[2] A recent review of current theoretical concerns will be found in Epstein, 1967; parts of this article read almost like a paraphrase of Balandier.

[3] Mitchell, 1966, contains a good recent survey of developments in this field.

[4] Forde (ed.), 1956, Part II.

and would do justice both to the sheer size and internal complexity of African towns, and to the unfamiliar aspects of their inhabitants' social life.

On these desiderata there was, at the time of the Conference, fairly general agreement; already earlier, Busia had 'tried to combine the methods of the survey with those of the social anthropologist'. The problem was—and remains—one of proportion and mode of combination; and since in the social sciences, method grows out of theory and 'feeds back' into it, each successive attempt to 'combine the methods of the survey with those of the social anthropologist' has tacitly demanded, at some level, a reformulation of anthropological theory on the one hand, the concepts of traditional urban sociology on the other.

First among the 'particular objectives for research studies' finally recommended by the U.N.E.S.C.O. Conference was 'a comparative study of new urban areas created by recent economic development under Western colonization and of African towns which had developed prior to Western colonization and economic activity.'[1] This recognition of the existence of indigenous African towns was a crucial one. It implied the rejection, not only of the view that in all discussions of African town life 'we are dealing with peoples who had no urban tradition', but rejected the quasi-identification of African town life with the sort of 'social change' brought about by colonial industrialization and the 'urbanization' of tribal peasants into a new industrial working class. In the last resort, this research recommendation re-opened the whole problem of what a town is, and of whether the kind of assumptions about the nature of urban life which had served well enough to underpin descriptions of industrialized cities in the West could be extrapolated, along with urban survey techniques, to the study of African towns.

II

The problem had by that time already been encountered in a practical form of several scholars. One of them was W. B. Schwab, who in 1949/50 was engaged in the study of Oshogbo, a Yoruba

---

[1] Forde (ed.),1956, Part I.

nucleated settlement of some 70,000 inhabitants. In 1954, Schwab wrote:[1]

There has been some discussion as to whether these Yoruba communities are indeed urban in the sense that social scientists commonly use the term. It is not my intention to become involved here in the various polemics regarding the necessary and sufficient determinants, and the social characteristics of the urban community. It is my impression that we have not yet arrived at an operational definition of the word 'urban' which is applicable outside the Euro-American city.

More than ten years later,[2] he still seems curiously uncertain as to whether he had been studying an urban community. On the one hand, he is cautiously prepared to concede that 'if we were to follow many of the typologies of urbanism, we would be compelled to admit that traditional Oshogbo satisfied most, if not all, the requisites for an urban community'. On the other, 'it is equally clear that the kinship system . . . has thus far prevented and opposed the fuller development of urban social characteristics'.[3] Despite his refusal to commit himself on the theoretical point, however, Schwab had found that in practice 'the structuralization of the community had those components that necessitated the utilization of controls, quantification, and other methodological procedures commonly used in the study of large urban-like aggregates'.[4] He accordingly devised a method of collecting information based on a 10 per cent random sample census drawn from a map, supplemented by a sub-sample of families whose economic and social organization was investigated more intensively over a period of one year. In other words, whether or not Oshogbo was an urban community, Schwab found he had to study it as if it were; although its unfamiliarity made it necessary to supplement the numerical collection of data by 'well-known anthropological methods' of 'intensive enquiry and first hand observation'. The implication is clear enough, even though Schwab makes it explicit only in his title: the article is called 'An Experiment in Methodology in a West African Urban Community'.

The U.N.E.S.C.O. Conference in its conclusions had opened the way for a typology of African towns that would include settlements like Oshogbo and, by implication, re-open the 'various polemics regarding the necessary and sufficient determinants,

---

[1] Schwab, 1954.   [2] Schwab, 1965.   [3] Ibid.   [4] Schwab, 1954.

and the social characteristics of the urban community'. Meanwhile, research proceeded on individual African towns; the theoretical framework remaining largely that implied by the specific problems listed by Balandier and more recently by Epstein: 'social change' as exemplified in the breakdown of the large kinship units characteristic of tribal Africa, the emergence of urban associations,[1] and the appearance of something that might, however distantly, resemble a class structure as it exists in European or American cities. These phenomena, all of them seen as processual, were taken as the most important aspects, almost indeed the 'necessary and sufficient determinants' of African urban life. At the same time, methodological experiment was proceeding; thus A. Southall and P. C. Gutkind, in their study of Kampala,[2] in a sense reversed Schwab's sampling technique: where he divided Oshogbo into four 'differentiated areas' and selected a 10 per cent random sample of the houses of each, they selected instead, on the basis of previous knowledge, two areas of Kampala: Kisenyi as representing 'the densest type of uncontrolled and primarily African settlement' within that city, and Mulago as 'an intermediate population representing the transition towards these conditions from a previously rural community'. In these chosen areas, however, they decided to interview every household.

The reason for this unusual and laborious procedure was the conviction that uncharted territory was being explored . . . The authors remain convinced that the 100% interviewing sample of type areas was the only practical initial means to their end. They consider that the studies of Kisenyi and Mulago revealed to them . . . the most important hypotheses to be tested in other areas of the town and in other categories of the population. This was because the interviewing of every household gave a continuous and intimate insight into basic social relationships in a manner which a random sample, with its subjects scattered about haphazardly, out of contact with one another, could not have done.

It was only 'armed with the confidence thus gained' that the authors proceeded 'to narrow down subsequent samples to a more normal basis of random sampling'. Like Schwab, they decided that 'the use of a questionnaire alone can never tell us how the individual or the family reacts in thought or action to the life of the town' and that, accordingly, 'a great part of the research would

---

[1] Banton, 1957, remains a classic in this field.
[2] Southall and Gutkind, 1957.

have to be along the lines of community and family participation';
like him, they used African assistants. Further ancillary techniques, such as the keeping of diaries and an essay competition
(both of which necessarily selected a sample of literates out of the
population) were used as cross-checks.

Southall and Gutkind's methods have produced a particularly
detailed and illuminating study of social life in one of the older
towns created by the 'colonial situation'; it is a pity that, since
Schwab has not so far published the complete results of his
Oshogbo study, it is not possible to compare the results of the
two different sampling techniques. Schwab was, indeed, working
in an older and ethnically far more homogeneous community,
where his straight 10 per cent random sample of the buildings
of each area may well have given the best statistical representation;
in any case, the absence of full publication creates a serious gap in
our knowledge of 'African towns . . . developed prior to Western
colonization and economic activity': a number of fieldworkers
have worked in Yoruba settlements, and argued as to whether or
not they could be regarded as urban,[1] but no monograph using
quantitative survey techniques has been published about any of
these centres. This in itself would seem to run counter to Schwab's
contention[2] that 'the question of whether or not Oshogbo can be
defined as "urban" is irrelevant to the methodological discussion'.
According to the evidence, the question would appear, on the
contrary, to be quite relevant.

In 1962, the first explicit attempt was made at an inclusive
typology of African towns. This was evolved at a symposium in
which many of those at that time engaged in African urban studies
took part—among them E. Ardener, D. Forde, J. C. Mitchell,
W. B. Schwab, A. Southall; and first published by Southall[3] in his
theoretical and critical introduction to a book which, under the
title of *Social Change in Modern Africa*, is in effect a reader on
African urban life. Southall draws a 'broad contrast' between
'old established, slowly growing towns' and 'new populations of
mushroom growth'; which he labels, respectively, Type A and
Type B. The distinction is crucial enough to deserve extensive
quotation:

[1] P. C. Lloyd, 1967, qualifies them as 'scarcely urban'.
[2] Op. cit.
[3] Southall (ed.), 1962.

Towns of type A are typically characterized by a more or less indigenous population core of considerable homogeneity . . . Subsistence agriculture still plays a part in the life of these towns, since surrounding land is used for subsistence crops as well as commercial production, and town dwellers also have farms even at considerable distances to which they go and work . . . Occupations are very diverse, in a setting which is predominantly clerical and commercial rather than industrial. Correspondingly, working groups are small and independent entrepreneurs numerous. There is also a continuous and very wide range of variations from wealthy proprietors of business, land, or property down to poor dependants, casual workers and beggars. Housing policy is marked by a permissive, *laissez-faire* attitude, accompanied by landlordism, extensive renting and taking of lodgers . . . accommodation for the masses . . . is provided by spontaneous economic reaction to opportunity from within the African community . . . rather than artificially from outside it . . . While an extensive and corporate kinship structure rarely operates in these conditions, they are sufficiently flexible to permit some tribal or kinship concentration. . . .

On the other hand, the newer centres of type B consist in the extreme case of a totally immigrant African population, which may be to a considerable extent of very distant origin. The break between town and country is sharp . . . Administrative control in towns of type B is close and appears to the immigrants to be exercised entirely by a dominant ethnic group of foreign origin and markedly different race. The African population is faced initially by a social vacuum without readily assimilable patterns or standards and this results in competition for status in non-traditional and extra-tribal terms. The occupational structure is based on clear distinctions between clerical, skilled, and unskilled workers and dominated by relatively few but large corporate organizations which are foreign to their African employees. African managerial, entrepreneurial, landlord and professional roles are little developed and independent African economic activity is slight . . . Aspirations of the African population find expression in trade unions, and political parties, as well as tribal welfare associations. There are no traditional institutions to provide a focus. The main income levels, like occupations, are sharply distinct, but the overall range is not great . . . The provision of housing is closely controlled and inflexible, being almost exclusively tied to large business concerns or to . . . government agencies . . . continued residence legally depends on proof of gainful employment. . . . The female population which these centres invariably attract . . . [is] . . . in a highly anomalous position. Tribal and kinship concentrations are even less possible than in the older towns. . . .

Some population centres conform fairly closely to one or the other of these polar extremes, but most probably show mixed features. Many West African towns show the characteristic features of type A. *This is especially true of places like Oshogbo which have not been greatly transformed.* On the other hand, in Ibadan traditional aspects have been modified by modern governmental functions, and in Lagos the presence of the port and of large-scale commercial activity has led to a more mixed situation. The same is true, *mutatis mutandis*, of Dakar, Abidjan, Kumasi, Accra, Freetown and many others . . .

Not only African towns, but African territories as a whole, can very largely be grouped according to this distinction. In the Union of South Africa, Southern and Northern Rhodesia, Kenya and the Belgian Congo, most towns belong to type B. In Tanganyika, Uganda, the former territories of French Equatorial and British and French West Africa, most towns belong to type A. It will immediately be seen that the most industrialized territories belong to type B and that this also means the territories with the largest white populations. Among those of type B it is some of the Belgian Congo towns which stand nearest to type A and among those type A some Tanganyika centres stand nearest to type B. . . .

In type A towns like Oshogbo, Koforidua, or even Lagos, there is considerable continuity of norms between town and countryside . . . In type B towns like Salisbury, Gwelo, or Nairobi there is great discontinuity. [Italics mine.]

Southall's range of African towns, in other words, explicitly includes near one of its polar extremes 'places like Oshogbo which have not been greatly transformed'. In effect, Southall is drawing the theoretical conclusion implicit in Schwab's method of research: that if Oshogbo is not 'urban in the sense that social scientists commonly use the term', then either 'the necessary and sufficient determinants, and the social characteristics of the urban community' will have to be re-examined and re-defined, or the use of the word 'urban' deliberately and explicitly restricted to those population centres where the ideas it connotes first arose.

III

The controversy, though at certain periods somewhat intermittently pursued, is hardly a recent one. M. Weber,[1] writing more than forty-five years ago, was well aware of the lack of a unified definition of the city; and nowadays, as H. Miner puts it,[2]

---

[1] Weber, 1921.   [2] Miner, 1967.

'everybody knows what a city is, except the experts'. Weber noted[1] that, in common-sense terms, the city 'is thought of quantitatively as a large locality. In itself this is not imprecise for the city often represents a locality and dense settlement of dwellings forming a colony so extensive that personal reciprocal acquaintance of the inhabitants is lacking. However . . . it would be ambiguous, for various cultural factors determine the size at which "impersonality" tends to appear.'

Weber attempts to get away from these 'ambiguous' quantitative and qualitative criteria, which he realized were culturally relative, to something more satisfactorily objective; and he accordingly lists a fortification, a market, and a degree of legal and political autonomy expressed in an *ad hoc* form of association, in an attempt to establish his own definition of what 'constitutes a full urban community'. But after all his pains, his new criteria are at least as culture-bound as those he has rejected; he himself is compelled to recognize that his discussion has been confined to 'historical localities' and is therefore of little use in analysing modern sociological phenomena; moreover, he believed that the city as he had described it 'appears as a general phenomenon only in the Occident' —i.e. in ancient and medieval Europe.

Theoretically speaking, Weber's book was thus a blind alley. L. Wirth, for his famous definition of a city,[2] returns to the initial common-sense concepts that Weber had rejected: size and impersonality. His initial definition, which has become almost Holy Writ for urban sociology, is 'a relatively large, dense and permanent settlement of socially heterogeneous individuals'. The 'relativity' specified is the cultural one, of which Wirth, like Weber, was well aware; the words 'village', 'town', and 'city' have no fixed meaning,[3] and are used quite differently, for instance, by different national authorities. In Britain, Census authorities define a 'town' as a place with a minimum population of 3,500; in the United States, the figure is 2,500; in the U.S.S.R., 1,000. This in itself suggests that where the definition is given by an absolute figure, that figure is determined by such non-statistical considerations as whether a national government chooses to define its population as predominantly rural or predominantly urban in character; and indeed, the use of numbers as a criterion in the first place is itself, as Weber had already noted, a cultural phenomenon.

[1] Op. cit.   [2] Wirth, 1938.   [3] Cf. Kuper, 1965.

Nonetheless, even with this caution, Wirth's numerical criteria of size, density, and permanence have never really been questioned since: whatever their limitations, they are far too useful. There has, however, been a good deal of debate as to what he meant by 'socially heterogeneous individuals'; whether the postulated heterogeneity had to be one of ranked social strata, or of ethnic affiliation, or whether a diversified occupational structure would satisfy the definition. Wirth himself assumes that 'the population of the city does not reproduce itself' and that it therefore 'must recruit its migrants from other cities, the countryside and—in *this country*[1] until recently—from other countries'. But 'heterogeneity' is not for Wirth identical with this ethnic diversity, or with the existence of social strata as such; rather its function is 'to complicate the class structure and thus induce a more ramified and differentiated framework of social stratification than is found in more integrated societies'. It is in fact equated with the differentiation of the individual's interests, and their expression through membership of a number of different associations:

No single group has the undivided allegiance of the individual. The groups with which he is affiliated do not lend themselves readily to a simple hierarchical arrangement . . . nor a concentric arrangement so that the narrower ones fall within the circumference of the more inclusive ones, as is more likely to be the case in the rural community or in primitive societies . . . By virtue of his different interests arising out of different aspects of his social life, the individual acquires membership in widely divergent groups, each of which functions only with reference to a single segment of his personality.

It is this many-sided group affiliation on the part of the individual that Wirth defines as 'social heterogeneity';[2] the whole point being that the criteria for membership of such groups need not be all of one character, whether ethnic, class, occupational, or any other.

The open character of Wirth's definition of heterogeneity appears to have largely escaped attention, which, instead, has become concentrated on what is in fact the most misleading part of his essay: the passages dealing with 'the urban mode of life'.

[1] i.e. the United States of America (italics mine).
[2] Nowadays we would be more likely to use the Parsonian terminology, and speak of 'role differentiation'.

C

IV

Wirth attempts to derive 'urbanism as a way of life' from his defined external criteria of size, density, permanence, heterogeneity; but this attempt soon breaks down, and what he in fact produces is an emotionally charged description of certain characteristics empirically observed by him in the social life of modern European and American cities:

The contacts of the city may indeed be face-to-face but they are nevertheless impersonal, superficial, transitory and segmental . . . The superficiality, the anonymity, and the transitory character of urban–social relations make intelligible, also, the sophistication and the rationality generally ascribed to city dwellers . . . The urbanite has lost the sense of participation that comes with living in an integrated society. This constitutes essentially the *anomie* . . . to which Durkheim alludes.

Such a description looks back beyond Durkheim to Rousseau; it is redolent with suppressed nostalgia for a subjacent 'integrated society' in which contacts were personal, deep, permanent, and involved the whole person. Even *anomie* implies that a *nomos* has, somewhere along the way, been lost. The urban model of social life, in fact, implies the existence of a rural model in the background; in terms of which it is judged.

A gloss on the assumptions contained in the common usage of the terms 'rural' and 'urban' is provided by A. L. Kroeber:[1]

It is customary to distinguish rural and urban components in modern populations. There are of course corresponding rural and urban facets or aspects in the culture of such societies. Moreover, while societies and cultures can be classified into those predominantly rural or predominantly urban . . . On the widest consideration, the rural–urban differentiation is a somewhat special and modern form of a more general distinction of societies and cultures into those that are more folklike, and those that are more sophisticated or civilized.[2]

This 'folk–sophisticate polarity' is, however, a common-sense one; and its roots go back very far in Western thought and emotion, well beyond Rousseau, certainly to the Renaissance pastoral poets and perhaps beyond them. It is part of the myth in terms of which Western man has seen his own social life; a dualist myth which

[1] Kroeber, 1948.
[2] For further discussion of the 'folk–sophisticate polarity', cf. Redfield, 1953.

acquired a measure of 'sociological' respectability under the guise of Tönnies's dichotomy between *Gemeinschaft* and *Gesellschaft*.

Kroeber goes on to give a general model for the 'rural' or 'folklike' pole of the dichotomy:

A characteristic folk culture or tribal culture belongs to a small, isolated, close-knit society, in which person-to-person relations are prevalent, kinship is a dominant factor, and organization both societal and cultural is therefore largely on a basis of kinship—sometimes including fictitious kinship ... By contrast, political institutions are weakly developed; 'primitive democracy' is the characteristic form ... Such a way of doing works because of the strong integration within the small group involved. Everyone knows everyone else, and many of them are blood or affinal relatives. It has long been noted that there seems to be a spontaneous upper limit to tribal size; probably about 5000 souls. ...

It is also the smallness of the maximal social unit which keeps folk populations homogeneous and uniform, with only slight division-of-labour specialization, beginnings of class divisions or slender concentrations of residence in permanent towns ... Folk cultures afford their individual members full participation in their functioning ... their functioning, however limited and inadequate, is therefore personalized and saturated. ...

This is, in effect, the classical functionalist model of the small face-to-face integrated community; and it is against this backcloth that Kroeber sets his contrasting model of 'urban' or 'sophisticated' society, defined by the familiar emotionally loaded, largely negative epithets: secularized, unstable, impersonal, and so on. He ends in what amounts to an admission of the culture-bound nature of the categories he has set up: 'It is evident that our present-day Western civilization is near one polar end—the most urbanized, lay, depersonalized, sophisticatedly civilized end—of an axis that can be traced through all societies and cultures.'

A certain style of social relationships, in other words—one which writers of this school regretfully attribute both to themselves and, by implication, to their readers, and which they describe largely by negative epithets[1]—is regarded, not only as associated with the pattern of large, dense, permanent centres of population, but as being an indispensable concomitant of such a settlement pattern; so that, if the 'urban mode of life' be absent, the settlement does not satisfy the necessary conditions of an urban centre.

[1] Cf. Kuper, 1965.

We have returned to the conception Weber[1] rejected, of some (theoretically determinable) 'size at which impersonality tends to appear', and disregarded his warning that 'precisely this impersonality was absent in many historical localities possessing the legal character of cities'. We have also come, as Miner[2] points out, to speak of 'the urbanisation of rural areas, bringing increasing urbanism (city-like life) to the farmer while the density of the farm population declines!'

Clearly, there is a need, as indeed many recent writers[3] have proclaimed, to redefine what we mean by 'urban' and by 'urbanization'. The related terminological confusion between 'city' and 'town' is probably irredeemable; but this seems less serious, since, if we once knew what we meant by an urban centre, 'city' and 'town' could remain as now, almost but not quite interchangeable common-sense terms.

V

This, then, is the background of common-sense assumption that underlies Schwab's doubts as to whether 'these Yoruba communities are indeed urban in the sense that social scientists commonly use the term'. W. B. Bascom[4] quotes him as saying, more explicitly, in his unpublished manuscript: 'If Oshogbo was viewed on the level of form, it was an urban community; if viewed in terms of social organization and process, it was folk' and 'folk' almost by definition equals tribal and therefore rural. By 'the level of form', Schwab presumably means that Oshogbo, a 'compact territorial unit' over 100 years old, with a population of 70,000, satisfies Wirth's quantitative criteria of size, density, and permanence; it is 'in terms of social organization and process' that it did not correspond to his qualitative model of urban life. Oshogbo, in fact, like other Yoruba towns, was, with its predominantly farming population and its large kinship units united by common residence and tenure of land, far too close to the 'rural model' of society. A similar malaise is more succinctly expressed by P. C. Lloyd[5] when he speaks of the Yoruba nucleated settlements collectively as 'tribal' towns and as 'scarcely urban'.[6]

---

[1] Op. cit.   [2] Op. cit.
[3] Kuper, 1965; Schwab, 1965; Epstein, 1967; Miner, 1967.   [4] Bascom, 1955.
[5] P. C. Lloyd, 1959(a).   [6] P. C. Lloyd, 1959(a) and 1967.

Bascom,[1] on the other hand, comes down squarely on the side of 'Yoruba urbanism'. After dealing with size, density, and permanence, he goes on to make a case for the 'impersonal, superficial, transitory and segmental' character of Yoruba urban social relations. The question of whether such characteristics are really an indispensable hallmark of urban society is raised by neither side in the controversy. Bascom ends by returning, though without formal acknowledgement, to Weber's political criteria of what 'constitutes a full urban community': the presence of a formalized town government with a certain degree of political and legal autonomy. This, he says, combined with the 'objectively measurable criteria' of size, density, and permanence, will provide a more readily transcultural definition of urban settlements than Wirth's notion of 'heterogeneity', which, he says, is not adequately defined.[2]

The non-numerical criterion of formalized town government has, for Yoruba towns, the advantage of coinciding with the way in which the Yoruba themselves conceptualize these settlements. Yoruba distinguish sharply between the statuses of *ará oko*, 'farm people'—most commonly used in contemptuous contexts where it could be translated as 'yokels' or 'country boors'—and *ará ìlú*—those who are by birthright members of an *ìlú*. *Ìlú* is the name they give both to their nucleated settlements and to the advisory and executive Council of chiefs which, in conjunction with the sacred king or *ọba*, constitutes the government of each settlement.

The concept of *ìlú* thus defines a mode of government rather than a settlement pattern: the Yoruba contempt for *ará oko* is related to that which they feel for neighbouring peoples who have no institutions of kingship. *Ìlú* accordingly defines, in terms of political institutions, the unit governed by these institutions: a unit which does not stop short at the mud walls which formerly

---

[1] Bascom, 1955, 1958, 1958–9, 1959, 1962.

[2] Mitchell, 1966, commenting upon Miner, 1953, and Sjoberg, 1960, says: 'Studies of [such] towns have been used to examine the generalizations developed by theorists such as Wirth (1938) on the basis of experience of American and European towns. This is possible because they provide an opportunity for testing the hypothesis that the features of the social system that may be characterized as specifically urban are due to the factors of economic differentiation, heterogeneity and mobility rather than the whole cultural complex of which they appear to be an integral part.' But in Yoruba studies at any rate, the theoretical problems never appear to me to have been quite as clearly set out as in Mitchell's formulation.

enclosed these towns, but extends into the farmlands beyond. These lands are cultivated by people who regard themselves as *ará ìlú*, members of the town—even though they may spend a considerable part of the year in hamlets near their farm, returning to their urban residence only for marriages, funerals, and the annual festivals of those deities (*òrìṣà*) that specially concern them. There is a sense, in other words, in which the boundaries of the *ìlú* do not coincide with the city walls, but are coterminous with those of the furthest plots farmed by men who are members of a 'compound' or residential unit within the clustered settlement. If *ìlú* refers both to the clustered settlement itself and to the Council of State through which it is administered, it also corresponds in some sense to what we could call the State. Conceptually, the city is not distinguished from its farming hinterland: the whole complex is seen as a unit, radiating out from a core consisting of the *ọba* and Council.[1]

Of course, this centralized pattern of government was not totally unconnected with demographic factors; rather, the two interacted on each other. Ojo[2] points out that the status accorded a Yoruba town depended not so much on its size and population as on the traditional prestige of its ruler; on the other hand, that prestige was itself affected by considerations of the size and population of the territory he controlled. The *ọbas* of the four largest kingdoms, i.e. the Oni of Ifẹ, the Alafin of Qyọ, the Alakẹ of Abẹokuta and the Awujalẹ of Ijẹbu, were *also* the most prestigious of the traditional rulers.

Ojo goes on to differentiate between 'crowned' or 'capital towns' (*ìlú aládé* or *olú ìlú*) which were believed to have been founded directly from Ilé Ifẹ̀[3] and whose rulers were accordingly entitled to wear crowns with beaded fringes; and 'farm-fringe' or subordinate towns (*ìlú eréko*), which were not direct offshoots from the sacred city, but either dependent on the *ìlú aládé* or directly deriving from them. These are towns governed, not by an *ọba*, but by a *bálẹ̀*; a ruler who may not wear a beaded crown (*adé*), but only a cap (*oríkògbófo*) or, in exceptional cases, a coronet (*àkòró*) without beaded fringes.[4] These subordinate

---

[1] We shall see in Chapter III that this is reflected in the actual lay-out of the older towns.
[2] Ojo, 1966(a), Chapter V.   [3] Cf. above, Chapter I, Section II.
[4] Ojo, 1966(b), Chapter II.

settlements are further classified into ọlọ́já (market towns), ìlétò (villages), abúlé (hamlets) and àgọ́ or abà (camp settlements).[1] Of these, only the first two categories, ìlú aládé and ìlú ọlọ́jà, 'crowned' towns and market towns, need concern us here.

On the whole, modern developments have followed the channels already cut by traditional arrangements. Lagos, as the most accessible port in Nigeria, formed an exception; another, as we have seen,[2] was provided by Ibadan. In general, however, the seats of the major ọbas became those of the early colonial District Officers and Travelling Commissioners. Similarly, further inland, the most central ìlú aládé tended to become the Provincial Head-quarters, while the others became divisional headquarters.[3] All this fitted in well with the British colonial concept of Indirect Rule; but the situation has not, as regards the relative importance of different towns, been substantially altered either by Independence or by subsequent administrative reorganization.

Thus, in native political thought, each clustered settlement is the residential expression of the political unity of a small State; an ideal which is in practice contradicted by the frequent relations of superordination/subordination existing even between ìlú aládé. This discrepancy between the theory of the ìlú and the realities of Yoruba politics is reflected in the always somewhat anomalous position of non-metropolitan 'subordinate towns'. Their existence is 'explained' either as settlements made by princes from the me-tropolitan town, or as formerly independent units conquered by the latter; they have the same ọba-and-Council structure of govern-ment as the metropolitan town, but were formerly subordinate to it in the conduct of foreign affairs including war, and expressed this subordination by the payment of tribute or tax. Even today they cannot claim a 'boundary' between their lands and those of the metropolitan town, as to do so would be tantamount to claim-ing independence from the latter.[4] (Where such claims do occur, it is usual for the subordinate town to alter its historical myths of origin, claiming to have been founded 'independently' and not by hiving-off from the metropolitan town).[5]

N. A. Fadipẹ[6] writes:

---

[1] Ojo, 1966(a), Chapter V.
[2] Cf. below, Sections VI and VII, and above, Chapter I, Section II.
[3] Ojo, loc. cit.   [4] P. C. Lloyd, 1962.   [5] P. C. Lloyd, 1959(a).
[6] Fadipẹ, 1939.

The government of the capital town presented one peculiar feature. Not only was it both the government of the town and the central government, but it did not visualize central administration as presenting a problem distinct from local government. This was largely because most Yoruba states partook to some extent of the character of the Greek city-State. The capital was the State, and the State the capital.

And all major settlements were, ideally, capitals. In modern usage, *ìlú* is quite often equated with nation or State; thus England is *ìlú òyìnbó*, the *ìlú* of the Europeans.

Yoruba in fact distinguish, rather as the Greeks did, between citizens and non-citizens; a distinction which does not coincide with that made by modern Western thought between townsmen and countrymen. The potential discrepancy between the two sets of conceptions raises a number of quite serious and genuine difficulties.

VI

First of all, the political–qualitative criterion of what constitutes a town, whether formulated by Weber or implicit in the Yoruba language, is potentially at war with the quantitative criteria of size and density, which, perforce, are those used by Census authorities. This conflict cannot but become actualized every time a Census is taken; that of 1952/3,[1] following the Census of India, defined a town as a settlement of over 5,000 people. This excluded several small *ìlú* and certainly included many settlements which the Yoruba themselves would regard as villages. The most glaring case is that of Ibadan, the largest of all Yoruba settlements (pop. 459,200 approximately, according to the 1952/3 Census), which has never had an *ọba* and is thus, by definition, not a town at all—except, of course, in the eyes of its own citizens.[2] Another instance is Ogbomọshọ.[3]

In 1952, some 46 per cent of the Nigerian Yoruba[4] were counted as living in settlements of 5,000 inhabitants or over. But many of the nucleations are far larger than this: 12 of them, in 1952,

---

[1] *Population Census*, 1953.   [2] Cf. below.   [3] Ojo, 1966(b), Chapter II.
[4] The Census, of course, excludes those Yoruba living in Togo and Dahomey, and—in smaller communities forming part of coastal towns—in other West African countries. Cf. below.

exceeded 40,000, and 31 per cent of the Yoruba population lived in these, distributed as follows:

Ibadan	459,200
Lagos	276,400
Ogbomọshọ	139,500
Oshogbo	122,700
Ifẹ	110,800
Iwo	100,000
Abẹokuta	84,500
Ọyọ	72,100
Ilẹsha	71,800
Isẹyin	49,700
Ede	44,800
Ilọrin	41,000

Below this magnitude, there are other sizeable settlements:

Ondo	36,200
Ikẹrrẹ	35,600
Ọwọ	30,700
Shagamu	30,100
Ado Ekiti	24,700
Ijẹbu Ode	24,600
Shaki	22,100.

Official figures for population densities are lacking except for Lagos; where the three wards of Lagos Island were, in 1950, calculated at densities of 67,000, 111,000 and 141,000 per square mile respectively.[1] In the interior towns, density appears to be very variable; thus on the basis of Land Survey Maps and 1952 Census figures, Ọyọ has about 20,600 inhabitants per square mile, Ogbomọshọ about 69,800 and Abẹokuta about 10,600. These figures cannot, of course, be taken literally; but they may serve to indicate something of the very wide range of variation to be found in this respect, and which itself corresponds to differences in material lay-out and history.

It will be seen that in 1952 Lagos, the capital city of Nigeria, was only a little over half as populous as Ibadan. Lagos is, for obvious reasons, ethnically the least homogeneous of the

[1] Bascom, 1955.

settlements;[1] in 1952 it was still counted, however, as 73 per cent Yoruba.

Anomalies of this type are simply the result of movements of population; before the nineteenth-century upheavals that transformed the face of Yorubaland[2] there was probably a fairly exact correlation between the population size of Yoruba settlements and the degree of development of their political institutions. Even now, Ibadan and Ogbomọshọ are the only large Yoruba towns which are not *ìlú aládé*. It is at the borderline between small town and large village that the other anomalies occur. Ojo[3] gives some examples from Ekiti division, where the traditional distinction is not yet blurred by modern developments, and where there are sixteen *ìlú aládé*. Of these Aiyede had 3,092 inhabitants according to the 1952 Census, Ọgọtun 4,468 and Ọyọ[4] 3,544; whereas Uyin, Ifaki, Ikoro, and Ipoti, all *ìlú eréko*, had population figures between 5,500 and over 8,500. Such anomalies are likely to increase rather than decrease in the future; just as, in Europe, chartered cities have dwindled almost to nothing, and villages reached urban proportions.

The second difficulty consists in assigning a given population figure to these settlements at all; in knowing which proportion of the total Yoruba population is 'urbanized' in the sense of 'living in towns'. In view of the identification of *ará ìlú* status with citizenship and indeed 'civility', all Yoruba will claim such status if they have any possibility of doing so;[5] and will substantiate this claim wherever possible by returning to the town compound of their descent group for important political, ritual, and social activities.[6] They regard themselves as *ará ìlú* much as an Englishman or American who commutes daily to an office in town regards himself as 'really' living in a garden suburb or 'in the country'. There is a difference, indeed, in the rhythm of the commuting: the Yoruba *ará ìlú* may spend weeks or months at a time at the farm that is his place of work—and in the nature of things, many of them will have been there at the time any given Census was

---

[1] But Ibadan, too, has relatively large, old, and stable non-indigenous communities. Cf. Mabogunje, 1967(b), Okonjo, 1967, Cohen, 1967.

[2] Cf. Chapter I, Section II.   [3] Loc. cit.

[4] Ọyọ Ekiti is not, of course, the same as Ọyọ the seat of the Alafin.

[5] Contrast the attitude of the 'Red' Xhosa, as described in Mayer, 1963.

[6] For a detailed documentation of this to-and-fro movement, cf. Goddard, 1965.

taken. Indeed, the Pax Britannica has made it possible, over the last fifty years, for more and more people to reside semi-permanently at their farms; and the rise in cocoa prices since the Second World War has made it profitable to do so. But this in itself does not make them *ará oko*. The status of *ará ìlú*, once acquired by birth into a descent group holding rights in a residential unit or 'compound' within the town walls, can be lost only by default—i.e. by failure to take part in the social, political, and ritual life of the *ìlú*; and such failure (unless one is known to be in temporary and profitable employment in another and larger town) is associated with bad debts and general shiftlessness. Even the town of employment is conceptually assimilated to the profitable but socially non-determinant farm-plot; thus P. Marris's informants in Lagos,[1] sociologically members of other Yoruba towns, told him: 'Lagos is only a farm to us.' A man's real life as a social being is in the town of which he is a member by birth, and in which he may well have a house that lies empty a good part of the year;[2] not in the *abúlé* (hamlet) or *agò* (farm camp) where he may, in sober fact, spend most of the time. This means that Census figures of 'the proportion of the population living in towns' are somewhat unreliable. In a largely illiterate population, where simultaneous enumeration is out of the question, there must be both many people missed out and others double-counted;[3] and since neither figure can be estimated, it cannot be assumed that they will cancel each other out. Lloyd[4] distinguishes between the population of a Yoruba town as given by the Census figures and its 'sociological population' as defined by all those who, if asked, would claim membership of it; and S. Goddard[5] has proposed a further refinement, namely a distinction between a fixed urban population, a farm-dwelling population, and an 'allegiant' population of persons who may, at any given time, be either in the town or at their farms, but who owe social, political, and often ritual allegiance to the town. In his case study of the movements of people in one Ọyọ compound[6] he found that its permanent town-dwelling population represented something like 40 per cent of its total allegiant population, which he believes to present a fairly accurate picture of the position prevailing in Ọyọ generally.

The 1952/3 Census listed 46 per cent of the Yoruba population

---

[1] Marris, 1961.   [2] Goddard, 1965.   [3] Op. cit.
[4] P. C. Lloyd, 1959(b) and 1962.   [5] Op. cit.   [6] Ibid.

of Nigeria as 'urbanized' in the sense of living in settlements of over 5,000 people; it is probable that a rather larger proportion would regard themselves as 'townsmen' in the sense of being *ará ìlú*.

In agreement with this situation, the population of most Yoruba towns seems to be to a large extent self-perpetuating or orthogenetic; this may, I think, legitimately be deduced from such information as is available about the sex and age structure of that population. The following figures are taken from the 1952 Census:

	Ibadan	Abẹokuta	Ọyọ	Ondo
MALES				
0– 7	81,682	10,118	10,409	4,001
7–14	49,475	8,852	6,181	3,410
15–49	86,664	16,675	17,220	9,433
50 and over	19,233	3,848	3,317	1,092
MALES TOTAL	237,054	39,493	37,127	17,936
FEMALES				
0– 7	78,252	11,014	9,424	4,152
7–14	44,054	8,016	5,077	3,159
15–49	81,694	20,468	16,874	9,550
50 and over	18,142	5,460	3,631	1,436
FEMALES TOTAL	222,142	44,958	35,006	18,297
TOTAL POPULATION	459,196	84,451	72,133	36,233

The Census figures would be more informative if the 15–49 age-group had been broken up into shallower units; as it is, no age-pyramids for the two sexes can be set up. It seems as if, for Ọyọ and Ondo, the male sex-ratio for the younger adult population were more or less normal; in Ibadan there are about 5,000 more men than women between 15 and 49, in Abẹokuta about 4,000 less. This may reflect in part the movement of young male literates, of whom Abẹokuta produces, and Ibadan employs, a great number. But even here the total male sex-ratios (107 for Ibadan, 88 for Abẹokuta) are far closer to normality than in most African towns for which we have figures; in Ọyọ and Ondo the ratios are 196 and 98 respectively.

The youth of the population of the towns—in all the towns the proportion of inhabitants under the age of 15 comes close to 50 per cent, and in Ibadan exceeds that percentage—simply reflects the high birth- and death-rates and low life-expectancies characteristic of tropical Africa. All in all, the demographic pattern of the towns is not substantially different from that of the countryside; if anything, the towns have a slightly higher proportion of people over 50. Lloyd[1] comments on this: 'To read any great significance in these slight differences is to credit the 1953 Census with far greater accuracy than seems warranted.'

The fact that the quality of *ará ìlú* is not affected by the prolonged absence of its holder in farm hamlet or town of employment does, in one sense, produce a situation not unlike that prevailing in other parts of Africa, where 'tribal areas', form the labour reserve of towns of Southall's 'type B':[2] there too, the men who spend a longer or shorter period as wage-earners in the big city do not on that account lose membership of their tribal community. Yet the attitude seems to be somewhat different: we have seen that the Yoruba—accustomed to a traditional situation in which a man lives his 'real' social and political life in a closely nucleated settlement and commutes into the countryside for a livelihood—say of Lagos: 'It is only a farm to us'[3]—meaning that they have come to make money and will return to the real town—their own—when they have harvested their fortune. Farm and big city or commercial port are both places to make money, which will be spent on their own urban life at home—on a fine house, or handsome clothes, or the feasts and payments required for membership of the associations which confer prestige in a man's own town. The intense local and tribal loyalties, widespread enough in Africa, are here attached to the town of origin.

Such an attitude not only makes for a core population with a normal and stable demographic structure; it also explains the comparatively low proportion of 'strangers' in most Yoruba towns. The 1952 Census did not, save in Lagos, record the place of birth of those enumerated, and it is therefore impossible to give exact figures; but Lloyd[4] calculates that in Iwo, for instance—which, although large, is poor and backward—strangers both

[1] P. C. Lloyd, 1959(a).
[2] Southall, 1962, cf. above, Chapter I, Section II.   [3] Marris, 1961.
[4] Lloyd, 1959.

Yoruba and non-Yoruba probably makes up less than 5 per cent of the population; in Ado Ekiti, the commercial and administrative headquarters of Ekiti Division, the proportion may be nearer 10 per cent; but that in prosperous Ijẹbu Ode, where there are plenty of educated local citizens to fill the available clerical posts, it is probably rather less than in Ado.

The exceptions are, naturally, Lagos and Ibadan, both of which afford exceptional job opportunities, particularly for educated men. Mitchel[1] calculates that 35 per cent of the population of Ibadan were not born there, 5 per cent of them being non-Yoruba (largely Hausa and Nupe) and 30 per cent Yoruba 'strangers'. In Lagos, only 40 per cent of the inhabitants were recorded as Lagos-born at the 1952 Census; of the remaining 60 per cent, over half (34 per cent) came from the Western Region, and can therefore be presumed to be predominantly Yoruba.

From the myths related by members of different descent groups, it would appear that the transfer of small groups from one town to another was not uncommon before the nineteenth century. The head of such a group would then swear political allegiance to the ọba of the town to which he had come, and receive land from him for himself and his descendants. In those days, when populations were smaller and farming was for subsistence, there was plenty of land for all, and strangers were quickly absorbed. During the nineteenth-century wars, immigrants came to the towns in immeasurably larger numbers; it was less easy to accommodate them into the existing pattern, and accordingly it often happened that incompletely assimilated groups were spatially segregated in a given quarter of the town, and received something less than the full political rights of ará ìlú. This was the case, for instance, at Iwo.[2] Nowadays, on the whole, strangers in Yoruba towns remain strangers, both in their own eyes and in those of the native townsmen.[3]

VII

Let us now consider the population size of the larger centres over time:

[1] Op. cit.   [2] P. C. Lloyd, 1954.
[3] Cf. below, Chapter III, Section VIII.

	1952 Census	1931 Census	1921 Census	1911 Census
Ibadan	459,200	387,100	238,100	175,000
Lagos	276,400	126,100	99,700	73,800
Ogbomọshọ	139,500	86,700	84,900	80,000
Oshogbo	122,700	49,600	51,400	59,800
Ifẹ	110,800	24,200	22,200	36,200
Iwo	100,000	57,200	53,600	60,000
Abẹokuta	84,500	45,800	28,900	51,300
Ọyọ	72,100	48,700	40,400	45,400
Ilẹsha	71,800	21,900	—	—
Isẹyin	49,700	26,800	28,600	33,300
Ẹdẹ	44,800	52,400	48,400	26,600
Ilọrin	41,000	47,600	38,700	36,300

These figures undoubtedly present anomalies (particularly those for Ifẹ); but these must be attributed to inaccuracies in all the censuses; some of the practical difficulties have already been mentioned in the previous section. What does emerge clearly is that, while all the centres have grown appreciably—recent growth having been, understandably, most remarkable in the case of Lagos—Census evidence indicates, in all cases except that of Ilẹsha, that their population was well over 20,000 in 1911; which by African urban standards is a respectable age. For Ilẹsha, while we have no earlier Census evidence, we do have the estimate of an early Governor of Lagos, C. A. Moloney,[1] who visited it in the 1880s; he calculates the population of 40,000. Moloney gives the population of Ilọrin at 100,000, and that of Abẹokuta at the same figure; no absolute numerical value can be attached to such estimates, which merely confirm that these were already populous centres in his time. The American Baptist missionary, T. J. Bowen,[2] who visited Yorubaland in the 1850s, quotes 60,000 for Abẹokuta; Bowen's figures in general are evaluated by Bascom[3] as 'conservative'. He did not visit Oshogbo, Ifẹ, or Ilẹsha, though he mentions the two latter as 'the countries of Ifeh [and] Ijesha' adding: 'We are assured that there are many large towns in the region.' He estimates Ibadan at 70,000, Lagos at 20,000, Ogbomọshọ at 25,000, Iwo at 20,000, and Ọyọ at 25,000. This takes the record of the principal Yoruba settlements

[1] Moloney, 1890.   [2] Bowen, op. cit.   [3] Bascom, 1955 and 1959.

back to the middle of the nineteenth century. Earlier evidence, where it exists, is non-numerical, and where exact local reference can be established, refers at times to centres of population which no longer exist. Thus Clapperton and Lander,[1] arriving in 1825, visited 'Katunga' (Old Ọyọ): but this is not identical with the Ọyọ described by Bowen as containing 25,000 people around 1850; the latter was not founded until about 1831.[2] In any case, these large population estimates given by the nineteenth-century travellers must not be taken too literally; they neither can, nor for our purposes need, be interpreted as meaning anything more accurate than 'a very large number of inhabitants'.

We are clearly very far here from Kroeber's 'spontaneous upper limit to tribal size . . . about 5,000 souls';[3] and equally so from Balandier's conception of the large African city growing up in direct response to a 'colonial situation'.[4] Nor have these settlements grown up in response to industrialization. Some light industry exists in Lagos, Ibadan, and Abẹokuta; it is small-scale and recent. Lagos and Ibadan are the two largest centres; Lagos is, in addition, as we have seen, the Federal Capital and the major port, and Ibadan was until recently a Regional Capital. But Abẹokuta comes only seventh in order of size; and Ogbomọshọ, Oshogbo, Ifẹ, and Iwo, all with populations of over 100,000, are none of them industrial towns.

It is clear, moreover, that the social life of Yoruba towns is, in certain important respects, different from either that of Western urban centres or African towns of the 'B' type defined by Southall. For one thing, there is not merely a 'continuity of norms between town and countryside' but to a large extent an identity of population: Yoruba farmers and Yoruba townsmen are, very largely, the same people—but they see themselves as townsmen who farm, rather than as farmers who come to town to sell their wares. For another, they acquire the sociological status of *ará ìlú* through membership of a large, highly cohesive kinship group which holds rights, both in an urban residential unit, and in farm land outside the walls—the kind of large corporate kin group, in fact, which has everywhere and always been associated with rural rather than urban life. It is hardly surprising that so unfamiliar a style of living in nucleated settlements should have given rise to an argument about nomenclature.

[1] Clapperton, 1829.　　[2] Johnson, 1921.　　[3] Op. cit.　　[4] Balandier, 1955(b).

It is the size and cohesion of Yoruba kinship and residence units, quite as much as the economic infrastructure of the towns, that has raised doubts as to whether these settlements can be described as urban; we are accustomed to associate town life with far smaller and shallower kinship and residential units. In certain Yoruba towns, these large kin groups are also the units in which political power is vested; membership of the *ìlú* Council of chiefs is by a series of titles each of which is held in one of the descent groups of the town. This segmentary[1] political structure has led Lloyd to describe the towns as 'confederations of lineages':[2] the conception that emerges is that of a congeries of large descent groups engaged in agriculture, each of them a 'community' in MacIver and Page's sense[3] of 'the members of any group . . . [who] live together in such a way that they share, not this or that particular interest, but the basic conditions of a common life', the communities being linked at the top by the political institutions of *ọba* and Council, but otherwise largely self-sufficient and bound to one another by merely mechanical solidarity.[4] With such a model, it becomes trivial that such descent-group communities should in fact cluster together in the middle of their farmlands instead of spreading out among them, as most of the nearby Ibo do: though it might still occur to us to wonder that societies with so demonstrably high a degree of material density[5] should remain so obstinately segmentary in character.

In fact, as I shall attempt to show, this model does less than justice to the complexities of social life as actually lived in Yoruba towns. Indeed, Lloyd[6] himself has shown that the political structure of the *ìlú* is not always that of a 'confederation of lineages' but exhibits, beneath an overall cultural similarity, a considerable range of variation. As will appear, other characteristics of the social life of Yoruba towns show a somewhat similar range.

In the following chapters, I shall discuss mainly the larger and better known Yoruba settlements, including some which are not *ìlú aládé* and therefore not 'towns' in the Yoruba sense at all.[7] I shall confine myself to that portion of the inhabitants' life which is in fact spent in town; which is in any case, to them, by far

---

[1] Durkheim, 1964. Cf. also Smith, 1956.   [2] P. C. Lloyd, 1955(a).
[3] MacIver and Page, 1949.   [4] Durkheim, 1964.
[5] Ibid.   [6] P. C. Lloyd, 1954.   [7] Cf. Table on p. 35 above.

D

the most important part. At the same time I shall attempt to give some idea of the actual quality of social life in these admittedly large, dense, and permanent clusters of population, and some reasons why I consider that the study of such towns continues to be relevant in the field of African urban studies.[1]

---

[1] For a different view, cf. Mitchell, 1966.

III

LAY-OUT AND APPEARANCE

I

THE classical plan of a Yoruba town resembles a wheel: the *ọba*'s palace being the hub, the town walls the rim, and the spokes a series of roads radiating out from the palace and linking the town to other centres. Beyond the walls lie the farm-plots; first the *oko etílé* or 'farms of the outskirts', then the *oko ẹgàn* or 'bush farms', merging imperceptibly with the *oko ẹgàn* of the next town.[1]

This form of town plan derives from the socio-political structure of each Yoruba kingdom, which, as Ojo[2] notes, 'imposes on Yoruba towns a more or less identical morphology'. The *ọba*'s palace is the converging focus of all interests; each road passes through a quarter under a quarter-chief, and all the quarters, as well as the compounds of their chiefs, look towards the palace. Similarly, within each quarter, the various compounds are as far as possible grouped around that of the quarter-chief.

Johnson[3] presents the traditional town plan as deliberate. Describing the mythical founding of Ilẹsha, he writes: 'It is also said that when the town of Ilẹṣa was to be laid out a special messenger was sent to the Alafin to ask him for the help of one of the princes to lay out the town on the same plan as the ancient city of Ọyọ.' Frobenius[4] indeed attempts to relate the Ifẹ town plan to Yoruba ideas of cosmology, as embodied in one of the creation myths he collected in that city. In this myth, the world in the beginning consisted of an island surrounded by water, on which the first chiefs wandered about aimlessly. To them descended *Ọlọrun*, the Yoruba High God who is generally seen as the ultimate Creator, with the other *òrìṣà*. *Ọlọrun* said:

---

[1] Johnson, op. cit.; Goddard, op. cit.; Schwab, 1965.
[2] Ojo, 1966(a), Chapter VI. Cf. also Schwab, op. cit.
[3] Op. cit.   [4] Frobenius, 1913, Vol. I.

Eshu,[1] sit thou behind me; thou Shango in front of me; Ogun sit thou on my right hand; Obatala thou on my left. Ye other gods, sit round me in a circle . . . This city shall . . . be called Ife. Sixteen gods have come with me. They will have children and they shall live around you. Thus will Ife have a great people. But thou Oni thou shalt here hold sway and tell the Alafins[2] the will of the gods.

Frobenius adds:[3] 'It is perfectly clear that the famous hill . . . in the centre of Ife was in ancient days the "navel" of the Yoruba idea of the universe. The descendants of the sixteen gods must have had their abiding places in the old sixteen divinations[4] of the compass, while the centre was occupied by the Oni's palace, which was regarded as the umbilicus of the world.' At the time of Frobenius' visit, Ife did have a governing council of 17 chiefs, though only 12 of them were quarter-chiefs, the other 5 being òrìṣà-cult associates of the Oni.[5] But Frobenius claims to have unearthed a tradition according to which

Ife in times of old . . . consisted of just seventeen town quarters, i.e. one central, four in the cardinal points of the compass, and twelve, made up of three to each of these four, inserted between them . . . The people themselves say that the cohabitation based on clanship is by no means as strictly regulated as it was. In the days of old the *enceinte* of the city was parcelled out among different *orishas*. Today the descendants of the various deities live among each other without any ordered distinction.[6]

This somewhat fanciful interpretation is, however, in so far as the significance of the number 4 and its multiples is concerned, taken up by a modern Yoruba authority,[7] who, moreover, states that Ibadan is reputed to have had 16 gates at one time.

Not all Yoruba towns, of course, correspond exactly to this

[1] For a further discussion of this òrìṣà and his significance in the ideology of Yoruba urban life, cf. below, Section II of this Chapter, and Chapter V, Section VI.

[2] This is a 'charter myth' for the spiritual supremacy of the Onis of Ifẹ, which contrasts in the traditional Yoruba scheme of things with the political and military overlordship of the Alafins of Ọyọ.

[3] Loc. cit.

[4] Frobenius is here relating the 16 gods not only to 16 points of the compass, but to the Ifa divination system (cf. below, Chapter V, Section VI) which is based on multiples of the number 16. Cf. also McClelland, 1966.

[5] This distinction may correspond to that later encountered by W. B. Bascom, between 'town chiefs', and 'palace chiefs'. Cf. Bascom, 1951, and below, Chapter VI, Section III.

[6] Op. cit.   [7] Ojo, loc. cit.

model. Where towns have moved from former hilltop defensive sites[1] to take advantage of modern road communications, they have often 'developed the typical belt pattern following the road, which was the dominant pattern in [their] movement.'[2]

In Lagos, even on the Island, where the oldest part of the town is situated, modern administrative and commercial development has swamped whatever original structure existed. Ibadan has no ọba's palace as centralizing focus; though Mapo Hall, the British-built centre of the Ibadan Native Administration, opened in 1929 and situated on a hill in the heart of the oldest part of the town, seems to fulfil a somewhat similar function. (The Olubadan, or Senior Chief [bálẹ̀] of Ibadan, not being an ọba, continues to reside in his own family compound after election; although proposals have been made for an official Olubadan's Residence, no such Residence has yet been built.) E. D. O. John,[3] himself an Ibadan man, writes: 'The Olubadan's house is almost certain to be in the centre of the town as the post may only be filled by members of noble families.' So potent is the pattern of the ìlú.

In Abẹokuta, on the other hand, the position of the Alakẹ's palace is, for historical reasons,[4] eccentric. Abẹokuta is said to have been formed by the amalgamation of over 150 small Ẹgba settlements, and the town to this day contains five crowned ọbas, each residing in his own palace, though the Alakẹ is generally recognized as paramount.[5] The same situation obtains in Shagamu, also a composite town, dating from the second half of the nineteenth century, where four different crowned ọbas reign over different parts of the town.[6]

Even where the kingship is single, there may be several palaces. In the Ijẹbu kingdoms, there are usually as many as there are branches of the royal descent group, between which the ọbaship rotates;[7] although the official palace at any one time is that occupied by the then reigning ọba, and there is a single sacred burial ground for all deceased kings.[8]

It will be seen that by no means all Yoruba towns conform to the 'more or less identical morphology' which seems to be postulated by the Yoruba themselves; the ideal model only

---

[1] For an account of such movements within one circumscribed area, cf. Gleave, 1963.
[2] Ojo, loc. cit.   [3] Biobaku, Dina and P. C. Lloyd (ed.), 1949.
[4] Cf. above, Chapter I, Section II.   [5] Ojo, 1966(b), Chapter II.
[6] Ibid.   [7] Cf. P. C. Lloyd, 1954.   [8] Ojo, loc. cit.

appears in those *ìlú aládé* within the spheres of influence of Ifẹ
and Ọyọ. But, whether or not the town plan really derives from
traditional cosmological ideas, it certainly reflects, with quite
remarkable fidelity, the pattern of political realities within each
settlement.

II

The central *àfin* or palace[1] with its surrounding land was traditionally thickly walled around, with only one main gate con-
necting its front, or public, courtyard with the market and the town
at large.[2] The surface thus enclosed may, even now, be quite
extensive: Ojo has calculated[3] that the proportion of walled palace
area to walled town area varies between 8·3 and 0·9 per cent.
Usually the walled grounds include a proportion of bushland; this
frequently contains shrines and burial places, whose exact location
may be known only to the palace servants.[4]

Access was typically through a huge porticoed gate; that of
the palace of Ifẹ is said to have been 300 feet long, 60 feet wide
and 24 feet high. However, there were also minor gates through
which the *ọba* could emerge secretly from the palace grounds.[5]

Internally, the *ọba*'s palace could best be described as a multiple
compound. Whereas most ordinary compounds have only one or
two internal courtyards, roughly rectangular in shape, surrounded
by a verandah on all sides on which the various rooms open, an
àfin had an indefinite number of such courtyards leading on to
each other. The front courtyard was regarded as a more or less
public place, and used for ceremonies; it was usually connected
with the town market through the main doorway. Opposite the
doorway, the verandah projected forwards into one or more porches
called *kòbì*, so as to allow the *ọba* to sit in state beneath a roof
while ceremonies or other meetings were going on. Such a *kòbì*,
like the high front portico, was regarded as a mark of rank;
commoners were not permitted to display these architectural
features.[6] The rooms abutting on this public courtyard were
generally occupied by the *ọba*'s drummers and trumpeters, slaves,

---

[1] Detailed descriptions of individual Yoruba *àfins*, together with plans and
photographs, will be found in Ojo, 1966(b).

[2] Ojo, 1966(a), Chapter VI.   [3] Ojo, 1966(b), Chapter III.

[4] P. C. Lloyd, 1962.   [5] Ojo, op. cit., Chapter VI.

[6] Ojo, op. cit., Chapter VI.

servants, and strangers;[1] until recently, they were often the sleeping quarters of casual Hausa labourers.[2] The ǫba, his wives, and other close dependants lived in the inner courtyards.

Frobenius[3] has left us an impressive description of the palace at Ifẹ before the First World War:

The palace of the Oni, whose massive walls meet the eye from whichever quarter one approaches it . . . Its front . . . with the fine open square on which it stands . . . The walls are mighty, over a yard broad at the base, and some eighteen feet high. The widely overhanging roof beams and the verandah covering . . . The mighty entrance is barred by a handsomely sculptured door . . . A narrow porch leads into a large open space . . . spacious, erstwhile court of reception . . . Colonnaded verandahs and passages surround this square, and the entrance to it is exactly opposite the throne . . . We cross the great, old, ceremonial piazza, pass through a doorway, along some passages and enter the first of . . . three small impluvial courtyards to the left. . . . A verandah projecting like a baldachino in the third . . . In front of us there is a recess, with a sculptured door in the centre, to which two high steps, running right along the entire wall, form an approach . . . From there the way leads to [the Oni's] private quarters . . . there is even a modern building in the West Coast style among them . . . Most of the even older walls of the buildings of the Oni's palace are evidently recently stuck on to its quite ancient, solid and firmly constructed foundations. It is improbable that its general plan has suffered any great change in modern times. A wall which fell to pieces was always replaced with one of clay.

But, aside from the new building in 'West Coast style', Frobenius also found evidence that he was already looking at a 'palace . . . shrunken to its original foundations and . . . besides, greatly decayed . . . The holes on which the crossbeams rested are still visible on the inside of its great enclosing walls. Lines of stables and servants' rooms ran along one side, the quarters of the women along the other and armouries, of which only sparse fragments now appear . . .'[4]

Today, the palace at Ifẹ contains, aside from the Oni's modern residence, a public Court, recreation ground, and the Ifẹ Archaeological Museum; and, indeed, many modern ǫbas have built themselves imposing personal houses, sometimes alongside the old àfin, sometimes incorporating it. The forest lands attached to the

[1] Ojo, 1966(a), Chapter VI.   [2] P. C. Lloyd, 1959(b).   [3] Op. cit.
[4] Loc. cit.

palace, on the other hand, have generally shrunk to make room for modern public buildings; Ojo[1] cites the encroachments made on the *àfin* of the Ewi of Ado Ekiti. These started in 1924, when a Native Court hall was erected within the palace grounds; there followed police barracks, a tax-collecting office, the stores of the United Africa Company and two other large commercial concerns, a public reading-room, a post-office plus post-master's house, a garage, a Local Authority school, Ado District Council Office, a Grade A Magistrate Court hall 'and other minor details'! Similar examples could be quoted from most Yoruba towns; the only major exception seems to be Ọyọ, where the palace, though built as a small-scale replica of the fabled original at Old Ọyọ, never had forested land with its walls, so that only minor changes could be accommodated on its territory.[2]

Before the 'storey-house' or *pẹ̀tẹ́sì*[3] made fashionable by the 'Brazilians'[4] in Lagos and Abẹokuta became a widespread form of prestige expenditure, the *ọba*'s palace with its characteristic high gabled thatch was the tallest building in town. Ojo[5] notes that many *ọba*s were concerned lest, with modern developments, their *àfin* should lose its traditional pre-eminence. They themselves were quick to adopt the new styles, as Frobenius' description shows; but they forbade their subjects to imitate them. Up to 1948 no one dared build a 'storey-house' anywhere in the vicinity of the palace at Ado Ekiti; and the Alafin of Ọyọ, having himself roofed his palace with corrugated iron, prevented any of his subjects from doing the same for some considerable time.

Often, too, the *ọba* controlled a further area outside the palace walls. Thus, in Ọyọ, all the compounds immediately adjacent to the *àfin* were occupied by people directly connected with the Alafin in some way: the *Àrẹ̀mọ* or crown prince, the chief eunuch and his lieutenant, the principal slave, and the seventh and last of the Councillors of State.[6] In some towns, members of the reigning *ọba*'s descent group inhabited a special area known as 'the *ọba*'s quarter'; but the land thus occupied is not usually included within the palace area. The somewhat anomalous position of the royal descent group in the political and social structure of Yoruba

---

[1] Ojo, 1966(a), Chapter VI.   [2] Ojo, loc. cit.
[3] This word is derived from the English 'upstairs'. Cf. Beier, 1958.
[4] Descendants of former slaves who returned to Yorubaland from Brazil and Sierra Leone. Cf. above, Chapter I, Section I.
[5] Loc. cit.   [6] Ojo, op. cit.

towns is spatially symbolized by this segregation outside the palace walls.[1]

III

In most Yoruba towns, the main market is located in front of the palace, where the ọba could watch from a reasonable distance the regular assemblage of his people.[2] Major markets could only, in traditional Yorubaland, be created by command of an ọba: their opening was usually heralded by the performance of appropriate rituals by the palace servants on his behalf. Nowadays these are frequently replaced by secular ceremonies.[3] The market is thus, in most cases, both spatially and ritually related to the ọba from whose existence, in Yoruba eyes, the settlement derives its status; or, in the case of a non-metropolitan town, to the bálẹ̀ ọlọ́jà, the 'bálẹ̀ who owns the market'. In either case, it is the ruler's function to preserve peace between the town's component segments, to symbolize its unity: this peace and unity are necessary requirements for market transactions in which strangers meet, but cannot be allowed to quarrel. The situation of the market in a metropolitan town, in the shadow of the palace, clearly expresses its relationship with the focus of political and ritual authority.[4] Burton[5] indeed was struck in Abẹokuta by the fact that markets were to be 'found even under the eaves of the palace'. This contrasts strongly with the situation described by Frobenius[6] for Ifẹ. After speaking of various 'small trading places' along the streets, he says specifically: 'There is no commerce at all in one very important quarter alone ... namely the square in front of the Oni's palace. No one may squat in front of the palace.' Today, people do buy and sell in front of the Oni's palace, but it is true that there is still no large market there: the absence of marketing in the past may have been due to the peculiarly sacred character of the Oni of Ifẹ, and thence of his palace, in the general Yoruba scheme of the Universe.[7]

In Ibadan, on the other hand, where there is no ọba and no palace,[8] the main market, Ọja Iba, has taken over some of the sociological functions of the palace in other Yoruba towns. Ibadan

---

[1] Cf. below, Chapter VI, Section III.   [2] Ojo, 1966(a), Chapter VI.
[3] Lloyd, 1959(b).   [4] Ojo, 1966(b), Chapter IV.   [5] Burton, 1863.   [6] Op. cit.
[7] Cf. above, Chapter I.   [8] Cf. above, Chapter I, Section II.

has many markets,[1] but it is Ọja Iba that remains the centre of traditional life. Every new Olubadan is installed there; it is surrounded by the compounds of earlier rulers, by the principal mosque, and by Mapo Hall, which contains the offices of the modern, main elective, City Council.[2] Since it functions as both a day and night market, Ọja Iba is also, at least for the more traditionally-minded inhabitants of Ibadan,

a centre of social intercourse. On an evening, a young man may attend the market in the hope of meeting a young lady who may appeal to him. He may also attend it to hear the latest in the politics of the city or even of the country, to share comradeship with his friends or even just to feel a sense of belonging. Besides, the market is the terminal point of many festivities in the older part of the city and one often notices a number of happy, dancing groups making their way to the market.[3]

But in Ibadan, where many modern influences have been at work,

the internal structure of the city shows the existence of two city centres —the older centre around Oja Iba and the new one around the railway station . . . The new centre is in many ways the converse of the old. Time and space have here acquired scarcity value often measured in pounds sterling. Trading is no longer an activity of the open space. It is properly housed in buildings whose growing height is one measure of the increasing scarcity of land . . . The central business district . . . performs some modest social functions. But in contrast to the old and traditional Oja Iba market centre, these functions are performed at a price. The dance clubs charge a fee for participation, and so do the cinemas. . . . [4]

But Ibadan, with its multitudinous morning, day, and night markets, quite aside from two eight-day periodic markets,[5] one of them specializing, on alternate market-days, in indigenous cloth and in black soap,[6] is, in this as in so many other respects, exceptional. More usual is the traditional *ọjà ọba* (*ọba*'s market)[7] in front of the palace in the centre of town:

an open clearing with no buildings. Normally trees with widespreading branches provided the shade. Blocks of stones about the size of small stools and smoothed boles of fallen market-trees were used as stools.

---

[1] Cf. Hodder, 1967.   [2] Mabogunje, 1967(a).   [3] Mabogunje, loc. cit.
[4] Ibid.
[5] For the periodicity of Yoruba rural markets, cf. Bohannan and Dalton, 1962. Cf. also below, Chapter V, Section IV.
[6] Hodder, 1967. Cf. also below, Chapter V, Section IV.
[7] Ojo, 1966(b), Chapter V.

Where constructed seats were used, these were made of light wood and raffia poles. Commodities exposed for sale were laid on the ground (yams, cocoyam, cassava, tubers) or in wooden or palm-woven trays (pepper, locust-bean, kolanuts, salt) or in calabashes (beans, cassava flour and yam flour).[1]

Night markets, whose function is primarily to distribute ready-made dishes, cooked meals, and small items of food to people living near the market site, seem (apart from Ibadan) to be mainly a feature of the northern Yoruba towns: Ilọrin, Iṣẹyin, Ọyọ.[2] But most urban markets take place daily, and in their busy gaiety have far more in common with the Ibadan Ọja Iba than with the somewhat dreary respectability of the shopping centre near the railway station.

Like Ọja Iba, most markets in provincial towns are important for celebrations and ceremonies. They have, too, a widely recognized ritual importance: a common feature of Yoruba town markets is a shrine housing a laterite pillar[3] over which cult officials daily pour palm oil on behalf of the whole town. This pillar betokens the presence of the òrìṣà Èṣù or Ẹlẹ́gba, the mischievous trickster deity of the Yoruba pantheon.[4] Èṣù, who is associated with no particular descent group, is specially connected with crossroads and markets, with all commercial transactions, with quarrels and trouble, as well as with uncertainty in general.[5] The presence of his pillar at all major traditional markets[6] may perhaps stand for Yoruba awareness both of the importance of the market and of its special dangers. The ọba's representatives are there to keep the peace; but it is obviously regarded as advisable to placate Èṣù all the same.

IV

Traditional public buildings other than the palace are not usually imposing. Frobenius[7] has indeed left us an impressive description, supported by Carl Arriens's drawing, of the Ṣàngó temple at Agbeni in Ibadan:

---

[1] Ojo, 1966(a), Chapter VI.

[2] Hodder, op. cit. Compare the description of Bida night market, Nadel, 1942. Cf. also below, Chapter V, Section IV.

[3] Wescott, 1962.   [4] Cf. below.   [5] Loc. cit.

[6] A distinction must here be drawn between recognized public markets created by an ọba and the countless sites where a few women will gather to sell their wares.   [7] Op. cit.

The exterior of the courtyard was characterized by some wooden pillars, embellished with carving, which supported the overhanging roof; the doorway, some nine feet in height, was boldly sculptured with figures in relief of a mythological character; . . . On entering, a spacious courtyard met our view in which the intermediate roofs, supported on carved beams, jutted out over a verandah . . . The originality of the building in front of me, whose straggling black façade was broken up with many colours, struck me dumb. A lofty, long and very deep recess made a gap in the row of fantastically carved and brightly-painted columns. These were sculptured with horsemen, men climbing trees, monkeys, women, gods and all sorts of mythological carved work. The dark chamber behind revealed a gorgeous red roof, pedestals with stone axes on them, wooden figures, cowrie-shell hangings.

Already in Frobenius's day, 'the fact that the door no longer hung upon its hinges, but was propped up against the lintel, was significant of decay.'[1] And a modern observer[2] adds:

The external courtyard described by Frobenius seems to have entirely disappeared. The modern temple is crushed in between shops and a shoemaker's room. When dances are held, the dancers jostle around in the cramped space between the vendors' stalls. The disused door has disappeared completely . . . There is an exiguous veranda, on the walls of which hang the sandals made next door.

According to G. Parrinder,[3] there are, in all, some fifty pagan temples and shrines in Ibadan, most of them small and neglected. Among the larger and better known is the temple to Odùdúwà below Ade Oyo:

The temple is built of clay, roofed with iron sheets. There is a veranda outside, on the walls of which are crude sketches of animals, men and women, in red, white, and black wash. A long frieze at the top of the wall represents a snake . . . A door gives off the veranda, and inquirers may be admitted into an inner room in which stand large drums which give their name to the cult . . . A further room, doubtless with an altar, has its doorway covered with a white cloth, and into this the priest . . . alone has the right to enter. Another room is reserved exclusively for men.[4]

In most Yoruba towns, there are small shrines, usually quite inconspicuous, to various òrìṣà; some of these were traditionally held by a single descent group within the town, either on its own

---

[1] Op. cit.   [2] Parrinder, 1953, Chapter II.   [3] Ibid.   [4] Parrinder, loc. cit.

behalf or on that of the whole community. Others were held to belong to the town as a whole. In Abẹokuta, the Olumọ rock constitutes such a shrine; priests from Itoko township offer sacrifices to the deity of the rock on behalf of the whole town. 'Abẹokuta' means 'under the rock'; Olumọ rock is said to 'belong to all the Ẹgba'. All other land in Abẹokuta is claimed by individual segments, townships, or descent groups.[1] In Ibadan, the female spirit of Oke'badan, the hill to which the first founders of the town came[2] seems to fulfil a similar function:

The Orisha Oke [hill spirit] may well be called the titular goddess of Ibadan. When the chiefs of that place were asked what animal or sign they would like as an emblem to figure on the medals to be given away at their agricultural show, they unanimously selected Oke. They had the photograph of a fine-looking woman taken, her breasts exposed and her arms raised towards heaven, as if to welcome her children. A picture of fruitfulness. She is the hill Orisha, connected with fire.[3]

Her shrine, however, 'consists simply of two large pots at the foot of a tree, and some small brick-like stones, all in the open air. Here kola nuts are placed by praying women, at any time of the year, and a bull is sacrificed at the annual festival.'[4]

In Ọyọ, the main temples of the different òrìṣà hierarchies were traditionally distributed throughout the various quarters; the principal temple of Ṣàngó (who, in one of his aspects, is thought of as a deified Alafin of Ọyọ) was in the royal quarter, others in the quarters governed by the different members of the Council of State. Lesser temples of each cult were sometimes set up within the compounds of titled priests; or the priest might set aside one room as a shrine. Most worshippers set up a small shrine in their own compound.[5] In Ifẹ, Frobenius[6] comments upon the dispersal of òrìṣà shrines: 'While, however, several Orisha shrines are situate near every market-place in Ibadan, this is not the case in Ilifé [Ilé Ifẹ̀]. The great and powerful deities dwell near the city walls within the outskirts.' In many towns, some of these shrines traditionally lay in forest areas towards the edges of the built-up land, near the walls or even beyond them: such forested areas, in addition to their use for defensive purposes and as emergency agricultural land to be farmed in siege conditions, tended to be

[1] P. C. Lloyd, 1959(b).   [2] Parrinder, loc. cit; Idowu, 1967.
[3] Bennett, 1910.   [4] Parrinder, loc. cit.   [5] Morton-Williams, 1964.
[6] Op. cit.

used to provide cover for semi-secret religious activities such as spirit-masquerades and the use of bull-roarers.[1] Nowadays, such forested areas have largely given way to modern religious, administrative, and educational buildings;[2] but many towns still have an area of 'bad bush' (*igbó burúkú*) which serves as a sort of spiritual and moral sewer, where the bodies of witches, executed criminals, undischarged debtors and those who died with bodily deformities were formerly thrown without burial. An aura of fear still lurks about such places.

In Ọyọ,[3] Abẹokuta,[4] and the Ijẹbu towns,[5] where the *ògbóni* and *òṣùgbó* associations had great political and ritual importance in the past, these associations have special meeting-houses, *ilédì*; in Abẹokuta, predictably, there is an *ilédì* for each of the constituent townships. These *ilédì* look like small compounds, but are distinguished by their colonnaded entrances; there seems to be a belief that they should ideally have a large open space in front of them for public meetings, but today, what with the overcrowding of the towns, and the decline in the functions of these associations, this is seldom the case.

In Ondo, there were formerly a number of 'title houses' (*ilé oyè*), the apanage of the senior non-hereditary chiefships; these, like the *ọba*'s palace, belonged to an office rather than a person, but in appearance they hardly differed, except perhaps in size, from the ordinary compound.[6] Most of these 'title houses', which were situated near the centre of the town, no longer exist, modern chiefs having preferred to build their personal houses, some on title land, and some elsewhere.[7]

V

We have seen[8] that the main roads of a traditional Yoruba town radiated out from the central area of the palace and market like the spokes of a wheel. These roads, which might be up to 30 feet wide, link the town with other, neighbouring settlements; where they intersect with the town walls, there were, in pre-British days, toll-gates, at which the *ọba*'s officials sat and col-

---

[1] Ojo, 1966(a), Chapter VI.   [2] Cf. below, Section VIII.
[3] Morton-Williams, 1960.   [4] P. C. Lloyd, op. cit.   [5] Ibid.
[6] Ondo compounds are rather small. Cf. below.   [7] P. C. Lloyd, op. cit.
[8] Cf. Section I of this Chapter.

lected toll from travellers, which formed part of the royal revenues. They also formed avenues of access to the centre of the town, along which dancers of various cults might move in procession to the market place in front of the Palace. Frobenius[1] describes the main roads of Ifẹ as

> broad enough to give the stream of agricultural life full play. Here and there they widen out to market places ... Although the principal commercial traffic is transacted on these wide highways, this does not mean to say that business is not done elsewhere. Small trading-places are found in the street of wells, on the road to Ebolokun, the Idena temple and on the way to Ilesha.

It will be remembered[2] that Ifẹ had no 'ọba's market' in the centre of town.

Along these roads, the compounds forming the residential units group themselves in wards or 'quarters',[3] the front entrance of the compounds facing the roads, and the back abutting either on land not yet built up or, more recently, on the compounds pertaining to other quarters. The backs of the compounds might be linked by footpaths, which often formed the boundaries between quarters. The quarter or ward grouped around a road was often, for some purposes, a subsidiary political unit within the town; we have already seen that in such cases the compound of the quarter-chief acts as a focus for the orientation of the dwelling-houses of his kinsmen and other dependants, much as the ọba's palace does for the town as a whole; the quarter-chiefs' compounds themselves looking towards the palace.[4] These quarter-chiefs' compounds, though smaller than the àfin, are generally larger than those of ordinary men, having at least two courtyards.

In a metropolitan town, a quarter-chief's responsibilities may extend beyond the town walls and adjacent farms, to the subordinate settlements lying in that direction, which are often believed to have been founded by men from that quarter. This follows from the fact that Yoruba political structure does not distinguish between urban and State administration.[5]

This wheel-shaped pattern of settlement—roads radiating out

---

[1] Op. cit.   [2] Cf. Section III of this Chapter.

[3] The term 'quarter', long discarded, seems once more to have come into use in post-war West African ethnography. D. Forde and S. F. Nadel prefer 'ward'.

[4] Cf. above, Section I of the present Chapter.

[5] Cf. above, Chapter I, Section V.

from the palace and market, with the quarters grouped around them—can still clearly be seen on the plans of such towns as Ifẹ and Ilẹsha. It is not, however, present in the same degree even in all *ìlú aládé* or metropolitan towns. Thus Ijẹbu Ode comprises over twenty quarters,[1] and Ondo has nearly forty,[2] each with its own chief; and in these towns the quarters, instead of radiating outwards from the centre, form a sort of chessboard pattern, divided by intersecting, approximately rectilinear streets. Here, the compounds—much smaller than those of northern Yoruba-land[3]—line the street, some facing it, while others are grouped in subsidiary courts or culs-de-sac. The pattern is not unlike that of Benin.[4] Quarters are still aligned with reference to the street; pathways running at their backs, rather than the streets themselves, form the boundaries between them.

The contrast between what might be called the 'radial' and 'chessboard' patterns of town settlement extends—in conformity with the Yoruba notion of the surrounding agricultural land as a sort of extension of the town—beyond the town walls. Contrast Types I and III in Lloyd's schematized diagram[5] expressing the relationship between metropolitan town and surrounding kingdom. Type I, exemplified in the Ọyọ and Ekiti towns, presents the same radial appearance as the Ilé Ifẹ̀ town plan. Here 'the boundaries of the compounds and quarters in the town extend into the farms so that, schematically, the farm areas appear as segments.'[6] Plots of land lying within three miles (say an hour's walk) from the town form the *oko etílé* or 'border farms', which are cultivated by men living in the town; beyond that are the *oko ẹgàn*, where distance requires their cultivators to live in small hamlets.[7] But, as Goddard has been able to show in detail for Ọyọ,[8] there is quite an exact relationship between the position of a particular compound in town and that of its farmland, as well as of the hamlets occupied predominantly by its 'allegiant' population.

Type III, on the other hand, resembles the 'chessboard' pattern of the Ondo town plan. Town compounds and quarters do not extend their boundaries outwards into agricultural land; instead, the metropolitan town is marked off from the relatively narrow

---

[1] P. C. Lloyd, 1966. [2] P. C. Lloyd, 1962. [3] P. C. Lloyd, 1962 and 1966.
[4] Bradbury, 1964. [5] Cf. Diagram I.
[6] P. C. Lloyd, 1962, Chapter III. Cf. also P. C. Lloyd, 1966(a).
[7] P. C. Lloyd, 1962, loc. cit. [8] Goddard, 1965.

strip of farmland which surrounds it, and in turn from surrounding subordinate towns and their land.

Lloyd correlates these differences with two corresponding ways of reckoning descent—agnatically in the north, cognatically in the south;[1] and these are also expressed in the differences in size and structure of the residential kin unit, which will be dealt with in the following chapter. It looks as if we were here dealing with two different types of *techniques d'aménagement de l'espace*[2]— almost, indeed, two different *notions* of social space, and, as we shall see in discussing the differences in descent reckoning, of social time as well. If this is so, it would go far to explain other sociological differences which the same author has pointed out between these two types of towns.[3]

Type II is attributed by Lloyd to 'a historical accident, albeit an important one'.[4] It corresponds to the 'new towns', Ibadan and Abẹokuta, where a large population was concentrated from the start in what was at the time devastated country. The newly founded descent groups staked out claims to land over a wide area, and built hamlets there, one of which might serve several descent groups. These hamlets, in contrast to the blocks of land themselves, were not associated with territorial boundaries.[5]

Within the town of Ibadan, on the other hand, land was given out in block grants to military and other leaders, who proceeded to settle there with their retainers and relatives. It was these blocks of land that provided the basis for the older of the present-day quarters; some of them bore the name of the chief prefixed by the most important topographic element, whether a hill (*òkè*), road (*òpó* or *pópó*) or minor market-space (*ìtá*).[6] Since, however, Ibadan chieftaincies, both civil and military, formed part of quasi-bureaucratic promotional ladders, no permanent link was ever set up between chiefly title, descent groups and responsibility for a quarter, as in certain *ìlú aládé*. The situation is, of course, different in Abeokuta, consisting as it does of 'townships'.

In these new towns, in other words, neither the 'radial' nor the 'chessboard' type of settlement pattern have had time to develop before modern pressures, e.g. for the commercialization of land, began to exert their own influence on town lay-out.

---

[1] P. C. Lloyd, 1962, Chapter III; P. C. Lloyd, 1966. [2] Balandier, 1955(b).
[3] P. C. Lloyd, 1959(a). [4] P. C. Lloyd, 1962, loc. cit.
[5] P. C. Lloyd, loc. cit. [6] Mabogunje, 1967(a).

E

VI

Formerly, all Yoruba towns were surrounded by mud defensive walls, often supplemented by ditches; only traces of these remain today. Some towns, such as Ọyọ, Oshogbo, Ifẹ, Ilẹsha, and Owo, are reputed to have had two or more rings of concentric walls, with a strip of forest between them.[1] Clapperton[2] describes the walls of Old Ọyọ as being 20 feet high; the height of the recently excavated city wall at Ifẹ, however, has been estimated at 6 feet, plus a ditch 6 feet in depth.[3] In a different category was the 80-mile-long rampart (ẹrẹdo) surrounding not only the town of Ijẹbu Ode, but its whole kingdom; this was in places about 20 feet high with the adjoining moat 25 feet deep.[4]

The town walls were intersected by the roads radiating out from the centre, at major and minor gates; as we have seen,[5] these served as toll-gates. Ibadan is said to have had sixteen gates at one time, and Abẹokuta twelve.[6]

As we have seen, the walls did not necessarily form the town's legal boundary. Especially is this so in the northern 'agnatic' type of town where there was traditional continuity between land tenure systems in town and countryside, and often, physically, in the blocks of land themselves held by the town-dwelling descent groups: 'the boundaries of the compounds and quarters in the town extend into the farms'. In Ondo, however, Lloyd[7] tells us that the wall and its ditch did until recently contain all the dwelling-houses of the town: inside the wall was the town, and outside, the farms. Moreover, customary law recognized that greater rights could be held in town land than in farm land; the wall formed the boundary, not only between farms and built-up area, but between two different tenurial systems. This corresponds to the difference we have already noted in settlement patterns. The cleavage between urban and rural tenurial system does not, however, appear to have held for Ijẹbu;[8] and even in Ondo, where ultimate rights in farmland seem to have been traditionally vested in the territorial community rather than the descent group, certain descent groups have now claimed an association of their ancestors with several areas of the valuable land on the perimeter of town; with the result

[1] Ojo, 1966(a), Chapter VI.   [2] Op. cit., p. 58.   [3] Goodwin, 1958.
[4] P. C. Lloyd, 1959(c).   [5] Cf. above, Section I.   [6] Ojo, loc. cit.
[7] P. C. Lloyd, 1962, loc. cit.   [8] P. C. Lloyd, loc. cit.

that this land is now considered to be vested in these groups.[1]

In both Ondo and Ijẹbu Ode, the town has now burst out beyond the walls; in each case, there is one new quarter. Lloyd[2] attributes this partly to the fact that the traditional compact 'chessboard' pattern of residence, with its smaller compounds, did not allow for the expansion of population within the town; and partly to the wealth of both these centres, which has led to a greater demand for the standardized plot, facing a main road, which is required for a modern two-storey house.

Elsewhere, although the built-up area frequently extends beyond the old walls, the extensions are mere prolongations of existing quarters. The walls have now outgrown their traditional defensive function; in former times, when a town expanded, its walls were simply rebuilt further outside, their sites thus forming a series of concentric circles. The process can still be traced in the traditions of the recently and rapidly expanded Ibadan, where the original town wall is said to have encircled an area of about half a square mile on Oke Mapo, the southernmost hill of the Oke Rẹmọ range, where Mapo Hall now stands. Ọja Iba market, already referred to, is also located within this area. The town subsequently spread towards the south and west, settlement in a north-easterly direction being impeded by the hilly ridges there.[3]

VII

The traditional standard unit of urban residence among the Yoruba is the compound, of which we have a number of detailed descriptions.[4] Essentially it consists of a rectangular mud structure of adjoining rooms, facing inward on to a common roofed verandah, which in turn surrounds an open space in the centre. The outer wall of mud has one main gate leading into the compound, and may have more; otherwise it is blank. The whole was formerly roofed with thatch, though now corrugated iron or 'pan' is becoming increasingly common. The small, dark rooms opening out on to the verandah are sleeping-quarters; normally one of them is assigned to each 'wife of the compound'; adult married men of the compound, normally members of it by birth, may also have

---

[1] P. C. Lloyd, 1966(c).   [2] P. C. Lloyd, 1962, loc. cit.   [3] Mitchell, 1961.
[4] Fadipẹ, 1939; Forde, 1951; P. C. Lloyd, 1955, 1959 and 1962; Ojo, 1966(a); Schwab, 1955 and 1965; Goddard, 1965.

rooms of their own allocated to them; or, if there is not enough space, may share with their wife, or wives in turn. Unmarried girls, as well as small children of both sexes, normally share their mother's quarters; unmarried youths may have a communal room assigned to them in the compound, or exceptionally a room of their own, or they may share with a father or elder married brother.

These rooms are used only for sleeping and storing personal belongings. Cooking and other daily activities are carried out on the verandah, each woman in front of her own room; she is normally responsible for keeping that part of the verandah clean. The central space is normally used for keeping small livestock; it may contain a well.

Facing the main entrance of the compound is the generally somewhat larger apartment of the compound head, *bálé*. This may consist of two rooms, one of them being used as a parlour for the reception of visitors; it may be distinguished from the rest of the compound by greater elevation. Nowadays the *bálé's* quarters in a prosperous compound often take the form of a 'storey' house of the 'Brazilian' type, loosely incorporated into the general structure of the compound; this may have European-type furniture in the downstairs parlour. Fadipẹ[1] tells us that formerly it was the custom for the sick of the compound to be nursed in the *bálé's* apartments.

Lloyd[2] distinguishes between two types of compound: a larger 'northern' type associated with the agnatic descent structure, and a smaller 'southern' variety housing a shallower, cognatically related kin group. The northern variety he sub-divides into Ọyọ and Ekiti sub-types:

In Oyo . . . compounds were in the past often very extensive (e.g. over 100 feet square), the male members of the agnatic lineage and their families living within a structure which had but one or two gates, the blank outer walls of the various courtyards forming an otherwise continuous perimeter. The open space of the courtyard was frequently very large; the inner roof of the courtyard was supported by a wall which enclosed the verandah. In Ekiti the individual structures were smaller, two or more separate ones forming the compound. The open courtyards were much less extensive (e.g. 20–40 feet square) and the inner roof was supported on posts, often carved, thus leaving the verandah open.

[1] Op. cit.   [2] P. C. Lloyd, 1962, loc. cit.

Both these types of compound are associated with the 'wheel-shaped' or radial lay-out of the northern Yoruba town, with plenty of space between the compounds for their expansion. Fadipę[1] has described how such expansion took place:

When the young men of the compound find themselves short of accommodation, as a result of marriage or because of the prospect of marriage, they put up an additional wing running parallel with the side of the compound, usually the side which faces the entrance. This additional wing will be complete with its own verandah and will communicate direct with the main entrance of the compound. Subsequent extensions are usually made in the same way, so that in some compounds there are three or four of these parallel lines of apartments. This system of extensions, known as *kara*, may be seen at its best in the Oyo-Yoruba town of Isehin[2] . . . More irregularly, addition to the living space of the compound may be made by building on any part of the quadrangular open space in the middle. . . .

He cites this second method as particularly characteristic of Ogbomǫshǫ—a town which received a very large influx of refugee population in the nineteenth century.

In the southern 'chessboard' type of town, however, the individual buildings are much smaller, not only having fewer courtyards but often substituting a small impluvium for the open Ekiti or Ǫyǫ courtyard.[3] This residential pattern is, as we have seen, associated with a different type of descent reckoning, inheritance law, and land tenure. With land rights in towns being vested in territorial units, it is the individual who is granted, by the quarter-head, a site on which he builds his house. After his death, the building passes corporately to all his issue,: but as it is usually too small to accommodate them all, some will have to build their own houses, either nearby or in another quarter. When the owners of these new houses come to die in turn, the cycle recommences. Thus the descent group segments at each generation, each segment being associated with a small amount of house property.[4]

This pattern also goes with the different style in urban expansion. Granted population pressure in both cases, granted also the superior wealth of Ijębu and Ondo—a radial segment can always, where the limiting wall is no longer required for defence, be prolonged indefinitely outwards, and will indeed grow wider as

[1] Op. cit. [2] Alternative spelling of Isęyin.
[3] P. C. Lloyd, loc. cit. [4] P. C. Lloyd, 1966(c).

distance from the centre increases; but a chessboard pattern of settlement can be extended only by adding further squares. This is what has happened in Ondo and Ijẹbu Ode, each of which has grown a whole new quarter to accommodate new housing needs; northern towns have merely, where necessary, prolonged the existing ones beyond the walls.

VIII

Today, the traditional pattern of Yoruba towns is more apparent from a plan or an aerial photograph than to the observer on the ground. Ojo[1] distinguishes three types of architectural growth and change in these towns: a filling up of the pre-contact part of the settlement within the walls, a peripheral expansion outwards, and 'a growth along the vertical', i.e. in the proliferation of two and three-storey houses.

The frequent siting of modern administrative buildings within the palace grounds has already been described.[2] Modern building techniques also made it possible to use interstitial open spaces between compounds and quarters, previously rejected as too steep, or rocky, or marshy for building.[3] Churches and mission schools, on the other hand, were frequently allocated land previously devoted to pagan ritual uses;[4] partly, it would seem, as a sort of ordeal or test of the spiritual strength of the new religion. Thus, in Ado Ekiti, the *Egúngún* (masquerade cult) grove afforded the land for the new buildings of the Anglican Church, the Anglican Girls' Secondary School and the Anglican Secondary Modern School.[5] The same may have been true of the first mosques.

Later, such public buildings had to find room at the periphery of the towns; most Yoruba settlements today are surrounded by a sort of ring of Government and Mission establishments. All this means that, to some degree at least, the palace and market have ceased to be the focus of the town; it has come to look outwards as much as inwards.[6]

Some of this peripheral growth may also, as Ojo[7] points out, be attributed to the Europeans' distaste for the congested centre of a Yoruba town, and consequent desire to build churches,

---

[1] Ojo, 1966(a), Chapter VI. Cf. also Schwab, 1963.
[2] Cf. above, Section II of the present Chapter.
[3] Ojo, loc. cit.   [4] Ibid.   [5] Ibid.   [6] Ibid.   [7] Ibid.

schools, Government offices and residential areas 'in places fairly remote, where an unlimited claim could be made on land, air, peace and quiet.' The Yoruba stereotype for those Europeans with whom he had the closest contact was òyìnbó orí òkè, 'the white man on the hill.'[1]

All these new types of building have greatly changed the appearance of Yoruba towns. Churches, mosques, and some Government buildings are, as much as 'storey houses', part of the 'growth along the vertical'; the traditional even skyline, dominated by the high gable on the ọba's palace, has given way to a highly accidented townscape, in which church tower and minaret combine with iron-roofed, often highly decorated pẹ̀tẹ́si, as well as with the new small rectangular houses and, of course, the remaining compounds. U. Beier[2] contrasts the appearance of a Yoruba town half a century ago, with its 'long, rectangular compounds with swinging grass roofs . . . [and] an appearance of aloof discreetness' with the present-day 'colourful painted cement houses and the "upstair" houses'. He also notes[3] how the 'Brazilian' style churches, and the mosques 'so utterly unlike the mosques of Northern Nigeria and . . . so remarkably like churches' (for the very good reason that most of them were built either by or in imitation of the same craftsmen that built the churches) fit into the Yoruba urban scene; whereas most of the Government buildings 'look rigid, uncomfortable and alien in their surroundings'. Most settlements, even quite small ones, have several churches (generally belonging to different Christian denominations), most of them with one or more schools attached; one or more mosques; sometimes a hospital; and a varying number of modern administrative buildings. In Ibadan, Parrinder[4] counted over fifty churches of varying size, aside from the meeting halls used by some smaller sects; and about 190 mosques.

'Brazilian'-style storey houses, too, which first appeared in Lagos and Abẹokuta, have increasingly spread inland with cocoa-based prosperity. The technique of building these houses, with their balconies, pillars, arches, and porticos, their cement sculpture and relief decorations, and their profiled window frames, was, as their name indicates, first brought by the returned 'Brazilians' around the turn of the century.[5] A handsome house has long been a

[1] Loc. cit.   [2] Beier, 1958.   [3] Beier, 1960.
[4] Op. cit., Chapters IV–VI.   [5] Beier, 1960.

coveted badge of prestige among the Yoruba; but formerly the ideal had been a large, solidly built compound, housing a populous aggregate clustering around the founder's lineage. Since the end of the Second World War, however, there is a fairly exact correlation between any town's cocoa wealth and its proportion of multistorey to one-storey houses.[1]

Marris[2] describes a large 'Brazilian' house in Lagos

built by a wealthy trader about a hundred years ago. It fronted on to a narrow lane, the walls patched with corrugated iron, the windows boarded with cream and black shutters grimed with age. Inside the door on the right, a passage extended past two rooms to an open yard, *where chickens and guinea fowls clattered in their pens.* A second passage facing the entrance led past three more rooms to *a larger yard at the back of the house, where the households cooked, washed and kept their stores.* Sheds lined the two sides of the yard, and lavatories were built into the corner. Inside the passage a narrow staircase gave access to the upper floor . . . On this floor were six more rooms, besides two small anterooms through which they were reached. *Altogether, the house contained eleven rooms, each occupied by a separate household . . . The head of each was a child (or his widow), grandchild or great-grandchild of the original owner of the house.* [Italics mine.]

Both in the composition of the group of inhabitants and in the use to which different areas of the house were put, this large 'Brazilian' house represents an adaptation of the compound pattern to a different architectural style. Such houses are comparatively rare in Lagos; Marris says that they are 'still usual' in other Yoruba towns. In other words, 'Brazilian' house-building may, but need not, involve a smaller unit of common residence.

More frequently, in the interior, the new 'Brazilian' house forms part of the larger compound; it may serve as the residence of its *bálé*, or it may face the street, the compound spreading out behind it, so that only an aerial photograph[3] will show its true relationship to the wider unit. Such a house will normally have been built for the wealthiest member of the old compound; if he is also an educated man, perhaps a Christian monogamist, it may represent an attempt at independence for himself and his immediate family[4]—an independence which does not, however, go so far as to express itself in segregation by distance.

---

[1] Ojo, loc. cit., gives an interesting chronological analysis of the spread of this style of building.

[2] Op. cit.   [3] Lloyd, 1959(b).   [4] Fadipẹ, op. cit.

In some towns, houses with no territorial reference to a parent compound have begun to appear. In wealthy Ondo and Ijẹbu Ode, the new quarter in each town is inhabited by the wealthiest among the citizens; and they have built themselves the fashionable two-storey houses, facing the road.

In Ibadan, where the immigration both of Yoruba and non-Yoruba soon obliged the colonial authorities to plan for new housing estates and regulate building, Native Administration Tax Returns for 1954 showed that, out of 19,000 dwellings of all kinds, only 2,000 were traditional compounds. In the new quarters, salary- and wage-earners not born in the town inhabit smaller, newer houses.[1]

In the remoter savannah towns, however, even the wealthy still build compounds, Lloyd[2] gives an example from Shaki—a house built for himself by the Onishaki (the local ọba) in 1951. It has twenty-seven rooms, arranged around a yard about 100 foot square, each adult man and woman having a separate room, and children sleeping with their parents in the usual compound style. It was inhabited entirely by members of the Onishaki's descent group, with their wives and children.

Even in central Lagos, at the time of Marris's study,[3] 'There were still several large compounds . . . One, for instance, had thirty-eight rooms, the other nineteen, both of one storey and built around a courtyard, in which was dug a now disused well.' In many towns it is possible to see, as in the older districts of Ibadan, examples of the compound in all stages of disintegration, from the old unbroken rectangle of apartments facing inwards on to the courtyard, to a collection of houses of varying size and apparent prosperity, still vaguely grouped around a central open space.[4] The compound's structure is still visible: but the whole has become literally *agbo ilé*—a flock of houses.

Until quite recently, Yoruba towns, essentially homogeneous ethnically, had no special quarters assigned to immigrants. In some towns, such as Iwo and Ogbomọshọ, which received large numbers of immigrants during the nineteenth century, there may be a tradition that the inhabitants of a given quarter are descendants of these immigrants, but such people are by now, for most purposes, regarded as full members of the town.[5] Others were

---

[1] Mitchell, op. cit. Cf. also Beier, 1958.   [2] P. C. Lloyd, 1955.   [3] Op. cit.
[4] P. C. Lloyd, 1959(a).   [5] Op. cit,

absorbed into existing compounds, resulting in the now fairly numerous 'mixed compounds' inhabited by members of two or more unrelated descent groups.[1] Somewhat later, with the spread of Christianity and of opportunities for travel, similar hospitality was often offered on a confessional basis.[2]

Somewhat different is the position of the immigrants attracted to Yoruba towns by present-day economic conditions. These fall, in the main, into two categories: Hausa or Kabba Yoruba labourers, poor and illiterate; and educated men from other Yoruba towns, or from the countryside, who have come to take posts as clerks or teachers. Both groups are regarded, and largely regard themselves, as transient. Hausa labourers are by tradition lodged in the ọba's front palace yard; but Schwab[3] mentions a special small Hausa quarter to the north of Oshogbo, confined to traders and cattle dealers; and the Ibadan municipal authorities found it necessary to build a 'Sabon Gari'[4] for Hausa immigrants as early as 1917—Nupe and Igbirra quarters being added in the 1930s.[5] These ethnic strangers' quarters in Ibadan formerly also contained quite a high proportion of Western Ibo.[6]

The newly arrived educated Yoruba 'strangers' have, in part, fallen heir to the Government Reservation Areas and the mission, school, and hospital staff housing facilities originally set up for Europeans. To some extent, however, they have also clustered together in new 'Foreign Quarters', such as that described by Schwab[7] for Oshogbo. These are made up almost entirely of 'Brazilian' multi-storey houses; the typical Yoruba compound structure is almost totally absent. Such foreign quarters are inhabited typically by Government clerks, teachers, shop owners and employees of European firms, though some of the transient Yoruba labourers may also find a lodging there. But most of the inhabitants of such quarters are in fact better educated and more affluent than the average citizen of their town of employment—a fact which is perhaps even more significant than their untraditional segregation by quarter

[1] Cf. below, Chapter IV, Section II: also Fadipẹ, op. cit.   [2] Ibid.
[3] Schwab, 1954, 1965.   [4] Cf. Cohen. 1965, 1967.   [5] Mitchel, op. cit.
[6] Okonjo, 1967.   [7] Schwab, 1965.

IV

KINSHIP, DESCENT, RESIDENCE, AND NEIGHBOURHOOD

I

WE have seen[1] that the quality of *ará ìlú*, member of a town, is normally acquired by birth into a descent group holding rights in one of the town compounds. The three statuses involved—membership of the town, of the descent group, and of the compound—are thus superposed: they are acquired simultaneously by a single ascriptive criterion, that of birth; and for a man—marriage being virilocal—they tend to remain superposed for life. Indeed, it is this link between descent group and compound, coupled with the fact that a man is a citizen by virtue of his membership of such units, that has led scholars to see the Yoruba town as a 'confederation of lineages', simply linked at the top of the political hierarchy by the institutions of kingship and council.

To see whether this is so, we must examine in detail the social life of the inhabitants of these towns, first in terms of the unit of residence (whose external morphology we have already considered in the previous chapter) and then in terms of those social ties which transcend it. Let us therfore turn first of all to the structure of the group of kin and affines normally inhabiting a compound.

The resident population of a compound can vary enormously, not only over time, as the 'allegiant' population[2] commutes between town and farm-hamlet, but between Yoruba towns with different kinship-and-residence patterns, and even in a single town between one compound and the next. Goddard[3] calculated for his Ọyọ compound (one of the large compounds found in the 'northern-agnatic towns' of Lloyd's classification[4]) a total 'allegiant' population of 204, of whom 85 were considered to have

---

[1] Cf. Chapter II, Section VI.
[2] Goddard, 1965. Cf. above, Chapter II, Section VI.
[3] Goddard, op. cit.
[4] P. C. Lloyd, 1962 and 1966(c). Cf. above, Chapter III, Sections V and VI,

'fixed urban residence'. Bascom[1] suggests for Ifẹ a range of 70 to 140; Schwab[2] found in his Oshogbo sample a variation between 15 and 450; Fadipẹ[3] proposes an 'average' of 40.

Thus, even the smaller compounds usually contain more than an 'elementary' or even a 'compound' family.[4] Since the Yoruba are a polygynous people, their smallest kinship unit is in any case not necessarily the so-called 'elementary' or 'conjugal' family of Western sociology,[5] consisting of father-mother-children, but the non-independent group consisting of one wife in a polygynous household with her children. Yoruba have no word for this group, though they refer frequently to the relationship between people who are ọmọ ìyá, children of the same mother, to one another. We shall here follow Lloyd[6] in extending the term ọmọ ìyá to describe the group of people standing in this relationship to each other; and further in restricting it, as the Yoruba do not, to a woman's children by the same husband.

Children of one father by all his wives stand in the relation of ọbà kan ('one father') to one another (here again, the term will be stretched to cover the group made up by those so related); the ọbà kan group, then, is subdivided into a number of ọmọ ìyá.

Yoruba state that their emotional ties with the mother are much stronger than with the father, relationship with whom is marked by reserve and distance.[7] In agreement with this, the ọmọ ìyá is a far more close-knit group than the larger ọbà kan. A woman's children eat together, and share their mother's sleeping quarters; it is held that 'the children of one mother should never quarrel openly but cooperate closely and not divide property rigidly.'[8] On the other hand, 'between the omoiya ... within the obakan there is hostility, competition and conflict.

---

[1] Bascom, 1942(a).   [2] Schwab, 1965.   [3] Op. cit.

[4] The difficulties inherent in the use of the English common-sense term 'family' to describe specific kin units are notorious, and have led to a number of ranges of classificatory epithets, none of which seems to enjoy general acceptance. The words 'elementary' and 'compound' are here used in the sense assigned to them in the sixth edition of *Notes and Queries on Anthropology*.

[5] For a criticism of the use of 'conjugal family' as a 'basic' unit in social organization, cf. Fox, 1967, Chapter I, Section IV.

[6] P. C. Lloyd, 1962.

[7] In P. C. Lloyd, 1966, it is maintained that the tie with the mother is even stronger among the south-western Yoruba, who have a cognatic descent group structure. For detailed descriptions of the father–children relationship, cf. B, B, Lloyd, 1967, and Levine, Klein and Owen, 1967,

[8] P. C. Lloyd, 1962,

Whatever a father has he must share equally between each *omoiya*; for instance, a father should endeavour to educate well at least one child in each *omoiya*—the mothers do their best to train their other children.'[1]

But at the same time as being a father, a man is, unless all his full siblings are dead, a member of the *ọmọ ìyá* group into which he was born; and in certain contexts, all the groups of *ọmọ ìyá* into which his own children fall will be regarded as forming part of that wider group. Similarly, his remoter descendants, seen from his own point in the line of descent, will fall into the groups of *ọmọ ìyá* corresponding to the children of each of his wives, no further distinction between them being required from his point of view.

The *ọmọ ìyá*, in other words, is not simply a close-knit group in the daily life of the compound, but the frame of reference through which a Yoruba views the structure of the kin group, both for purposes of inheritance and to reckon descent.

As regards inheritance, 'At a man's death most of his statuses— and thus his rights to property—remain within his own *ọmọ ìyá*— a group comprising not only himself and his brothers and sisters but also their children.'[2]

Fadipẹ[3] states specifically that a deceased man's children had no rights in his personal property that could be asserted against the members of his *ọmọ ìyá*; but 'As a rule, the children were left in undisturbed possession of their part of the compound . . . Although in theory the rights of a deceased man's siblings extended even to his own farmland, they nevertheless usually left his children in undisturbed possession of it.' Lloyd[4] suggests that in any case this system of inheritance caused little conflict in the past, when men married later and died younger; a man's children were unlikely to have reached adulthood at his death, and in taking over his property, his junior brothers also took over responsibility for his widows and their children. The ideal at any rate is clear: the largest *ọmọ ìyá* known to the actors remains a unit, and so does each smaller and shallower *ọmọ ìyá* within it.

Both the northern and the southern Yoruba have corporate descent groups associated with rights in land.[5] The northern Yoruba use the term *ìdí'lé* (literally, 'root of the house') to refer

[1] P. C. Lloyd, 1962.   [2] Ibid.   [3] Ibid.
[4] P. C. Lloyd, 1962.   [5] P. C. Lloyd, 1966(c).

to their large agnatic descent groups; the term *ẹbí*, usually translated into English as 'family', may refer to a descent group of
any type or, according to context, a kindred (in the sense of an
ego-centred, non-exclusive group).[1] Rights to land derive from
membership of one's descent group, which is ascribed by birth;
however, agricultural land held in this way cannot, by traditional
law, be said to be transmitted by inheritance. Inheritance does,
however, apply to self-acquired property; and here the general
principle is that a man's property is divided into as many equal
parts as he has wives who have borne him children. Non-divisible
property is held in rotation between these stocks of *ọmọ ìyá*. The
same principle of segmentation operates at higher levels; the
descent group is divided into two or more segments, each con-
ceptualized as having been founded by a child of the total group's
apical ancestor by a different wife. Thus, a chieftaincy title held
by the group rotates among the segments in turn; and if the group's
land comes to be divided, it will be shared out equally between the
segments.[2] In the case of the agnatic *ìdí'lé*, the ancestors of the
different segments are, of course, always described as males; such
a segment is called an *ìsọ̀kọ*.[3]

Idí'lé are generally large groups:[4] membership of 1,000 living
persons (i.e. about 200 adult men) is not unusual in some northern
towns. In such towns, the adult men of the descent groups, with
their wives and children, traditionally live in a single compound,
a series of linked courtyards forming one residential unit;[5] the
descent group corporately holds rights both to the town land on
which the compound is built and to one or more large blocks of
farm land.[6] The group may also hold a chieftaincy title, which
rotates between the segments into which it is divided; in the past,
members were also collectively responsible for the debts of any
of their number. Various diacritical marks, such as worship of a
common *òrìṣà*,[7] food taboos often associated with such worship,
identity of facial marks and praise-names (*oríkì*), further serve to
emphasize the *ìdí'lé*'s unity and distinctness.

Above all, the *ìdí'lé* is an exclusive group. Membership is
determined at conception, when the mother (who normally ob-

---

[1] Cf. Goodenough, 1961.   [2] P. C. Lloyd, op. cit.   [3] P. C. Lloyd, 1955.
[4] P. C. Lloyd, 1955, 1962, 1966(c); Schwab, 1955, 1958.
[5] Cf. above, Chapter III, Section VI; and Goddard, 1965.
[6] Cf. Goddard, 1965.   [7] But cf. below, Chapter V.

serves only the food taboos of her own *idi'lé* of birth) begins to observe those of her legal husband also, for the benefit of her un-born child. And normally, for both men and (for most purposes) women, such membership lasts for life. A man may, indeed, choose to throw in his lot with his mother's descent group, even (in some cases) to the extent of taking up residence in their compound. But while he may successfully 'beg' a piece of agricultural land from his mother's group while still primarily farming with his own, the grant of an area of town land by the mother's group generally im-plies residence with that group, and ultimately absorption into it. So does acceptance of a chieftancy title held in the mother's descent group, which they may have granted to a daughter's son for lack of a suitable candidate among themselves. The chief so chosen will take up residence in the compound of his mother's descent group, and his descendants will probably in time come to constitute a separate segment of it.[1]

But such a choice—not, in any case made usually more than once in any one lifetime—does not affect the essential exclusiveness of membership of agnatic descent groups. Once a man has, for whatever reason, taken up residence in his mother's compound of birth, membership of the group into which he was born will almost automatically lapse.[2]

In south-eastern Yorubaland, however, cognatic descent groups are found,[3] in which land, certain titles, and such hallmarks of descent as facial marks and praise-names, are inherited bilineally. In a recent article,[4] Lloyd classifies these cognatic groups into an Ijẹbu and an Ondo type (though the 'Ijẹbu' type is also found among certain Ondo descent groups). In Ijẹbu, the apical ancestor of the descent group is also the founder either of a village or of a compound or quarter of the town. In this settlement there live at present a proportion of those descended from him in both male and female lines; almost all of the (usually male) household heads claim such descent. All the compounds in the town, and most of the villages, are believed to have been founded long ago; so that the settlement pattern seems to be fairly stable. But the territorial units it comprises, containing in each case only a proportion of the descendants of the founder, are much smaller than the compounds of the agnatic descent groups of northern Yorubaland; thus

[1] P. C. Lloyd, 1966(c).   [2] Ibid.
[3] P. C. Lloyd, 1955, 1966(c).   [4] P. C. Lloyd, 1966(c).

Ijẹbu Ode (population in 1952: 25,000) comprises over twenty small quarters, each containing the compounds of some two to seven descent groups. In such a situation, even where land—and, occasionally, a title—are still corporately vested in the descent group, it is hardly surprising that both compound heads and title holders are overshadowed by the *olórítún* or quarter-head.

In most Ondo descent groups, the situation is still more fluid. As we have seen,[1] it is the quarter-head that grants the individual land to build his house; which is generally too small for all his issue to live in after his death, so that some will have to build elsewhere, quite likely in another quarter. Thus, there is no large core of descent group members resident on the land of the apical ancestor; the latter is not associated with land at all, save perhaps the house he originally built, or its successor on the same site. His descendants live dispersed all over the town, or even elsewhere in the kingdom. Land being vested in the territorial unit (quarter, town or village, or the whole kingdom) rather than in the descent group, the latter segments at each generation: there are groups within groups, and apical ancestors (each associated with a small amount of house property) at each generation. Moreover, descent being traced through both males and females, no group is exclusive; and, over time, a group can easily grow so large that it ceases to be effective as a unit of social organization. Accordingly, chieftaincy titles are not vested in descent groups, but granted by the *ọba* on the advice of his senior chiefs.[2]

In such a system, every person is at birth theoretically a member of as many cognatic descent groups as he has ancestors at the highest generational level known to him. Thus at a mere seven ascending generations (and on the assumption that marriage prohibitions have been strictly observed) he would have 128 ancestors, and belong to the groups descended from each of these. On the other hand, it is clearly impossible for anyone to participate in the rights of, or fulfil his duties towards, more than a few of these groups. In practice, a man will probably identify himself with those groups with which his parents were most closely associated; it is to these groups he will tend to turn in seeking new land or selecting a new residence: and—even in Ondo—he is most likely to have grown up in his father's house, to follow him to the farm, and to participate in the ritual of those groups in which his parents

[1] Op. cit.   [2] Ibid.

were active members. In the circumstances, it is not surprising to find that a majority of men in fact live in the same compound as their fathers' fathers; or that the 'cognatic' groups of the south-eastern Yoruba have a in fact 'a strong agnatic bias'.[1]

Yet, despite this bias, and despite the fact that, through the foreshortening and simplification of genealogies, the effective choice of descent groups is numbered in tens or less rather than hundreds, the individual still appears to have considerable freedom of choice. Moreover, there does seem to be a genuine structural difference between the exclusive and agnatically conceived *idi'lé* of northern Yorubaland, and the more loosely defined, non-exclusive Ijẹbu and Ondo descent groupings; particularly the second type. The difference, from the actors' point of view, would seem to lie in the possibility of multi-membership of the latter; and Lloyd shows that a number of people do exploit these wider and more flexible opportunities of choice.

We have already seen that these two different descent structures correspond, on the ground, to two types of compound, of town lay-out, and of relationships between town and countryside which have been noted above. The segmented *idi'lé* spreading out from an apical ancestor goes with large rambling compounds, with quarters spreading out radially from the centre of town, and with deep blocks of lineage land conceptually continuing the quarters beyond the walls. The smaller compounds of Ijẹbu and Ondo are the material expression of the much smaller cognatic groupings into one of which the individual will insert himself; the quarter and the town itself, instead of extending indefinitely like an ideal genealogy, come to a sharply defined end in space, as the shallow cognatic group does in time. Nor need administrative territorial units be exactly coterminous with descent groups.

As has been noted, the agnatic descent system of the northern Yoruba goes also with a type of segmentary political structure in which chiefs tend to be selected by and out of the members of the descent groups that go to make up each town; whereas, with cognatic descent groups, other methods of recruitment must be employed, notably the title associations,[2] and direct appointment by the ọba to certain offices.[3]

It also seems at least possible that the *idi'lé*, the 'root of the

---

[1] Op. cit. [2] P. C. Lloyd, 1954, 1962, 1965, 1966(c).
[3] P. C. Lloyd, 1966(c).

F

house' stretching back into the past—a type of descent reckoning where the emphasis is strongly on ascribed status—goes also with a certain conservatism. Lloyd[1] notes that the popular stereotype of the Ijẹbu is that of a man dominated by high achievement motivation; which could perhaps be correlated with a social structure which permits the exploitation of varied kin ties. However, the stereotype is not applied to the Ondo, where, on Lloyd's own showing, the social structure is even more permissive in this respect; and, as he himself says, the pushful enterprise generally associated with the Ijẹbu might equally well be attributed to their land hunger, and consequent inclination for trade and emigration.[2] In the absence of satisfactory psychological tests to determine the personality differences, if any, between northern and southern Yoruba, such interpretations must remain highly speculative.

II

In daily life, the ọmọ ìyá group consisting of a woman and her children forms the smallest unit into which the population of the compound can be divided. While the children are small, they share their mother's room; girls normally continue to do so until marriage. A woman also cooks for her own children and (since nearly all Yoruba women have some independent gainful occupation) helps her husband to provide for them.

To Yoruba themselves, the term ọmọ ìyá denotes not a group but a relationship; the smallest unit they recognize within the compound is the ilé tèmi ('house of mine', defined by reference to the speaker), which occupies several adjoining rooms, and may comprise a man, his wife or wives, their children, and perhaps his mother and younger, unmarried brothers and sisters. It thus consists of several groups of ọmọ ìyá with their mothers and common father, plus any members of his own ọmọ ìyá group (including his mother) who may be dependent on him. We shall refer to this group as the domestic family. It may vary from two to forty persons.[3]

The domestic family is, very largely, an economic unit; although in this respect it falls into sub-units corresponding to the different ọmọ ìyá groups within it. It is a man's business to provide, whether by farming or other work, for the subsistence of members

[1] P. C. Lloyd, 1966(c).   [2] Ibid.   [3] Forde, 1951.

of his domestic family; and, as we have seen, to share out any surplus, such as money available for education, equally among the
different groups of *ọmọ iyá* to whom he stands in the relation of
father (*baba, bálé tèmi*). A woman's business, aside from cooking
and cleaning for her own children, and taking her share in the
work of seeing to her husband's comfort, is to supply any 'extras'
she or her children may require. Thus in Lagos, S. Comhaire-
Sylvain[1] notes that it is regarded as proper for a man to present
each of his wives with a new cloth once a year, at Christmas;
other clothes and jewellery she supplies herself. A father will pay
for a child's food, basic clothes, and school fees; but textbooks
and other equipment are regarded as the mother's responsibility.
This division of budgetary responsibilities is not confined to
Lagos.

Some women engage in craft occupations; but most acquire
the extra income required for such expenses by trading. Of
Comhaire-Sylvain's[2] sample of 207 mothers of schoolgirls in
Lagos, 170 worked outside the home (those who did not came
mainly from the higher income groups and from monogamous
households); and of these 170, 144 were traders.

It is customary for a man to give his wife, shortly after their
marriage, a capital sum, which seems to vary between £5 and £50,
to initiate her trading activities; and it is not exceptional for him
to re-finance her once or twice if she fails, assuming that he is
able to do so. Normally, however, the two keep separate purses.
In Lagos, the wife's earnings are often, as Marris[3] has shown, a
form of insurance upon which a man can fall back in time of need.
One of Marris's informants, a mechanic, is quoted as saying of his
two wives, one a trader in cloth and the other a telephone operator:
'At times when I lay down, they carry me up. The reason I can
manage is because I gave them capital to trade. When they see the
money is not sufficient for chop, they help me out until the end
of the month. Or when my money is not enough for me, they might
help me and I pay them back.' An interesting distinction here is
drawn between 'the money'—the necessary budget of the household—to which the informant's wives feel an obligation to contribute in time of need, and 'my money'—i.e. what he used for his
own personal expenses—where he may receive temporary help
from his wives, but must repay them.

[1] Comhaire-Sylvain, 1951.   [2] Ibid.   [3] Ibid.

Such a situation is, of course, more likely to arise in Lagos or Ibadan, where the domestic family may be 'strangers', isolated from the wider circle of kin and from the 'family land' which in other towns provides a cushion in times of economic distress. Nonetheless, this separate economic activity of husband and wife or wives is worth noting as one of the features of Yoruba social life which is congruent with an urban situation—the more so as the wife's work is almost always 'urban' in character—i.e. not only performed within the town, but intrinsically dependent on the large market of cusomers that only a nucleated settlement will furnish.

Within the compound, then, the *ilé tèmi* forms a residential and economic unit, though it is subdivided into its component *ọmọ iyá* for many purposes. In their economic activities, the *bálé tèmi* and each of his wives may individually be members of wider groups, often not recruited by kinship or compound membership (cf. Section III of the present Chapter).

A larger unit, known as *ilé* ('house') or *ilé tìwa* ('house of ours') extending over two to five generations, is based on either the cognatic or the agnatic descent reckoning. In the latter case it may correspond to an *orígun* or *isọ̀kọ* segment; the domestic family or *ilé tèmi* is sometimes called the 'small *orígun*'. Such an agnatically based *ilé tìwa* may consist of a head (*bálé tìwa*), his wives, his younger brothers and sons and their wives and children, his unmarried sisters and daughters, and sometimes the sons of his father's younger brothers with their wives. This is the group to which Fadipẹ[1] refers as the 'extended-family'. It may or may not comprise the whole population of a compound.

Within the *ilé tìwa*, a distinction is drawn between members by birth and the 'wives of the compound' who have joined the unit only by marriage. The first group is known as the *ọmọ'lé* ('children of the house');[2] the male *ọmọ'lé* constitute the permanent agnatic core of the group, but the daughters, who are expected to marry away, are also members. Seniority[3] is the principle by which the compound is governed, and the details of its daily life regulated: among the *ọmọ'lé* it goes by order of birth, among the 'wives of the compound' by order of marriage. A wife is junior to even the youngest child born in the compound before her own entry

---

[1] Op. cit. [2] Schwab, 1965.
[3] Fadipẹ, op. cit.; Bascom, 1942; Schwab, 1955.

into it; senior to all those who, whether by birth or marriage, enter it thereafter.

Many compounds, however, contain a third group of people aside from the *ọmọ'lé* and their wives: the *àléjò* ('strangers' or 'guests'—the word will bear both senses) with their own wives and children. Fadipẹ[1] explains these 'strangers' within the compound as being partly, in former times, the descendants of freed slaves who had been absorbed into the compound though not into the founding lineage (there is no Yoruba ceremony of adoption into a lineage); and partly as freemen who had arrived as refugees from other towns, whether as losers in contests for the *ọba*ship or various chiefly titles, or as offenders who had had to leave their own town as an alternative to the death penalty, and who were received into compounds elsewhere as a matter of hospitality. Later, the number of such mixed compounds increased as a result of the nineteenth-century wars:

The intertribal wars, which entailed . . . wholesale forced migrations, threw friends and their families, or the remnants of their families, together in localities where they eventually settled. The most outstanding example is in Abeokuta, which received several waves of immigration after the first wave which resulted in its settlement had ended. Among the Oyo-Yoruba of Ago Ijoye in that town, for instance, many compounds were founded by two or even more friends; others received men belonging to different families after they had been founded. Many towns which either had escaped . . . these intertribal wars, or had been settled by refugees . . . later received many waves of refugees from other towns and villages which had suffered the ravages of war, and many compounds containing composite elements were the result. Two such towns were Ibadan and Ogbomosho.

Fadipẹ further cites the advent of Christianity—with hospitality often offered on a confessional basis—and 'the greater opportunities for the movement of population which trade and the building of roads generally have introduced' as factors in the generalization of these 'compounds containing composite elements'.

The only difference made between the *ọmọ'lé* of a compound and the 'strangers' within it is that only an *ọmọ'lé* can become *bálé* or head of the compound as a whole; or, where the compound was founded by two unrelated friends in the nineteenth century, the *bálé*ship is transmitted in rotation to their two lines of descendants.[2] Normally, the *bálé* or *olórí ẹbí* (roughly: 'head of the family')

[1] Op. cit.   [2] Fadipẹ, op. cit.

is the eldest male among the *ọmọ'lé*; but the criterion of seniority by age may be displaced by such considerations as good character, wisdom and tact in settling disputes, wealth (necessary to keep up a *bálé*'s duties of generosity and hospitality), and even, Fadipẹ[1] tells us, political prominence in the town.

There are unfortunately no figures documenting either the frequency or the distribution in different towns of these composite compounds; although authorities agree that they are fairly common,[2] and Fadipẹ[3] adds that 'even in those communities which have . . . escape[d] being abandoned or sacked during the intertribal wars . . . compounds which contained more than one extended-family were not unknown before the establishment of British rule.' It seems probable, however, that their number increased as a result of the nineteenth-century wars.

But if the compound may be shared between more than one descent group, a single descent group may also grow too large for its compound, and one segment—usually an *ọmọ ìyá* group with their affines and children—may have to move elsewhere; or the same decision may be the outcome of strain and conflict in the compound. If the separation is amicable, members of the new 'daughter compound' will still feel themselves as belonging in spirit to the descent group and compound of their origin; and, ideally, should build the new compound alongside it. This is practicable in the loose 'radial' settlement pattern of the northern towns; if even the huge compound of Ọyọ can no longer contain the descent group, it is at least likely that 'hiving-off' segments will not go far, but will continue to build at any rate in the same precinct (*ògbón*) or quarter (*àdúgbò*). In the tightly packed chess-board pattern of settlement that corresponds to cognatic descent, an *ọmọ ìyá* group is unlikely to find room to build near its compound of origin: its members, if crowded out, may either re-allocate themselves among their paternal and maternal *ọmọ ìyá* groups; or, if they stay together, build where they can, often on the other side of the town. If this happens, sheer geographical distance will soon enough attenuate the ties between the two compounds.

The situation may be summed up as follows: Yoruba themselves, especially northern Yoruba, like to think of compound and descent group as being coterminous; as the expression 'root of the house' to define the latter clearly shows. This ideal comes nearest to

[1] Fadipẹ, op. cit. [2] Ibid; Bascom, 1942; Forde, 1951; Schwab, 1954. [3] Op. cit.

complete fulfilment in the Ọyọ towns, where the descent group
is reckoned by agnation, and therefore kept together over time:
and where the radial settlement pattern allows room for expansion
in space. Elsewhere, a number of different factors—the effects
of the nineteenth-century wars in some cases, of cognatic descent
and a more compact lay-out in others, in Ibadan and Lagos the
abundance of recent immigrants attracted by job opportunities,
have produced enough deviations from the 'one-compound-one-
descent-group' rule to cast some doubt on its validity as a statistical
norm. Descent group and unit of residence overlap; they cannot
be regarded as strictly coterminous.[1]

III

Whether agnatic or cognatic, and even where it does not form
a residential unit, the Yoruba descent group remains a potent
force in the lives of its members. We have seen that the individual's
status as *ará ìlú* is determined by membership of his descent
group; and that, in a composite compound, the identity of the
core of *ọmọ'lé* is maintained by that group's exclusive rights to the
headship of the compound. In the north, moreover, the patrilineal
ìdí'lé asserts its corporate nature also by the transmission of a
number of identifying characteristics; members of a patrilineage
share facial marks, food taboos, *oríkì* or praise names, devotion to a
particular *òrìṣà*, and traditionally, a single craft occupation. The
ìdí'lé is here also the group in which both land and political titles
are held.

Further south, where the *ìdí'lé* loses its identity, these attributes
and possessions are transmitted by other channels. The same
facial marks are, in Ijẹbu and Ondo, shared by all *ará ìlú* of a single
town, only the royal lineage bearing additional distinguishing
scars; *oríkì* and food taboos, along with land and priestly titles,
descend through women as well as men; political title and *òrìṣà*
affiliation, as well as the newer crafts practised in these richer
towns near the coast, are organized along associational lines.[2]
In other words, powerful interests which in the Ọyọ and to a lesser
extent the Ekiti towns are kept within the descent group and serve
to strengthen it, here look beyond it into the wider community
constituted by the town as a whole.

[1] Cf. Schwab, 1965.   [2] Cf. Chapter V.

This contrast is, naturally, over-simplified; it would be truer to say that the social and political structure of every traditional Yoruba town was a delicate, variable balance between its component descent groups with their sectional interests and those elements making for town unity (represented, at one level by the ọba, and at another by the associations which, in southern towns, assume many of the functions performed by the descent groups further north). It is legitimate to present the balance as tending to favour the descent group in the north, the town in Ijẹbu and Ondo; but even in the Ọyọ towns, the descent group is subordinate to the town in the sense of having no history before its arrival there: at most, the descent-group's myth may mention the town of its origin. Conversely, even in Ijẹbu Ode and Ondo, one or two of the highest political titles were always vested in a descent group, and others, in principle assigned by ọba or association, showed a tendency to be 'absorbed' by a descent group that had managed to restrict them to its members for a couple of generations. Today the increased value of land, whether for cocoa or building, also tends to stiffen the structure of the descent group in these towns:

The building of modern houses in the towns has created permanent rights . . . Slowly Ondo men are becoming aware that similar rights might be claimed over farm land, and especially over commercially valuable sites . . . To the west of the town . . . rumours that a new road to Ijebu and Lagos will pass this way have led many men to recollect that their great-grandmothers farmed hereabouts! As the built-up area extends it begins to encroach into proper farms; here the descent group currently farming the area is usually recognized, at least by prospective purchasers, as the owner of the land with the power to sell it as building plots . . . One might generalize that while land has little scarcity or commercial value it will be described as communal; but as soon as it becomes valuable, the descent groups currently using it will begin to claim rights amounting to full ownership.[1]

But, whatever the balance, in different Yoruba towns, of the individual's allegiance between sectional descent group and wider groups coterminous with the town, the loyalties and obligations of kinship everywhere remain both wide and strong. Conceptually, as we have seen, the groups of varying extension and depth to whom such loyalties and obligations apply, are seen as ọmọ ìyá

[1] P. C. Lloyd, 1962; cf. also Schwab, 1965.

groups; and 'the children of one mother should never quarrel openly but cooperate closely and not divide property rigidly'.[1] Where descent group and compound are co-extensive, such unity is expressed in the informal compound meeting, where matters affecting the lives of its members are discussed under the *bálé*'s presidency; on certain occasions, the *ilé tìwa* may also assemble as a religious group, to pay honour either to genealogical ancestors or to its *òrìṣà* patron.

But even where the wider descent group is scattered over several compounds throughout the town, a surprising degree of cohesion persists. The extreme example of dispersal is, of course, Lagos, where even the *ilé tèmi* is often prevented, by sheer congestion, from living together.[2] Yet Marris[3] statistically documents the close relations that prevail between spatially scattered relatives.

Of his sample of central Lagos householders ('all the households ... who lived under the same roof, "ate from the same pot" and kept house together ... in a group of streets at the heart of the slum clearance area'), only 16 per cent had their mother living in the same building, 3 per cent their father, 29 per cent a brother and 9 per cent a sister of the same *ọmọ ìyá*. Yet 38 per cent stated that they saw their mother daily, 48 per cent a brother, 27 per cent a sister (but only 7 per cent saw their father daily, which probably reflects, among other things, the greater social distance of that relationship). 70 per cent of the sample habitually gave financial help to relatives; the average monthly amounts varied from under £1 (16 per cent) to over £6 (11 per cent) the largest group giving between £1 and £2.

These are informal contacts. But 52 per cent of the sample attended 'family meetings' up to three times a month, a further 9 per cent up to eleven times a year. Such meetings, aside from serving, as do traditional compound meetings, as forums for discussion of members' affairs, often channel financial contributions; in those towns where the wider kin group is scattered, they serve to hold it together and keep it alive. The frequent kinship celebrations—weddings, funerals, naming-day ceremonies, welcomes to young relatives returned from study abroad—also express such solidarity; which is further externalized by the womenfolk, or sometimes both sexes, donning the *aṣọ ẹbí* or 'family cloth'; a habit costly as their purse can buy, the same for all and chosen

---

[1] P. C. Lloyd, op. cit.   [2] Izzett, 1962.   [3] Op. cit.

by common agreement some weeks in advance. A group of such women dancing, all in identical handsome wrappers and blouses and smartly knotted head-ties, perhaps with a hired drummer to accompany them, is one of the most characteristic sights of a Yoruba town.

In sophisticated circles, 'family meetings' are often formalized on the model of English committee procedure; the group often has a literate secretary and a common purse or even a bank account. The most elaborate organization along these lines is that described by Lloyd[1] for a large, prosperous, and highly educated kin group in Ondo, which has gone to the length of drawing up a written constitution:

The association is open to any member of the family and its purpose is to 'foster relationship between the five families, i.e. segments of the group, so that they can unite for the progress of the families'; an executive committee of which the *olori ebi*—the eldest member—is chairman, is elected to represent the five segments; Secretaries and Treasurers are appointed . . . Members are entitled to financial benefits from the association when they marry, take a chieftaincy title, die, or send a son to England for education. Land vested in the group can only be sold by the executive committee. The association manages a school on its own land. Although Ondo political chieftaincy titles are (with one exception) not hereditary, this kin group endeavours to ensure that one or perhaps two of the most senior titles are always held by members of the group; this they achieve by supporting the campaigning for their own candidate whenever a title falls vacant.

Such organization was, apparently, exceptional in Ondo at the time when Lloyd encountered it; but the idea enjoyed general approval.

Fadipẹ[2] also describes how small disparate segments of the same *ìdí'lé*, together in the same town, will fuse into a single segment:

When two or more individual families belonging to the same extended-family find themselves fellow immigrants in the same town, even when they are not in close geographical contact with one another, they generally combine to constitute . . . a branch of the extended-family in that town, with the oldest member of the combination acting as the head. Such a combination acts in absolute independence of the main body left at home. Many such fragmentary extended-families in Lagos . . .

[1] P. C. Lloyd, 1959; cf. also P. C. Lloyd, 1962.   [2] Op. cit.

carry on as though, for all practical purposes, they were the entire extended-family to be found anywhere.

This tallies with what we know of the lack of interest of members of a descent group in the history of their descent group before it arrived at its town of settlement, and gives an illuminating picture of how large descent groups may have been formed in each town in times for which we have no record. The possibility of such fusion seems, however, to be correlated with geographical proximity; Marris[1] records the greatly decreased attendance at 'family meetings' of those members who had been rehoused at Suru Lere by the Lagos Executive Development Board's slum clearance scheme, and who were isolated from their kin by the sheer distance of the new estate from central Lagos and the consequent transport costs.

One further instance of the vitality of descent group values is provided by the 'Brazilians'[2] who arrived in Lagos and Abẹokuta after several generations in Brazil or Sierra Leone, and who in some cases, appear to have 'succeeded in re-establishing contacts with some members, though not with all, of their extended-families'.

IV

It follows from what has been said that, in the northern towns, the large, segment-shaped quarters along the towns' major roads will largely be composed of compounds linked by a recognized agnatic relationship between their members. In such a situation, political responsibility for the quarter will also devolve upon an office held in the descent group in question; modern territorial voting procedures hardly affect such a situation.

In Ondo and Ijẹbu, the quarters are smaller and may contain compounds belonging to more than one group. Here territorial political authority is quite separate from authority over a descent group; we have seen that traditionally the quarter-chief, who overshadowed the heads of the descent-groups inhabiting the quarter, was chosen by the ọba in consultation with his senior chiefs; this meant in practice that the quarter-chiefs, like other political title-holders, were chosen within the ògbóni-type associations. Nowadays, they, too, are elected territorially; which means in

[1] Op. cit.   [2] Fadipẹ, op. cit; Biobaku, 1957; Verger, 1953.

practice that the candidate of the largest descent group will win.[1]

Historical developments have given Ibadan a less coherent quarter organization than the majority of Yoruba towns, and Abẹokuta a more highly developed one. In Ibadan, the titles of the hierarchically promoted political chiefs carry no special quarter responsibilities or powers. In Abẹokuta, on the other hand, the situation is complicated by the internal political structure of the sectional 'townships' of which the settlement is composed, each of which has its own chieftaincy and association system.[2] The five sectional ọbas[3] appear to function more or less as quarter-chiefs, with the exception of the Alakẹ himself, who, as already stated, seems to be more of a *primus inter pares* than a true symbol of town unity after the style of more traditional ọbas. The sectional ọbas are supplemented in the government of the town as a whole by 'general titled chiefs' whose offices, like those of the Ibadan chiefs, are based on the military organization required by nineteenth-century conditions.

In the northern towns, the quarter was thus more or less coterminous with the maximal descent group, and had the same degree of cohesion. Elsewhere, though the quarter seems to have had considerable political importance, no very great social solidarity seems to have obtained between its inhabitants. Fadipẹ[4] notes the casualness with which the territorial boundaries between quarter and quarter—as distinct from those between compound and compound—were delimited; and certainly there never seems to have been anything like the intricate quarter-based politico-ritual organization described by D. Forde for the Yakö.[5] One has the impression that the traditional àdúgbò, considered as a territory, was a somewhat prosaic administrative unit, less important in the values and attachments of its inhabitants than descent group, compound, association, or ìlú.

The situation seems, however, to be rather different in the new 'foreign quarters'. Schwab[6] finds in Oshogbo that

in the Foreign Quarter the ties of neighbourhood are a significant source of interaction. The area is characterized by one or more nuclear families living in single modern dwellings. Although most of the people living in the Foreign Quarter are Yoruba, few have operative kin ties in Oshog-

[1] P. C. Lloyd, 1962 and 1966(c).   [2] P. C. Lloyd, 1962.
[3] Cf. above, Chapter I, Section II.   [4] Op. cit.
[5] Forde, 1964.   [6] Schwab, 1965.

bo to fall back upon for support in the routines and crises of life. Most are better educated, have more skills, and are wealthier than the average person in Oshogbo. The social as well as physical separation of this section of the Oshogbo population has promoted close and strong neighbourhood relationships.

Schwab contrasts this situation with that prevailing within the traditional core of Oshogbo, where 'kinship or *omole* ties virtually preclude other ties based merely on physical proximity'.[1] In the new 'foreign quarters', in other words, it looks as though a genuinely new basis for social interaction was coming into being.

But membership of descent group, compound, and quarter do not, in any case, account for more than a part of the Yoruba town-dweller's interests. Many others are catered for by a multitude of associations of various kinds, which, at many different levels, cut across residential and kinship boundaries.

[1] Schwab, op. cit.

V

INTEREST GROUPS AND ASSOCIATIONS

I

MacIver[1] defines an association as 'a group organized for the pursuit of an *interest or group of interests* in common'.[2] Such groupings may, but need not, be face-to-face; their membership will normally transcend the units of kinship—but even where it does not, the criterion of membership is no longer being kin, but the specific common interest of the members.

The abundance and variety of associations in Yoruba town life reflect the same qualities in the interests served by them. These include both modern and traditional economic, political, and religious interests, as well as purely social and recreational ones.

Associations serving economic interests can be subdivided into those concerned with production, those concerned with distribution and trade, and those concerned with the accumulation of capital.

Political and religious interests formed in the past an undivided cluster, as indeed they do in many non-Western societies. The *ọba*'s was among other things a ritual office; and Bascom[3] records that, upon asking one of his informants, an Ifẹ chief, 'What are the duties of a chief?' he received the answer: 'To make festivals for the *òrìṣà*'. The older associations we shall be describing under this heading, therefore, whether *òrìṣà* cult groups or closed associations, can best be defined as politico-ritual; though it should be understood that the two elements, the political and the religious or ritual, are not always present in the same proportions. With the coming of colonial rule, the political functions of these various associations largely lapsed, and in so far as the associations themselves still flourish, it is almost entirely as religious and social groups. At the same time, new

---

[1] Op. cit.   [2] Italics in the original text.   [3] Bascom, 1944.

associations have evolved to cater for these political interests which did not devolve upon the official institutions of colonial and post-colonial local government; and the spread of Islam and Christianity has called forth new associations based on mosque and church. The more recent of the associations grouped under this heading can therefore be divided, as the older ones cannot, into the political and the religious.

As for associations serving mainly social and recreational interests, these are represented chiefly by the voluntary social clubs known as ẹgbẹ́, which seem to have developed out of the traditional age-sets whose name they bear. The associations primarily serving economic, political, and religious interests sometimes also have recreational aspects; what distinguishes the ẹgbẹ́ is that they usually have none but social and recreative functions.

II

Associations serving interests of economic production fall into two main categories; the first comprises work groups operating mainly in agricultural situations, and which therefore need not concern us here. Of these groups, the àró was based on the relationship between members of the same age-set; the ọwẹ̀ on the obligations of sons-in-law to work for their father-in-law at certain specific tasks.[1] One of these was house-building, now organized by entrepreneurs and carried out by paid specialists.[2]

The second type of association organizes urban production, both of goods and services, into specialized craft occupations. We must here distinguish between an older type of organization, connected with traditional craft specialists, and a modern type, evolved in response to the different organizational needs set by the new crafts that have appeared in the last half-century.[3]

Yoruba have a large number of traditional craft skills, of which some are declining as a result of recent changes, whilst others, such as the weaving of costly traditional gowns, seem to have taken on a new lease of life from the changes in fashion brought about by nationalist politics and independence.[4]

Most of these crafts appear to be fairly ancient. In the days when Ibadan was known as the 'city of sixteen gates' it was also

---

[1] Fadipẹ, op. cit.   [2] Cf. below.
[3] P. C. Lloyd, 1953(a).   [4] Ibid.

the 'city of seventy blacksmiths' (today, A. Callaway[1] has counted 246). We know that Yoruba slaves were already prized for their skill in weaving and dyeing by the rulers of Nupeland in the 1840s.[2] Such crafts were, too, specifically urban, not only in that they are in fact practised in the towns, but in that the degree of economic specialization which they imply requires the market facilities that can only be afforded by large, dense clusters of population. The smaller population centres (around 5,000 souls) have at most two or three local craftsmen, and these are not usually full-time specialists, but rather farmers who do a few emergency jobs for their neighbours in their spare time.[3] A. H. Leighton and T. A. Lambo[4] noted the dependence of Ẹgba villagers on Abẹokuta for specialized goods and services. People would go to town to 'buy clothes, engage a tailor, visit a hairdresser, or seek the aid of a carpenter, smith or healer'. This essentially urban dependence on specialists for the production of various goods and services is, of course, congruent with the pattern of 'commuting' between farm-hamlet and town compound, with the typical Yoruba contempt of 'the bush' and 'bush people', and indeed with the whole complex of Yoruba attitudes towards towns and town life. Goddard[5] has recently pointed to the fact that, for all the dependence of Yoruba towns on their rural hinterland, the excess of food produced on the farms is not taken to town to sustain the urban-dwelling members of the descent-group; it is sold, first in the periodic rural market to middlemen, and then to women who retail it in the town market, often after some further preparation; and it is in the town market that townsmen obtain their food.

Indeed, Fadipẹ[6] derives the whole of Yoruba craft diversification from the combination of the nucleated settlement pattern with the traditional sexual division of labour in which men grew the food and women prepared it for consumption. In farm settlements, he reasons, every woman had to process and conserve food for her own family. But in towns, the same necessity does not obtain; there is both the opportunity and the incentive to specialize: 'There one woman takes maize as her raw material, and specializes in preparing it for consumption in one of about half a dozen different forms in which it is consumed. Another specializes in preparing the same raw material in still a different form.

---

[1] Callaway, 1967.   [2] Nadel, 1942.   [3] P. C. Lloyd, op. cit.
[4] Leighton, et al., 1963.   [5] Op. cit.   [6] Op. cit

Another woman takes one kind of beans for her raw material, and prepares it for consumption . . . Each of these occupations is a full-time job.'

This somewhat Durkheimian derivation of craft specialization from sheer population density is, of course, speculative; but it is true that most crafts are practised in town[1] and that those concerned with the preparation and sale of food (with the exception of butchering, a modern occupation) are still in the hands of women. So are dye-making and the dyeing of cloths—two separate occupations—pottery, and a number of cosmetic arts. Weaving is a feminine speciality in some areas (Ekiti), a narrow vertical hand-loom being used. In Qyọ, on the other hand, weaving is a masculine occupation, performed on a horizontal loom worked with both hands and feet. In Shaki, both sexes weave.[2]

As for men's crafts, those already mentioned by Clapperton[3] in the early nineteenth century include: blacksmith's work (manufacture of bolts, pins, stirrups and bits, hoes and cutlasses, axe-heads, several types of bells, chains, and ornaments); smith's work in brass and lead; carpentering (including both the manufacture of domestic utensils such as bowls, mortars and pestles, and the carving of ritual images); calabash-dressing; leather-working; leechcraft and herbal medicine, combined with magical techniques; surgery. There were also ritual specialists of various types, drummers and bards[4] generally attached to the ọba's court, and those who made a living by selling the drinking-water from wells dug within the compound.[5] Callaway[6] adds: 'Baskets were fashioned from palm leaves and cane from waterside areas. Mats and hats were woven from grass and plant fibres. Black soap was made from palm kernel mixed with ash, and later from cocoa pods . . . Beer was brewed from plantain and banana; palm wine was tapped from the palm tree in the same way as is done today.'

Fadipẹ[7] points out that this economic specialization was 'horizontal' rather than 'vertical', i.e. the division of labour was not between successive stages of transformation from raw material to finished product, but between the different fairly simple techniques

[1] Goddard, op. cit.   [2] P. C. Lloyd, op. cit.   [3] Op. cit.
[4] For a description of the conditions under which this trade is plied in the case of ijalá-chanting, cf. Babalọla, 1966, Chapter IV.
[5] One of the finest 'Brazilian' houses in Lagos is still called 'the Water House' because it is said to have been built on the proceeds of this sort of transaction.
[6] Op. cit.   [7] Op. cit.

G

whereby a limited stock of locally available raw materials could, by the use of equally simple and local tools, be transformed into a number of different and exchangeable end-products. There was thus no differentiation, in principle, between 'rougher' and 'finer' trades, occupations requiring greater or lesser skill. To use Durkheim's terminology,[1] the division of labour that has grown up in the material and moral density of Yoruba towns is 'elementary' rather than 'complex'. In the same way, within the town itself, production and sale remained largely in the same hands; the only exception being agricultural production, where the farmer's wife marketed the foodstuffs grown by her husband. (Inter-town trade, of course, always required middlemen, and its increased volume has almost certainly swollen their numbers.)

This mode of economic specialization does not, either in techniques or capital, require large units of production. The skills involved are, like agricultural skills, transmitted within the units of kinship and residence. In pre-British times, the *iwòfà* system of debt-peonage meant that occasionally children pawned by their parents for service into another compound would learn the craft practised by their masters; Johnson[2] indeed claims that

The system is used also [i.e. in addition to being a method of paying a debt or raising capital] for apprenticeship. A man who wants his son to learn a particular trade would put him under the craftsman for the purpose, and obtain from him a certain amount of money; the master, wishing to get his interest out of the boy will see that he learns speedily and well, so as to be of some use to him.

The *iwòfà* system, was, however, made illegal under colonial rule; so that on the whole traditional craft skills passed from father to son and mother to daughter.

In the case of women's traditional crafts, the combination of mother-to-daughter transmission with virilocal marriage means that adult women in the same compound rarely practise the same craft. Spinning, weaving, the cosmetic arts, and the preparation of food are practised privately and at home; potters, dyers, and dye-makers tend to congregate at public work places, but each woman attends to her own job, and there seems to be no organization in pursuance of common interests.

For masculine crafts, transmission from father to son tends to

[1] Durkheim, 1964.   [2] Op. cit.

result in specialization by compound. Traditionally, the descent group held rights both in a block of farmland and in a town compound; not all compounds had a craft specialization but, where this was the case, an individual member could to some extent choose which of the group's two occupations—farming or urban craft—he would predominantly follow; though a prosperous craftsman might have a farm as well, worked by junior relatives, or by slaves and debt pawns acquired through his craft gains. Or where, as in Ondo and Ijẹbu, the individual could in any case choose between several kin groups as regarded his main affiliation, one of the factors of his choice might be a desire to follow the craft practised by one of the groups, rather than to farm with another that might have surplus land to allocate.[1]

In Ọyọ country, large compounds of blacksmiths and male weavers are common; ideally, the craft, like the compound itself, is identified with a lineage or a major segment thereof. Often such lineages claim descent from an ancestor who migrated from Old Ọyọ; if such claims are founded on fact, it would indicate the existence of considerable craft specialization in that vanished metropolis. Woodcarvers, and also drummers and praise-singers (two aspects of the same occupation) are likewise organized in compounds; the latter appear to be a speciality of Ọyọ country, the tradition of praise-singing being perhaps correlated with the strength of lineages.[2] In Ekiti towns, such craft compounds are poorer and smaller; weaving is generally a women's craft, carried out individually, and drummers and bards do not exist as specialized crafts.[3]

In those villages where an occasional craftsman, e.g. a part-time blacksmith, serves local needs, such a man will not usually be a member of a specialized descent group of this type. He is more likely to be a local man who does emergency work to oblige neighbours, and who will train only one of his sons to succeed him. Neither will a town descent group send out one of its members to supply village needs; there is a strong feeling that the craft should be 'kept in the compound'.[4]

Within such craft compounds, actual production processes are carried out within very small units, each consisting of a man with

---

[1] P. C. Lloyd, op. cit. Cf. also P. C. Lloyd, 1966(c) and Schwab, 1965.
[2] Babalọla, op. cit., Chapters II and III.
[3] P. C. Lloyd, 1953.   [4] Ibid.

one or two assistant-apprentices (generally younger unmarried male dependants, whether brothers or sons). No wider co-operation is required; though kinsmen practising the same craft in the same compound perform small casual services for each other, there is nothing corresponding to the Nupe lineage-based *efakó* craft unit.[1] A traditional craftsman, like a farmer, has a responsibility to train his sons and give them a start in life; this, for the traditional craftsman working in his own compound, involves the provision of training, the first set of tools, and bride-wealth for the son's first wife. A young craftsman is likely to 'leave' his father earlier than a farmer's son; though this involves neither ritual nor residential separation, nor any great enhancement of status.[2]

In craft-specialized compounds as in others, the *bálé*'s word is law:[3]

His authority extends to all matters affecting the craft industry as well as the social life of the lineage. At the same meeting the craftsmen will decide about their marriage disputes, farmland, prices, the maintenance of high standards of work, or the repair of the common workshop . . . There is no division in the minds of the craftsmen between their social and economic activities . . . The structure of these organizations was the lineage structure, the lineage meeting was the craft meeting; the craft head was the compound head, the oldest man in the lineage.

Despite this patrilineal ideal, however, craft training did, even in the past, sometimes descend to the son of a daughter of the compound; it was felt in such cases that the boy 'must have craft-blood in him'. The training, however, was still familial in character, no fee being charged; but these exceptions to the patrilineal transmission of a craft may, along with the institution of *iwòfà*, have paved the way to the non-kin-based organization of apprenticeship in modern crafts.[4]

Those crafts for whose products there is a large and constant demand (e.g. blacksmiths) are in fact unlikely to be confined to a single descent group or compound: thus Iwo's forty blacksmiths were in 1953 organized into six compounds.[5] In this case, the *bálé* of one of the compounds concerned acts as head of all the craftsmen in the town or even the district concerned—e.g. in channelling the relations of the craft corporation with the *ọba*,

---

[1] Nadel, op. cit.   [2] P. C. Lloyd, op. cit.   [3] Ibid.
[4] Cf. below, Section III.   [5] P. C. Lloyd, op. cit.

to whom a tribute in kind was often due in the past. Normally, the writ of such a craft head is coterminous with that of the ọba (an exception occurs in the case of calabash-carvers, whose craft is said—like others—to have originated in Ọyọ and been brought elsewhere by descent groups migrating from that town; but in this instance the Ọyọ craft *bálé* still has jurisdiction over the calabash-carvers of Iwo and Ibadan, his authority being seen as analogous with that of a descent group head). Such a craft head was rarely a titled chief, though he did enjoy some privileges, including direct access to the ọba; most craft heads bore titles that reflect the basically familial organization of the crafts, e.g. *baba alágbèdẹ*, 'father of the blacksmiths'. Such titles were generally kept in a single lineage, the practice being justified by saying that the original title had been granted by the ọba to that lineage.

Meetings of craft members took place regularly every 16 days or four market-weeks[1] (nowadays the European month is more often used as a period) in the compound of the craft head; they discussed only matters affecting the craft. Such inter-compound meetings were more common in some professions than in others; e.g. among blacksmiths (perhaps, as Lloyd suggests,[2] because of the military importance of their craft), hunters (who also functioned as police and night-watchmen, and as *ijalá*-chanters[3]), and wood-carvers. Other trades, such as weavers, drummers, and herbalists seem to have confined themselves to the compound unit of organization.

Craft compounds seem to be distributed all over town; Yoruba towns have no 'craft quarters' such as exist in the towns of northern Nigeria.

Some craft-specialized groups unite in traditional *òrìṣà* worship. Thus, smiths, hunters, and woodcarvers have a special devotion to Ògún,[4] the *òrìṣà* particularly connected with iron, which is important in their crafts (in this capacity, Ògún has been inherited as patron by such modern occupational groups as mechanics and lorry-drivers). Other craft groups seem to have had *òrìṣà* patrons less explicitly connected with the nature of their work. 'In both cases the deity is regarded as beloning to the lineage and . . . rites . . . are carried out by the *bálé*.'[5]

---

[1] On the periodicity of Yoruba market-weeks, and the system of time-reckoning associated with them, cf. Hodder, 1962.

[2] Op. cit.

[3] Babalọla, 1966, Chapter II.

[4] Ibid., Chapters I and II.

[5] P. C. Lloyd, op. cit.

Certain traditional crafts have weathered recent changes surprisingly well. A survey[1] carried out in Ibadan in 1961 and 1963 showed the existence of 246 blacksmiths' shops, mostly still owned by members of the same lineages and clustering around the original blacksmithing area. Apprentices were mostly young relatives of the master craftsman, and were generally living in his house. However, 'in some cases the old blacksmith's yard has been transformed into a modern foundry producing such items as photographers' stands, barber's chairs, iron bedsteads, iron chair frames, and a wide variety of farm tools. Here are the beginnings of a light engineering industry.'[2] Spinning, weaving, and àdìrẹ dyeing are also still carried on in the same Ibadan compounds: 'close together in Oke Oluokun and Oke Foko and less closely together in Oja Iba'[3] traditional methods still being used.

But

the more traditional crafts . . . are not expanding at the same rate as the newer, more mechanised industries. The oldest businesses in Ibadan are found among the goldsmiths, weavers and blacksmiths; in some cases the businesses were inherited and the dates of their establishment are not known . . . There are few partnerships. Some craftsmen, however, form loose cooperative groups to buy materials jointly and to share work.[4]

On the whole it would appear that, although traditional crafts still manage to hold their own in the greatly changed environment offered by Ibadan, the old craft association, based on the lineage or the compound, has largely been eroded away. It is the more modern crafts that have managed to organize themselves in a pattern suited to the new conditions.

III

'Brazilian'[5] and British cultural influences, together with the new prosperity created by cash cocoa and the improvement of communications, have brought a number of new crafts to Yoruba towns. The 'Brazilians' brought the technique of building two-

---

[1] Callaway, op. cit.   [2] Ibid.
[3] Ibid.   [4] Ibid.
[5] The term 'Brazilian' is here used to include, not only the Yoruba-descended liberated slaves actually returned from the New World, but also the Creolized 'Aku' Yoruba of Sierra Leone (cf. Banton, 1957; Biobaku, 1957).

storey houses, and with it, house-building as a specialized occupation, or rather group of occupations: wall-makers, plasterers,
painters; to these were added a new type of sawyer-carpenters,
now differentiated from the old inclusive groups which not only
made doors and roof-beams, but household utensils and religious
images as well. Tailoring as a specialized occupation seems to
have been a 'Brazilian' import also; nowadays, sewing machines
are used and there are sempstresses as well as tailors. Shoemaking
owes something, not only to changes in fashion produced by
cultural influences and growing prosperity, but also to the possibility of obtaining abundant leather from northern Nigeria.
Barbers using scissors and comb, washermen, bicycle repairers,
and mechanics are also among the new craft specialists; public
letter-writers (who often act as 'bush lawyers' in drawing up
deeds, conveyances, and the like) could perhaps also be included
here, since their occupation seems to carry a similar status to that
of the properly manual crafts. A whole group of occupations has
emerged by specialization within the old blacksmiths' craft;
there are tinkers, gunsmiths, silversmiths (in some towns separately
organized, in others belonging to the blacksmiths' organization),
and goldsmiths who have diffused from the original home of that
craft in Ijẹbu Ode.

Today, most Yoruba towns are, like Ibadan,

alive with the activities of craftsmen . . . tinsmiths hammer out metal
cases and containers in intricate tones and rhythms. A tailor on the
veranda of his house sews the seams of an *agbada* (traditional gown) on his
treadle machine. At the side of a main road, a carpenter and his apprentices are sawing boards and building the body of a *bolekaja* (a passenger
and produce lorry). A mechanic works in an area under the trees
between two buildings; his apprentices cluster round the vehicle being
repaired.[1]

In Ibadan, it has been possible to document the approximate
chronology of the establishment of modern crafts.[2] After the old-
established goldsmiths, weavers, and blacksmiths,

Tailors and carpenters form the next wave, with some businesses dating
from the 1920s. Enterprises that were not found before 1940 include
corn-milling, printing, photography and, surprisingly, tinsmithing.
Ninety per cent of the small businesses have started since 1945; 75 per

[1] Callaway, op. cit.   [2] Ibid.

cent since 1950 . . . Explanations for this can be found in the business optimism during the . . . fifties resulting from high government expenditure on construction works, and from high returns to the cocoa farmer. Of the few businesses started in 1961 and after, 10 photographers and 33 dry cleaners predominate.

These crafts resemble the traditional ones in that production techniques are still fairly simple and do not (except in the house-building trades and carpentering) require the work of more than one man at a time. Disposal, too, is still largely in the local market. However, whereas the tools of traditional crafts were cheap and made locally, those required for the new occupations are nearly all imported (mainly from England) and are comparatively costly. Thus, a shoemaker will need leather, needles, and blocks; a laundryman, an iron heated by burning charcoal; a bicycle repairman, tools for mending punctures. A carpenter's set of tools cost about £5 in 1953;[1] so did a barber's equipment of combs, clippers, razors, etc.; while the cost of a sewing machine was as high as £25.

The cost of such equipment effectively precludes the setting up of a labour unit larger than the technology of the craft requires; and this, as we have seen, remains very small except for builders and carpenters. Nonetheless, when the new crafts first appeared, demand for their products, in the general climate of increasing prosperity, expanded rapidly; accordingly, there was room for a great many practitioners. Even Iwo, a large (100,000 in 1952) but poor and backward town on the northern fringes of the wealthy cocoa belt, had in 1953 about 400 tailors, 120 carpenters, 80 barbers, 50 shoemakers, and 40 goldsmiths.[2]

The rapid introduction of these new skills, coupled with the large and immediate market for their products created by cocoa prosperity, posed a number of new problems. There was no ready-made machinery, such as specialization by descent group and compound provided in the more long-standing crafts, for the transmission of skills and the recruitment of new practitioners; no craft-compound *bálé* or town craft head to settle disputes, maintain standards of workmanship or regulate relations with the political authorities. Moreover, most of the practitioners of the new crafts were young, too young to have sons of a suitable age for

---

[1] P. C. Lloyd, op. cit,   [2] Ibid,

training so as to perpetuate the traditional mode of transmission of skills.

In response to this situation, the new urban craftsmen evolved an original type of organization which, while fulfilling the economic functions of the compound-based organization of traditional crafts, in structure and constitution resembles the *ẹgbẹ́* social clubs.[1] English-speaking Yoruba often use the term 'union' to refer to these modern craft associations, although they differ both in aims and structure from trade unions as known in industrial countries: 'There are unions of corn-millers, bakers, tailors, mechanics, shoemakers. (Such unions are also familiar in trading,[2] and even include an Association of Worn Out Tyre Traders).'[3] Lloyd[4] has given these associations the name of 'craft guilds' by analogy with European medieval craft guilds, which these Yoruba associations do in some respects resemble. This seems a more appropriate use of the term than Nadel's,[5] who uses 'guild' for the *efakó*-type of craft unit recruited by descent.

Membership of these guilds is both unrestricted and compulsory: all practitioners of a craft within a given town must join the appropriate guild. This includes 'strangers'; those who are only in the town for a short time join on a short-term basis. In Iwo, where Lloyd[6] made a special study of such guilds, his informants told him that infractions of this rule were exceedingly rare: there had been one case in 1930, and the *ọba* had expelled the offender. The guild head or President (*baba ẹgbẹ́*, 'father of the association' or simply *bálé*), is, in the more conservative Ọyọ towns including Iwo, either the oldest craftsman or the longest established in the town; except, apparently, in those guilds where most of the members are themselves young. In Ekiti towns and further south, he is more likely to be elected by the guild members on the basis of personal qualities or achievement. The secretary is normally the most fully literate member of the guild; there may also be a treasurer, but there is not usually any great proliferation of offices, such as has been noted in other types of African urban associations;[7] the reason is probably that the guilds are strictly economic in function, so that neither membership nor office

---

[1] Cf. below, Section XI.

[2] Cf. below. Some authorities consider that the market-women's associations provided a model for the modern craft guilds. Cf. P. C. Lloyd, 1967.

[3] Callaway, op. cit.   [4] Op. cit.   [5] Op. cit.   [6] Op. cit.

[7] Banton, 1957; Balandier, 1955(a).

carries any great prestige in the town. It is noteworthy, even so, that though the office of *bálé* may be ascribed by age or seniority in the craft, it is in no case ascribed by birth into a descent group, or even by membership of the town: even a stranger may become craft *bálé* or secretary if his experience or ability seems to warrant it.

The rule that all practitioners must be guild members includes apprentices and journeymen as well as established masters (*ọ̀gá*) with apprentices of their own. Indeed one of the chief functions of the guild is to regulate training in, and access to, the craft concerned. Training is by apprenticeship against a fee paid by the apprentice's father; access appears, so far, to be unrestricted, the number of apprentices a master takes being limited only by his prosperity.

Since production units, because of the cost of equipment, remain small, the main work relationship is that between master and apprentice. It is a personal, face-to-face relationship, but essentially a transient one: most apprenticeships last from three to five years, the usual age of entry being about 16.[1] This contrasts with the long slow training given in an old-time craft compound, which started as soon as the growing boy was able to do a few odd jobs for his father; moreover, the modern craft workshop is more likely to be in rented accommodation than in the master's familial compound.

Despite its removal from the kinship sphere, however, the master-apprentice relationship is quite unlike that of employer and employee in a factory: not only because of the smallness of the unit and the consequent intimacy of contact, but also because the apprentice has every hope of becoming, in the not-too-distant future, a master with apprentices of his own. Callaway[2] notes that

A general rule emerges: the greater the capitalization of a firm, the greater the likelihood that the master–apprentice relationship will approximate to the apprentice-contract conditions of government and of the large firms, particularly in money payments from the master to the apprentice. Examples . . . are found among the printing establishments, the modern blacksmiths' and mechanics' workshops, and the improved furniture works.

More usually, the guild regulates the rates of apprenticeship fees or premiums; these are often on a sliding scale varying

[1] Nowadays in Ibadan, over half the apprentices have completed at least primary schooling (Callaway, op. cit.)
[2] Ibid.

inversely with the length of the apprenticeship. The reason for this is that the boy becomes more useful to his master the longer he stays, and, until the termination of the apprenticeship, all his work belongs to the master.[1] Thus in the Iwo Bicycle Repairers' Union, the fee in 1953[2] was £3 for 6 months, £2 for a year and £1 for 2 years; no fees being payable for an apprenticeship of 3 years or more. (This recalls the *ìwòfà* system under which payment was made, or a debt remitted, by the master to the boy's father). In theory, the guild is responsible for seeing that apprentices are well-trained; they are not allowed to change masters casually. Disputes arising out of the relationship are referred to the guild. At the beginning of apprenticeship, a contract covering fees and conditions (in accordance with guild regulations) may be drawn up between the master and the boy's father by a public letter-writer; the master then presents the new apprentice to the guild meeting for registration. The apprenticeship is concluded by a small 'freeing' ceremony, for which the boy's father invites the guild members to his home and entertains them with beer or palm wine, kola, and cigarettes; he also usually provides his son with his first set of tools (in accordance with a father's traditional duty of setting his sons up in life, whether in farming or urban occupations). In some trades, however (carpenters, goldsmiths), the master may provide the tools. The guild head blesses the new journeyman, and he or the secretary reads the guild laws to him. No clear distinction is made between the statuses of journeyman and master: a master is simply a journeyman grown rich enough to own more than one set of tools, and therefore to employ apprentices.

The guilds also control prices of workmanship in a given town (owing to under-capitalization, the customer generally pays for the raw material as a separate item). These may be adjusted upwards for a rich client or downwards for a friend, but only within certain limits; such control is generally possible to maintain within a given town. The wages of a journeyman working for a master after the completion of apprenticeship are also regulated by the guild; they depend both on the type of work and on whether or not he uses his own tools; but no large class of tool-less craftsmen has so far arisen.[3]

[1] P. C. Lloyd, op. cit; Callaway, op. cit.   [2] P. C. Lloyd, op. cit.

[3] Even in Ibadan, 14 per cent of those employed by modern craft entrepreneurs are 'in some form of journeyman or employee relationship with the master'; the rest are apprentices (Callaway, op. cit.).

Craft guilds are also supposed to be responsible for maintaining standards of workmanship. This is acknowledged to be a problem, chiefly because of unrestricted access and the lack of a clear distinction between journeyman and master. Even the end of apprenticeship involves no test of skill; there is nothing corresponding to the 'masterpiece' of the European craft guilds. Nor is there any inspection by the guild authorities; the only sanction appears to be the censure of fellow members.

Disputes, both among guild members (e.g. over 'work-stealing') and between these and their customers, also fall within the province of the guild authorities. The sanction here, if a guild member is held to be in the wrong, is a fine, which is spent on beer for the other members. On the other hand, members are protected against unreasonable customers, the *bálé* if necessary taking the case to court on their behalf.

The *bálé* in general represents guild members in those of their relations with authority which arise out of their work. He is responsible, for instance, for bringing members before the tax assessment committee, ensuring that a fair assessment is made, and that the tax is thereafter paid. Like the traditional craft *bálé*, he enjoys direct access to the *ọba*, though like him he holds no political office or right of membership in the town's ruling Council. Appeal from a guild *bálé*'s rulings lies direct to the *ọba*, the ultimate sanction being expulsion from town. The modern guild pays no tribute in kind to the crown, since taxation is now compulsory and the *ọba*'s salary is paid out of taxes; but the *ọba* may order work from guild members without paying for the craftsmanship; though, like other customers, he pays for the raw materials.

As a sample of guild organization the rules drawn up in 1945 by the literate secretary of the Iwo Carpenter's Union[1] may be quoted:

1. To meet every 8 days [a week in the Yoruba reckoning].
2. To meet from 10–12 a.m.
3. To fine a member 1s. if he is 20 mins. late.
4. A carpenter who starts work on a house must pay the *Bálé* 1s.
5. A carpenter who steals another man's work [i.e. seeks to obtain contracts on which the other has defaulted] must be fined £2 10s. 0d.

---

[1] P. C. Lloyd, op. cit.

6. A carpenter who goes to the house of a deceased person [i.e. to seek an order for a coffin] must be fined 10s.

Guilds thus regulate entry into a craft occupation, exercise variable degrees of control over training, standards of workmanship, and economic rewards, restrict competition, exercise a measure of social control, and represent members in matters arising out of their occupation. They do not provide political representation for their members, nor offer in any other sense an alternative form of social grouping to those provided by descent group or compound; nor do they offer their members any form of social security or financial benefits, or function as social clubs for them. The former function, where organized beyond descent group or compound, is performed by a type of association known as *èsúsú*;[1] the latter, by the voluntary social clubs also called *ẹgbẹ́*, which, though they share with the guilds a generic native term and certain organizational characteristics, are quite different in function and atmosphere.[2]

The guilds appear to represent a 'grass roots' development; they were not organized from above, either by traditional *ìlú* government or by the British colonial authorities. Parallel developments have arisen in Calabar and elsewhere in the former Eastern Region of Nigeria. The idea may have been carried inland, with the crafts themselves, from the towns near the coast: Lagos, Abẹokuta, Ibadan, Ijẹbu. The first Iwo guild, formed in 1925, organized a craft of 'Brazilian' origin, the carpenters; the second was that of the goldsmiths, a skill known to have originated in Ijẹbu Ode.[3]

Nearly all guilds are coterminous with the town in which they are organized. The most notable exception is the Motor Transport Union, with headquarters in Ibadan, a guild of lorry owners and their employees, which formerly regulated fares and freight rates for the entire Western Region.[4] The explanation here probably lies in the essentially inter-town nature of the work involved.

The strongest guilds seem to be those pertaining to occupations which necessitate a co-operative effort: notably the house-building trades. The weakest organization is among tailors: there are too many of them, each with an expensive machine to

[1] Cf. below, Section VI of the present Chapter.   [2] Cf. below, Section XI.
[3] P. C. Lloyd, 1959(a).   [4] Ibid.

amortize, and only just before Christmas or Sallah (the main Muslim festival) are all of them likely to be in work.

The transition from the traditional to the modern type of craft organization represents a change-over from a situation in which craft occupations, though urban, were still transmitted, like a stake in land, from father to son, to one in which craftsmen are recruited and trained on a non-kinship basis, and work relationships, though still face-to-face, are based on contract. Such relationships are no longer all-embracing or multiplex but in Wirth's sense[1] 'segmental'; they concern a situation corresponding to only a limited part of a man's life.

At the same time the organization of the new crafts allows the individual to choose his own occupational role—a freedom strictly limited in traditional craft organization. In Ondo and Ijẹbu towns, indeed, the potential area of choice was, even for traditional crafts, rendered somewhat wider by the existence of alternative kin groups with which a man might elect to cast his lot. This tradition of looser recruitment may, with the cocoa-based wealth of these towns and the probably earlier emergence there of the modern guilds, partly explain the far higher proportion of craftsmen among the adult male population: according to the 1952/3 Census, Ijẹbu Ode (population 28,000) had 19 per cent to Iwo's 8 per cent in a population of 100,000. Conversely, 68 per cent of Iwo's adult males were farmers, as against only 20 per cent in Ijẹbu Ode. It is on the basis of occupational structure that Lloyd[2] calls Ijẹbu Ode and Ondo 'more urban' than the Ọyọ towns.

In other words, the proportion of urban craftsmen in the population of a town is not directly correlated with the size of that population. In Ibadan 65 per cent of the adult men were farmers in 1952—a proportion which, along with its lack of the *ilú* type of government, explains its description as a 'city village'. The proliferation of craft occupations seems rather to be correlated with wealth, a cognatic type of kinship and the corresponding shift of emphasis from descent group to association as a framework for craft organization.

V

We have already noted[3] the central position occupied by the

---

[1] Op. cit. Contrast Durkheim's 'segmentary' (Durkheim, 1964).
[2] P. C. Lloyd, 1959(a) and 1962.   [3] Cf. Chapter III, Section III above.

main market-place in the traditional Yoruba town plan. This corresponds to the great importance of trade in traditional economic and social life, an importance which the introduction of coined money, improved communications, and cocoa prosperity have certainly done nothing to diminish—although, of course, the nature of trading has changed to some extent. With agriculture and craft production, it constitutes the third mainstay of the Yoruba economy.

Town markets must be distinguished from rural ones, which operate in various smaller localities with 4-, 8- or 16-day periodicity, different 'market weeks' being so calculated as to set up a 'ring' of markets in different places, thus enabling a trader to visit each in turn.[1] Within each 'ring', there is some degree of commodity specialization; and there also seems to be some specialization between the five 'rings' surrounding Ibadan, which supply farm produce and other locally produced commodities to the large urban population.[2]

Ibadan itself, with its multitudinous markets,[3] is of course exceptional; quite aside from the many morning, day, and night markets, it also has two periodic markets, one of which still bears traces of its rural origin. Both are held at 8-day intervals; they take place on successive days, so that Ibuko market always immediately follows Oje market day. But whereas Ibuko remains primarily a wholesale collecting point for foodstuffs, Oje market is nowadays very much a specialized market for indigenous cloth. Up to the middle 1930s it was like Ibuko in being primarily a collecting and distributing centre for food crops and the products of various craft industries; and a small part of it still functions in this way. But in the late 1930s, people from Iṣẹyin, Oshogbo, and Ọyọ came to settle nearby and introduced into Oje market the products of their traditional weaving; and gradually the trade in Yoruba cloth came to dominate the market.

But Oje is a specialized market in a unique way, in that the indigenous cloth 'fair', as it is usually called, takes place only every 16 days, i.e. every other market day, while on the intervening market day Oje operates as a specialized 'fair' for Yoruba black soap. So that, whilst Oje is, strictly speaking, an 8-day market, it operates as a dual-purpose specialized market, each of two

---

[1] Hodder, 1962 and 1967.   [2] Hodder, 1967.
[3] Ibid. Cf. also Chapter III, Section III above.

products of local craft industries—cloth and black soap—dominating on alternate market days.[1]

This degree of specialization is, on the whole, rare in Yoruba urban markets. Most towns have at least one daily all-purpose market; Ibadan and some of the northern Yoruba towns have night markets[2] as well, which, more than others, specialize in selling cooked food. The women buy the raw materials for this— maize, yams, rice, cassava flour, beans, palm oil, firewood, leaves for wrapping—from the morning feeder markets and large day markets; and may spend the rest of the day transforming them into àkàrà, èkọ, èbà, dùndú and other delicacies. Or they may simply break up their purchases of fruit, cigarettes, or kola into small units for resale at 1d., 3d. or 6d. a unit.[3]

Where there is a night market, the commercial importance of the town can often be gauged by the development of this kind of trade. For instance, Ilọra has two day markets and a night one; but the latter is small and sluggish because of the competition of the much larger one in nearby Ọyọ.[4]

The antiquity of Yoruba markets is documented by Clapperton,[5] who describes that of Old Ọyọ:

In returning we came through the old market which, though nearly sunset, was well supplied with raw cotton, country cloths, provisions and fruits, such as oranges, limes, plantains, bananas and vegetables such as small onions, chalotes, pepper, grown for soups; also boiled yams and acassous. Here the crowd rolled on like a sea, the men jumping over the provision baskets, the boys dancing under the stalls, the women bawling and enlisting those who were looking after their scattered goods ...

The traditional pattern of trade seems to have been largely internal to the political unit formed by a town and its agricultural hinterland; though the Landers,[6] in the first half of the nineteenth century, met 100 wives of the Alafin of 'Katanga' (Old Ọyọ) trading for him as far afield as north of Ilaro. The pattern and volume of this traditional long-distance trade seems to have been largely determined by the slave-trade; many famous markets collapsed after the end of the nineteenth century wars and the beginning of British rule, which finally enforced the termination

---

[1] Hodder, op. cit; Aremu, 1963.   [2] Cf. above, Chapter III, Section III.
[3] Hodder, op. cit.   [4] Mitchell, op. cit.
[5] Op. cit.   [6] Lander, 1832.

of the latter.[1] Meanwhile, modern 'legitimate trade' based on tropical vegetable produce spread slowly inland from Lagos; in most districts, it really only began to gather momentum with the introduction of cash cocoa; near the coast wealthy middlemen appeared somewhat earlier.[2]

At present, the markets offer, not only locally produced food-stuffs and craft products, but also imported goods, both from other regions of Nigeria and from Europe. Thus, the Hausa-speaking areas of the north send down leather, citrus fruits, kola-nuts,[3] as well as cattle on the hoof *en route* for Lagos, some of which are slaughtered on the way as and when market opportunities offer.[4]

There is, in addition, a considerable volume of internal trade between different parts of Yorubaland. In the case of Oje 'cloth fair', already mentioned,

The cloth comes from Ilorin, Oyo, Iseyin, Ede and Oshogbo, and the market is attended by up to 1,500 traders from as far away as Ghana to the west, Ilorin to the north, and Enugu to the east. The two main types of cloth are *ofi* (locally woven cloths) from Iseyin, Oyo, Ogbomosho and Ilorin districts, and *adire* (traditional patterned fabrics) from Oshogbo and Ede. From Oje the cloth goes into other Ibadan markets and through a chain of intermediaries to other parts of Yorubaland and beyond. . . .

The local weavers in Iseyin, Oyo or Ilorin have their work very much tied to the Oje market circle. Most of them are full-time weavers who work only to the orders of Oje market traders; so that their incomes from the weaving industry and the extent to which they have time for occasional farming depends on the demands of Oje market.[5]

The black soap 'fair' which alternates with the cloth market draws from a smaller area; mostly the palm-oil producing centres in the vicinity of Ibadan, such as Akanran, Araromi, Lalupon, Lagun, Egbeda and Jago.[6] Again, in addition to its cloth, Oyo sends down yams, maize, bananas, dried meat, calabashes, and some iron work into the cocoa belt, where they are paid for with money earned from the sale of that crop; dried fish (together, of course, with imported goods) travels up from the coast; the region west of Abeokuta supplies Lagos with such foodstuffs as maize and cassava.[7]

---

[1] Newbury, 1961. [2] P. C. Lloyd, 1958. [3] Cf. Cohen, 1966.
[4] For a description of how this *ad hoc* slaughtering and the consequent meat trade function in Ibadan, cf. Cohen, 1965.
[5] Hodder, op. cit. Cf. also Aremu, op. cit. [6] Ibid.
[7] Forde and Scott, 1946.

H

The markets also act as centres for small-scale produce buyers (of cocoa and palm kernels). These 'pan buyers', as they are called from the local measure of volume used, are the first link of a chain which goes through as many as three or four increasingly large-scale middlemen until it reaches the licensed buying agents that sell at controlled prices to the Cocoa and Palm Kernel Marketing Boards. These licensed buying agents are, in the case of cocoa, either private firms or the Association of Nigerian Co-operative Exporters (ANCE); the system of prompt payment on declaration of grading, instituted by the Marketing Boards during the war, has tended to favour small Yoruba firms, since not much capital is required. Each of these employs a number of local intermediaries, either as middlemen proper or as commission agents, who in turn use sub-buyers known as 'scalers' (because they use weighing machines). 'Scalers' operate at town markets, buying from 'pan buyers' or from the 'runners' who visit farmers in remote areas. 'Pan buyers' and 'runners' tend to specialize in either cocoa or palm kernels; but most intermediaries deal in both.[1]

This complex pattern of trade is, in part, quite highly specialized. In the smaller urban markets, traditional craftsmen still largely sell their own wares; and locally produced foodstuffs of vegetable origin, whether raw or cooked, are, in accordance with the traditional sexual division of labour, largely in the hands of women. Even in Ibadan, women remain the chief retailers of consumption goods, including fish and cloth; but in supplying the markets of most of the larger cities, the profitable middleman's trade is now largely done by men, often through a very extended network. Thus, for Ibadan,

Travelling merchants, each attached to a group of traders specializing in one or two particular commodities, collect and bulk the foodstuffs from periodic markets or other marketing centres and transport them by lorry or train into Ibadan's Gege-Oritamerin market where the goods are deposited at the stores of individual wholesale traders. The goods are then sold to bulk purchasers in bags and standard measures of one kind or another. Whereas most of the travelling merchants are men, most of those selling in the market itself are women.[2]

For the Oje 'cloth fair' too 'Most of the selling is wholesale, often on a credit basis, and the larger wholesale traders—some 300 of them—are all men.'[3] It is most often women, however, who actu-

[1] Galletti et al. 1956.   [2] Hodder, 1967.   [3] Ibid. Cf. also Aremo, 1963.

ally sell the cloth (whether indigenous or imported) to consumers. 'Pan buyers' are about equally divided between the sexes; but again, middlemen dealing on a larger scale are generally male.[1] Imported hardware is a male speciality; so are butchering and the sale of meat, whether locally produced or imported from the north.[2] This division of labour, between male wholesalers and female retailers, would seem to be traditional, based perhaps on the rural system of sexual specialization, in which the man grows the food and his wife or wives process and market it. Formerly at Abẹokuta, Ifẹ, and Ijẹbu Ode, guilds of male traders held monopolies of imports, both from Europe and from other Yoruba towns; such goods were bought wholesale and distributed to women retailers.[3] Nowadays, it is quite usual for both sexes to travel up and down from the coast with their goods, and women are beginning to be important in the long-distance cloth trade.

We may accordingly classify Yoruba urban interest groups especially concerned with markets and trade into the following main categories:

  (i) Market-women's guilds.
 (ii) Guilds of male traders, both local and concerned with long-distance trade.
(iii) Trading partnerships (with reference particularly to long-distance trade).

Market-women's guilds are described by Lloyd[4] as having a structure similar to that of the craft guilds,[5] for which they may have provided the model.[6] The most detailed study published so far is that made by S. Comhaire-Sylvain[7] for Lagos. On the basis of a 1950 survey, Comhaire-Sylvain states that of 60,000 Lagos women over the age of fifteen, 29,600 were traders of various kinds; about 8,000 of these were market-women holding permits for stalls (since there was much illegal speculation on market stalls, the actual number of market-women was probably considerably higher). These women were organized in different associations according to their specialities (e.g. fish, *gàrí*, yams, cloth); the sectors were spatially segregated within each market. Most highly organized was the fish sector, where all transactions passed through a woman known as the 'fish broker'. Shellfish, on the other

---

[1] Galletti *et al.*, op. cit.   [2] Cf. Cohen, 1965, and Comhaire-Sylvain, 1951.
[3] Bascom, 1955.   [4] P. C. Lloyd, 1953.
[5] Cf. above, Section III of this Chapter.   [6] P. C. Lloyd, 1967.   [7] Op. cit.

hand, were separate: the mussels known as *ìṣére* were a feminine speciality and their sale regulated accordingly, while trade in the *ìṣán* variety was free to all. Meat remained in the hands of men; a few Ibo women dealt in it, but no Yoruba women. The guilds, which controlled prices, were organized largely on a gerontocratic basis, though with considerable allowance for personality and achievement. They had recreational as well as strictly professional and commercial functions. A Market Women's Party had existed since 1944, and was able to exercise considerable political pressure.

Fadipẹ[1] further mentions the existence, 'in most towns', of an association of rich women, but does not give details; such an association might have been based on the more prosperous women retail traders in the markets. It may have been identical with the *ìyálóde* society mentioned by Abraham[2] for all Ẹgba townships, and which certainly seems to have been associated with authority in the markets. *Ìyálóde* was the title of the head of this powerful association; it seems to have been a civic title conferred by the *ọba*. The famous nineteenth-century *Ìyálóde* of Abẹokuta, Madam Tinubu,[3] was the niece of *ọba* Akitoye of Lagos; the trade network controlled by her was so powerful and extensive that she was able to equip the entire Abẹokuta army with guns against the Dahomeyans.

Guilds of male traders may be subdivided into the traditional *pàràkòyí* association which exercised social control in the markets, having first-instance jurisdiction over disputes and cases of theft occurring there;[4] and the recently constituted guilds of butchers and small-scale produce buyers, which are similar to the craft guilds.[5] The *pàràkòyí* has disappeared except in Abẹokuta,[6] its functions of local control having passed to modern local Government authorities.

The traditional male guilds controlling long-distance wholesale trade to certain towns have already been mentioned; they appear to have withered away in recent times in favour of smaller-scale partnerships. It is not clear whether or not they were connected or articulated with the *pàràkòyí*.

Trading partnerships tend to be informal and loosely structured: 'connections' would perhaps be a more descriptive term. The

[1] Op. cit.   [2] Abraham, 1958.   [3] Biobaku, 1957.
[4] Fadipẹ, op. cit.   [5] P. C. Lloyd, 1953.   [6] Forde, 1951.

chain of intermediaries from 'pan buyer' to Licensed Buying Agent is by no means firm; at each level, the trade may buy from, and sell to, a number of different persons, and shift allegiances between them in accordance with relative commercial advantages at any given time.[1] The development of partnerships in other sectors is hampered by lack of capital and of formal business organization; the old guild monopolies have been broken up by easier rail and motor transport, and no comparable structure has arisen to replace them.

Long-distance trading partnerships seem, however, to be slightly firmer among women. These may be based on family connections;[2] a woman who has, as often happens, trained her daughter in trading and set her up in business on her own at the age of 10 or 12, will have a ready-made partner if the girl marries a man from another town and moves there. Such networks extend well beyond Western Nigeria, going as far as Ghana, Gambia, Sierra Leone, and Fernando Po.[3] In Lagos, women's firms consist mostly of women born in other Yoruba towns; their activities are often regulated by written contract. One such firm finances several weaving-sheds in Ijẹbu Ode, employing about twelve workers in all.[4]

VI

The intense and long-standing Yoruba preoccupation with trade early required a standard, easily accumulable medium of exchange. This was, in the days before European-introduced money became common, provided by cowrie shells. Opinions differ as to when and by whom these were introduced;[5] what seems well established is that they were in use for several centuries before the beginning of the colonial period.[6] Cowrie shells were used in a similar way by several other West African peoples.[7]

As with other forms of 'primitive currency', the question remains open as to how far these cowrie shells could be regarded, as Bascom[8] holds, to be 'true money', valuable only as a medium for exchange and the convenient accumulation of wealth, and not for ritual or decorative purposes. Certainly cowries were used in

---

[1] Galletti et al., op. cit.   [2] Comhaire-Sylvain, op. cit.   [3] Ibid.
[4] Ibid.   [5] Bascom, 1955; Fadipẹ, op. cit; Johnson, op. cit.
[6] Bascom, op. cit.   [7] Nadel, 1942.   [8] Op. cit.

connection with the worship of several of the òrìṣà;[1] in the case of Èṣù,[2] who has a special connection with commerce and money matters, his more modern images are indifferently adorned with strings of cowries and with coins[3]—which would seem to indicate that these two forms of wealth have at any rate become inter-changeable in the minds of his worshippers, whether or not they were so originally. When European currency first began to trickle into the Yoruba hinterland, people readily used both media of exchange; cowries, being less valuable, retained their usefulness for very small commercial transactions, and were exchangeable for English-style money at known, though variable, rates. In Ọyọ country, both media were still being used in this way less than ten years ago.[4]

The Yoruba, therefore, have long been accustomed to the pre-sence of an accumulable medium of exchange. They are, more-over, one of the richest peoples in Africa; and wealth is important in their hierarchy of social values. But, to gain prestige for its possessor, it must be wealth well and lavishly spent, not hoarded; and the ideal of polygyny as well as the manifold obligations of kinship and hospitality provide many opportunities for dissipating it. The only form of wealth that cannot be so alienated is land, which is held in the descent group; on the other hand this mode of tenure effectively prevents the land from being used as security to obtain bank loans.[5]

Despite cocoa prosperity, then, capitalization presents a diffi-culty, some of whose effects we have already noted in the small size of craft production units and trading ventures. In the past, one way of obtaining either ready cash or remittance of a debt was to pawn either oneself or one's child under the ìwòfà system.[6] This, however, was made illegal under colonial rule. As a result money can only be obtained either as a loan from kinsmen, from professional moneylenders charging high interest, or through the revolving-credit association known as èsúsú.[7] The briefest de-scription of èsúsú is given by Johnson:[8]

Esusu is a universal custom for the clubbing together of a number of persons for monetary aid. A fixed sum agreed upon is given by each at a

---

[1] Parrinder, 1949.   [2] Cf. above, Chapter III, Section III, and below.
[3] Wescott, op. cit.   [4] E. C. Rowlands: personal communication.
[5] P. C. Lloyd, 1962.   [6] Cf. above, Section II of the present Chapter.
[7] Ajiṣafẹ, 1924; Bascom, op. cit.; Johnson, op. cit.   [8] Op. cit.

fixed time . . . and place, under a president; the total amount is paid over to each member in rotation. This enables a poor man to do something worth while where a lump sum is required. There are laws regulating this system.

In Yoruba terms, 'something worth while' may be a costly wedding or a handsome gown as easily as a new set of tools for a craftsman; the *èsúsú* system offers a means whereby a fairly large sum can be accumulated to meet either type of expense. It is not quite clear what Johnson means by 'laws'; certainly nowadays the operations of *èsúsú* funds are not regulated by either traditional or statutory law: each fund makes its own rules.

There are two main types of *èsúsú* fund:[1]

(1) 'Unrestricted' *èsúsú* may have a large and scattered membership, generally of men; often a condition of membership is wage-earning or salaried employment of some kind, to ensure regularity in the payment of contributions. The president or head is known; generally he is chosen because of a reputation for efficiency and probity—a fairly common scandal is the absconding of an *èsúsú* head with the members' money! (In some *èsúsú* it is either openly provided or tacitly accepted that the head is entitled to one or two 'rounds' of the *èsúsú* for his trouble in organizing it.) Otherwise, however, members of a large *èsúsú* often do not know one another; nor need the number of *èsúsú* shares (which, of course, determines the number of 'rounds' or times the total sum will be paid out) be the same as the number of individual members. A rich man will take two or three shares; two less prosperous men may take half a share each.

In a very large unrestricted *èsúsú* the head may delegate some of his duties to sub-heads responsible, e.g. for particular quarters of a town; these will then be responsible for seeing that members resident in those quarters pay their dues, and receive their benefits, at the right times. Non-payment of dues normally involves corresponding loss of benefits, though a man may plead a special emergency and beg to be allowed another week to pay. Some effort, too, is made to time the benefits so that a member can receive the lump sum that is due to him at a time when he may particularly need it; though as a rule an agreed rotation is observed.

Different *èsúsú* vary in number of shares, periodicity of payments and benefits, and sizes of dues: there are rich men's and

[1] Bascom, op. cit.

poor men's *èsúsú*. The same individual may, if he can afford the dues, join several at the same time. Altogether, *èsúsú* arrangements are about as anonymous, impersonal, transitory and segmental as anything the most modern western Megalopolis can show. Ajişafę[1] says quite specifically that 'this society deals with money matters only'. It never functions as a social club.[2]

(2) There is a somewhat different type of *èsúsú* that is often organized among the daughters of a compound. This is like the first type as regards general structure, but the number of people concerned is usually rather smaller, and of course there is considerable personal contact between them. It is interesting that the men of a compound—its agnatic core—never form an *èsúsú* among themselves; Bascom[3] suggests that the possibility of cheating and consequent quarrels involved in this type of organization would militate against the ideal of unity within the descent group, who will normally have to spend much of their lives together in the same compound. This may be contrasted with the organization of traditional crafts, where the men of a compound are always fellow craftsmen, the women rarely or never: the same principles—patri-local marriage and the ideal of compound unity—are at stake in both cases, but they operate to produce contrary effects. A common occupation is held by the actors to be a cohesive factor; the *èsúsú* credit fund, a divisive one.

Both types of *èsúsú* are, for obvious reasons of ensuring prompt payments, confined to a single town.

Institutions similar in type to the *èsúsú* exist in many parts of the world.[4] Two African urban examples are those described by E. Hellman[5] for Johannesburg and by Balandier[6] for Brazzaville. The Yoruba themselves claim that *èsúsú* existed and functioned with cowrie shells before the introduction of European coined money; Balandier makes a similar claim for the *temo* practised by the Bakongo of Brazzaville and adds:[7]

Our investigation has shown us that we are here dealing with a survival from a period at which it was groups and not individuals that entered into relationship within the *temo*. The institution must originally have made it possible to establish peaceful and commercial relations between formerly antagonistic elements . . . thus constituting one of the

---

[1] Op. cit.   [2] Bascom, op. cit.   [3] Ibid.   [4] S. Ardener, 1964.
[5] Hellman, in Forde (ed.), 1956.   [6] Balandier, 1955(a) and (b).
[7] Balandier, 1955(b).

attempts, perhaps one of the most ancient, to break down the isolation of lineages. . . .

It is a pity that he does not specify on what data this interesting conclusion is based.

VII

Associations serving political and religious interests will be classified here, for the reasons suggested in the first section of this chapter, into traditional and modern; the latter category, though not the former, will again be subdivided into religious and political.

Traditional politico-religious associations fall into two main categories: òrìṣà-worship groups each comprising the devotees of a particular divinity, and the more or less closed associations connected with less particularized objects of worship, whether of the earth or of the collective male dead.[1] The latter, like similar associations in Benin,[2] undoubtedly had important political functions in the past.[3] It would seem that in Ọyọ at any rate, the same was true of òrìṣà-worship groups: 'Each cult was organized round a hierarchy of titled priests, whose offices had political aspects of varying importance.'

Traditional Yoruba religion postulates a Supreme Being, Ọlọ́run or Olódùmarè, who is thought of as living in the sky. It was he who sent down Odùduwà, ancestor of kings, to create the world at Ilé Ifẹ̀. Yet Ọlọ́run remains something of a *deus otiosus*; divine intervention in the world of man takes place through a number of beings known as òrìṣà.[4]

There are a great many òrìṣà, male, female, and androgynous;[5] some of them are highly localized in their influence, others quite widespread throughout Yorubaland (Èṣù, Ògún, Ṣàngó, Ṣọ̀pọ̀ná); in no two regions is the pantheon quite the same. Many of them are connected with natural phenomena (Ṣàngó with thunder; Ṣọ̀pọ̀ná with smallpox) or with geographical sites (Ọsun is the òrìṣà patroness of the river of the same name, and special honour is paid to her at Oshogbo). Nonetheless, òrìṣà are thought of as having lived on earth in human form in some remote past, and as having engaged in human activities; Ọrànyàn, Ògún, and Ṣàngó are reckoned among the sons of Odùduwà, who set out from Ifẹ̀

---

[1] Morton-Williams, 1960, 1964, 1966 and 1967.   [2] Bradbury, 1967.
[3] Morton-Williams, 1960 and 1967.   [4] Parrinder, 1961; Idowu, 1962.
[5] Morton-Williams, 1962; Parrinder, op. cit; Idowu, op. cit.

and founded the ancient *ìlú*. Bascom[1] says of the *òrìṣà* that they are regarded as superhuman 'only in that they came from heaven above, that they turned to stone or disappeared into the ground [instead of dying] and that some of their magic was more powerful than any known today.' *Òrìṣà* are thought to be powerful, for good and evil, in the lives of men; accordingly, they have special shrines, are honoured at rites and feasts and propitiated by animal and vegetable—in the past, also human—sacrifices.

Now there are clearly too many *òrìṣà* for a man to pay due devotions to them all: one might just as well ask an Ondo man to fulfil the duties of a descent group member in all of the descent lines that converge on both his parents. And, just as an individual from one of the 'cognatic towns' will live and act principally as a member of one group, with perhaps subsidiary ties with one or two others, so a traditional Yoruba will pay particular honour to one *òrìṣà* with perhaps a minor devotion to one or two others. Devotees are spoken of as being 'born by' or being 'a child of' the *òrìṣà* of their devotion. It is in this sense that Bascom[2] says that devotion to an *òrìṣà* is 'conceptually' identified with the honour paid to lineage ancestors at their shrine in the compound.

The two types of rites, however, differ appreciably in their external form. Ancestor rites within the compound are modest and private, an affair for the localized descent group only, with perhaps some members from a 'daughter' compound which still retains its ties with the parent one. *Òrìṣà* festivals are public affairs, usually celebrated annually and lasting about seven or eight days; the cult group consisting of the devotees of the *òrìṣà* that is being honoured will dance through the whole town, perhaps wearing special costumes, and sing songs appropriate to the occasion; the climax of the festival being the rite performed by the *òrìṣà*'s priesthood at a special sacred grove (*igbó*) or shrine (*ilé òrìṣà*).[3] It is a time for feasting and drinking, and for paying visits to relatives and friends. We may safely conclude that *òrìṣà* cults are not, in fact, the same sort of thing as rites in honour of ancestors; and this is further confirmed by the composition of the cult groups.

Frobenius[4] thought of the *òrìṣà* as a 'Sippengott', 'sib-god';[5] and

---

[1] Bascom, 1944.   [2] Op. cit.   [3] Cf. above, Chapter III, Section IV.   [4] Op. cit.
[5] 'Sib' in the old English sense rather than that used in modern American anthropology.

it is true that the most usual way of acquiring a devotion to an
òrìṣà is by inheritance, either through one's father or one's mother.
A man or woman devotee whose òrìṣà has watched well over the
family may bring up one, or several, or all of his or her children
to honour that òrìṣà. Since any given individual may honour more
than one òrìṣà, there is no conflict between devotion to the patron
of either parent; if one such patron is preferred above the other,
the choice may be affectionally motivated, or be an affair of
temperament, or the outcome of the individual's fortunes in later
life. A husband and wife are expected to pay some honour to
each other's special òrìṣà, but not to abandon any previous
devotion. There is no compulsion in the matter; an individual
may well abandon his parental òrìṣà when he grows up; Yoruba
say that even before the advent of Islam and Christianity there
were a few who honoured no special òrìṣà at all.[1]

However, it is quite possible for the individual to acquire
an òrìṣà devotion belonging to neither of his parents. This may
happen at birth, if the mother prayed to a particular òrìṣà (not
the one of her usual devotion) to get a child, or if the birth itself
was accompanied by unusual circumstances (caul births, albinos);
in this case, it is said that the child 'came from heaven' already
honouring a particular òrìṣà. Or an òrìṣà may 'call' him at any
time in later life, either by appearing in a dream (there have been
instances of people abandoning Christianity for this reason),[2] or
if some crisis in the individual's affairs—illness or other unexplained misfortune, marriage, house-building, a journey, financial
need, a chieftaincy contest, desire for a child—leads him or her to
consult an ifá oracle.

The ifá[3] oracle is a Yoruba method of divination by a trained
priest—babaláwo—who throws kola nuts or seeds upon a special
board and interprets the resulting pattern in terms of a set of 256
sacred verses of pronouncement and advice applicable to different
situations.[4] This is related to Yoruba ideas of fate in the sense of
an external, unknown but knowable, order. Ifá consultation thus
enables people to 'put their lives in order' when in special and
puzzling circumstances the known rules of behaviour are felt to be

[1] Bascom, op. cit.   [2] Ibid.
[3] Parrinder, op. cit., and 1953; Idowu, 1962; Bascom, 1966; McClelland, 1966;
Morton-Williams, 1966.
[4] On the significance of this number, cf. McClelland, 1966.

inadequate guides. Most *ifá* verses simply recommend a sacrifice, without specifying to which *òrìṣà* it should be offered—presumably one already honoured by the person concerned; there are nine of them, however, which command the client to honour a particular *òrìṣà* as the way out of his perplexity.[1]

This is the type of situation which may lead an adult to change his *òrìṣà* allegiance, or to acquire a new one; the *babaláwo* and other people usually offering the explanation that the *òrìṣà* in question must have been honoured by someone in that individual's family, but so long ago that the devotion has been forgotten. Bascom[2] comments:

The statement . . . of laymen and some *babalawo* that '*Ifa* would not tell a person to worship an *orisha* that was not already in the family' can be taken as nothing more than a reflection of the native's stereotype that *orishas* worshipped in a given family should be transmitted in that line. . . . The insistence on the ideal pattern probably reflects as well the importance of inheritance as a method of obtaining an *orisha*. In this case the *orishas* follow the bilateral pattern of descent which defines the exogamous group . . . Omitting the factor of 'calling' . . . the selection of *orishas* to be worshipped probably reflects their relative importance to his parents, the affection felt towards the parent, and also to a certain extent the patrilineal emphasis . . . As the family name and the sib make it easier to keep track of the ancestors in the male line, so also do they facilitate remembering the *orishas* that these ancestors worshipped. . . . *There is, however, no identity between the sib and the worshipping group, Frobenius and the ideal pattern to the contrary notwithstanding.* [Italics, except for Yoruba words, mine.]

This lack of actual identity between the descent group and some other group 'ideally' identified with it is, of course, common enough in all societies where the actors themselves see their social structure as defined by the descent system, and adjust any anomalies that occur during a period of time to fit this construct.[3] What is interesting, though, is that the *òrìṣà* cult group in its method of recruitment recognizes that the individual's personal destiny, as symbolized by the *òrìṣà* who watches over him and to whom he pays special honour, offers a number of possible alternatives, which are by no means exhausted by the known *òrìṣà* destinies of parents or ancestors. In his religious devotions, and as a member

[1] Bascom, 1941, 1942(b), 1966.   [2] Bascom, 1944.
[3] L. Bohannan, 1952; E. Ardener, 1959.

of the group based on them, a man may 'belong' with and to a set of people previously unconnected with him by any ties of kinship—even if such 'belonging' is rationalized in kinship terms.[1] (The priesthoods of the different *òrìṣà*, and also the *ifá* body of priest-diviners, are similarly recruited.)

We have already noted[2] that a craft body, whether traditional or modern, may have a collective *òrìṣà* cult: Ògún, the patron of the 'iron trades'—smiths, hunters, warriors, barbers, scarifiers, lorry-drivers—is the most frequently cited example. So may a compound containing more that one descent group; or a town quarter; or a whole town—any social group, in fact, whose members are felt to share a destiny in important aspects of their lives. Lloyd, in discussing the concept of 'public land' in traditional Yoruba towns,[3] says:

Shrines are another form of public land; here one must distinguish between those shrines which belong to the whole town and those which are held by a single descent group. In the case of the latter the worship of the deity concerned may be by a certain descent group but for the benefit of the whole town; the destruction of the shrine by the group may be met by considerable opposition from the community . . . The shrines of some deities are obviously attached to the whole community. . . .

It is suggested that the very variable width of *òrìṣà* cult groups, the looseness of modes of recruitment, and the ease with which an individual can pass from one to another are features well in agreement with the mentality of a people whose lives are spent in large, closely nucleated settlements, where it is impossible for a descent group to keep its ideological boundaries unblurred, as it might hope to do in geographical isolation. In this connection it would be interesting to know whether membership of an *òrìṣà* cult group is—like land, titles, and craft occupations—inherited more strictly along agnatic lines in the Ọyọ towns: on the face of it, this would appear likely.

There is one *òrìṣà* whose devotees do not form a group, but perform their devotions individually; Èṣù.[4] We have already noted the special connection of Èṣù with markets, crossroads, quarrels, money, chance, and change; he seems to represent in Yoruba life

---

[1] Schwab, 1965.   [2] Cf. above, Section II of this chapter.
[3] P. C. Lloyd, 1962.   [4] Parrinder, 1961; Idowu, 1962.

the principle of uncertainty, the mischievous quirks of life against which no man can provide in advance.[1]

In this sense he complements the *ifá* divination system, which, precisely, enables a man to deal with an unforeseen emergency by taking appropriate action. Parrinder writes:[2] 'Ifa is closely associated with Eshu, for both are intermediaries between the gods and men, and Ifa declares the divine will. According to myths it was Eshu who first taught Ifa the use of the palm nuts for divining.' The *ifá* revelations thus represent the part of uncertainty and contingency which Èṣù will allow men to know.[3] Yoruba sometimes speak of Èṣù as 'the anger of the *òrìṣà*'; some say he does not exist at all as a separate being, but is simply a name used by devotees to any *òrìṣà* at times when they are particularly afraid of him.

He appears, in a word, to symbolize all that is 'impersonal, superficial, transitory and segmental'—and, it may be added, potentially dangerous—in the many contacts between strangers that must occur in a large nucleated settlement. It is significant that in his case there is not even any pretence that he was once the patron of a descent group like other *òrìṣà*. Èṣù is, in Wirth's sense, the most recognizably 'urban' of all Yoruba divinities.

VIII

Bascom[4] treats all closed ritual associations as variants of *òrìṣà* cult groups, and regards them as forming an internally undifferentiated category. He recognizes that in Ifẹ 'the *Egungun*, *Oro* and *Ogboni* . . . perform important political functions'; but adds: 'That these political functions are secondary is seen in the fact that no one ever joins *Ogboni* to "have a voice" in the affairs of the town'. Moreover, he maintains that in Ọyọ, *ògbóni*, *egúngún*, *oró* and *agẹmọ* were all of them cult groups sociologically indistinguishable from those made up of the devotees of a particular *òrìṣà*.

A totally different picture emerges from the more recent studies effected in Ọyọ by P. Morton-Williams.[5] According to Morton-Williams,

From the political point of view . . . there is no doubt that the Ogboni

---

[1] Wescott, op. cit.   [2] Parrinder, op. cit.   [3] Morton-Williams, 1964.
[4] Op. cit.   [5] Morton-Williams, 1956, 1960, 1964, and 1967.

cult of the Earth was of prime importance in moderating the relationship between Alafin and Ọyọ Mesi [the Council of State of Ọyọ] since
it could impose ritual sanctions on both . . . As far as the general public
was concerned, the known function in government of this cult was to
punish the shedding of human blood . . . The cult was believed, too,
to perform vitally important rites for the king and the community in
the secrecy of its lodge in the palace forecourt . . . But, politically
speaking, those of its activities that were most important to keep secret
were its deliberations on government policy.[1]

The *ògbóni* association (in Ijẹbu: *òṣùgbó*) is also known to have
been of cardinal political importance in the traditional government of Ẹgba, Ijẹbu and Ondo towns.[2]

Many West African societies in which lineage is an important
principle of political structure have, counterbalancing the power of
the descent groups, some form of earth-worship, which cuts
across lineage ties and cleavages, complementing lineage values by
those of the earth in both her local and universal aspects. Such a
cult is often associated in myth with the 'original owners of the
soil', thought to have inhabited a region before it was overrun by
its present occupants.[3]

These, we have seen, are in Yoruba myth the sons and grandsons of Odùduwà—conceived as the founder of a large patrilineage
of which all existing royal lineages represent segments—who
migrated from Ilé-Ifẹ̀, each with his followers, and founded cities
wherever they settled. Some Yoruba towns have very sparse
traditions of previous inhabitants of the region; both Ondo and
Ijẹbu Ode, however, tell of pre-existent settlers who accepted the
rule of the prince from Ifẹ in recognition of his divine birth.[4]
Both Ijẹbu and Ondo are towns in which the political functions of
the earth-cult seem to have been well-marked; but the same,
according to Morton-Williams,[5] is true of Ọyọ, the central political
stronghold of the descendants of Odùduwà, which seems to have
no particular traditions concerning former autochthonous inhabitants. Morton-Williams's Ọyọ findings also disprove Fadipẹ's
thesis[6] according to which the power of the *ògbóni* association
varied inversely with the size of the political unit.

---

[1] Morton-Williams, 1967.   [2] P. C. Lloyd, 1954 and 1962; Fadipẹ, op. cit.
[3] Parrinder, op. cit; Fortes, 1945; Forde, 1964; Little, 1951; Horton, 1956.
[4] P. C. Lloyd, 1960.   [5] Morton-Williams, 1960, 1964, and 1967.
[6] Op. cit.

Descriptive accounts of *ògbóni*-type societies[1] also vary considerably, particularly as regards the breadth of the recruitment base. This may be partly due to a confusion between the lower ranks of the association, which may in most towns have been open to all male *ará ìlú* of good character, and its upper ranks, membership of which seems in all cases to have been fairly restricted; or the situation may in fact have varied between different towns.

What does seem to have varied were the *criteria* for membership. In Ọyọ, with its large powerful agnatic descent groups, 'The fully initiated members . . . were recruited partly by hereditary right, partly by invitation from the Ogboni priests from free Ọyọ lineages on a basis of age, presumed wisdom, and some prominence in secular or religious life.'[2] In Ijẹbu and Ondo, on the other hand, the 'mix' appears to have contained rather less ascription and more achievement—concretely in the form of wealth— i.e. the candidate had to make various payments and offer feasts to *ògbóni* members of the rank to which he aspired.[3]

Membership of the highest rank of all seems usually to have overlapped with membership of the *ìlú* Council of State, though not necessarily in such a way that the highest statuses in the two bodies were held by the same persons:

All members of the Ọyọ Mesi [Ọyọ Council of State] were *ex officio* admitted to the senior grade of the cult, but were debarred from the highest ritual offices, which were vested in certain lineages (though successors had to be acceptable to the Ogboni and the king, and the choice confirmed by the Ifa oracle). The Alafin, too, was represented in the cult by a woman who heard all that was said and reported to him, but could not herself take part of the discussions. Thus, while they attended the plenary meetings that were held at sixteen-day intervals, the Ọyọ Mesi did so in circumstances that placed them to some extent under the discipline of sanctions vested in a priesthood from which they were excluded and which bound all Ogboni members to accept decisions taken at the meetings, even though the decisions might not have been unanimously reached . . . It is also of significance that the Ogboni leaders were shielded from undue pressure from the Ọyọ Mesi because the holders of the highest [*ògbóni*] titles . . resided in the royal sector of Ọyọ and so were not subordinate chiefs of any of the Ọyọ Mesi.[4]

---

[1] Frobenius, op. cit; Fadipẹ, op. cit; Bascom, op. cit; P. C. Lloyd, 1954; Morton-Williams, 1960, 1964, and 1967.
[2] Morton-Williams, 1967.   [3] P. C. Lloyd, 1954.   [4] Morton-Williams, 1967.

In Ijẹbu Ode, on the other hand, some of the seniormost òṣùgbó titles were filled from amongst the palace slaves.[1]

In Qyọ, the òghóni association appears to have maintained the always somewhat delicate balance of power between the Alafin and the Qyọ Mesi (which represented the major descent groups);[2] in Ijẹbu Ode and Ondo, and to a lesser extent in Abẹokuta, the higher ranks of the corresponding association seem in effect to have governed the town, the ọba in each case simply confirming their decisions.[3] While the higher ranks of the association were thus concerned with policy decisions, its rank and file exercised functions of social control.[4] They were much feared, there being no appeal from their judgement.

Today, with their religious aspects frowned upon by both Islam and Christianity, and their political functions taken over by modern local government institutions, the old òghóni-type associations are moribund in the towns; though in Ijẹbu villages the òṣùgbó is still a respected judicial power, hearing disputes before they come to the customary courts.[5] Some of their ceremonial and prestige-conferring aspects have been taken over by the Reformed Ogboni Fraternity, set up by a Yoruba clergyman, the Revd. T. A. J. Ogunbiyi, in 1914, in order to provide an alternative form of prestige association to the old pagan òghóni.[6] Members of the Reformed Ogboni, like those of the higher ranks of the old òghóni-type associations, tend to constitute an economic élite; the difference is that no political power attaches to membership. Rather, the Reformed Ogboni constitutes a social club offering certain facilities for a new style of urban life: that of wealthy, literate professional and business men who move readily from town to town. The Reformed Ogboni, which has incorporated certain features of English freemasonry, has lodges in all Yoruba towns: a man simply joins the lodge in the town of his temporary residence. A sophisticated, inter-urban association of this kind also channels some economic functions; membership of the Reformed Ogboni is often taken by fellow-members as a guarantee of trustworthiness for credit.

All in all, the Reformed Ogboni is an example of how completely

---

[1] P. C. Lloyd, 1954. This situation is not unlike that formerly existing at Benin (cf. Bradbury, 1967).
[2] Morton-Williams, 1967.   [3] P. C. Lloyd, 1962.
[4] P. C. Lloyd, 1954; Morton-Williams, 1967.
[5] P. C. Lloyd, 1962.   [6] Parrinder, 1953.

an institution can change in function while retaining the same name; another instance is the number of different senses now attached to the word *ẹgbẹ́*, which originally denoted Yoruba age-sets.[1]

Aside from *ògbóni* and *òṣùgbó*, there were in Yoruba towns a variety of male closed associations, some of them with regulatory functions of a type fairly common in West Africa, in which masqueraders represented the spirits of the dead; in some cases, these seem to have been articulated on to the lower ranks of the *ògbóni* associations, which delegated to them certain policing duties such as the execution of witches. The best known of these is the *egúngún* society;[2] other variants are *orò* and *agẹmọ*.[3] None of them seems ever to have retained important political functions.

Membership of these associations seems to be acquired in the same way as for *òrìṣà* cult groups, i.e. either by inheritance or by 'calling'. Nowadays, the functions of *egúngún*, are, in many towns, largely recreational; though the masqueraders are still feared by women and children, their appearance is also an occasion for merriment.[4] In this way, *egúngún* still exercises certain functions of social control, though the sanctions are nowadays very diffuse.

Unfortunately there is very little information about closed associations for women. Abraham's '*ìyálóde* society' or Fadipẹ's 'rich women's association' may have had ritual or regulatory aspects;[5] we also know that the Ọyọ *ògbóni* had a women's section.[6] The Reformed Ogboni Fraternity has some women members.

IX

Over the last hundred years, and particularly over the last fifty, two major influences have tended to disrupt the ancient unity between political and religious interests for the inhabitants of Yoruba towns. On the one hand, two major world religions have spread over the country: Islam from the north, brought not so

---

[1] Cf. below, Section XI of the present Chapter. The term *ẹgbẹ́* is also used of the modern craft guilds described in Section IV above.

[2] Morton-Williams, 1956: Parrinder, 1953; Idowu, 1962 and 1967.

[3] Bascom, op. cit.; Idowu, 1962.   [4] Cf. Beier, 1959.

[5] Abraham, op. cit., Fadipẹ, op. cit. Cf. above, Section IV of the present Chapter.

[6] Morton-Williams, 1967.

much by the Fulani conquerors of Iḷọrin as by the peaceful penetration of individual Hausa travellers and merchants; Christianity from the coast, brought by the missions of the different churches that established themselves in nearly all the major towns. On the other, the coming of British Colonial government deprived *ògbóni* and *òṣùgbó*, as well as the lesser *orò* and *egúngún*, of their former political functions. No present-day Yoruba urban association serves the whole cluster of political and religious interests, as did the old *ògbóni*; instead, there are a number of mainly religious, and a number of mainly political associations.

Very few town-dwelling Yoruba, nowadays, practise exclusively the religion of their ancestors. In most towns, Islam predominates; thus Iwo (metropolitan town) was, in 1952, 82 per cent Muslim; Ijẹbu Ode 69 per cent;[1] Abẹokuta, according to Leighton and Lambo's more recent random sample of dwellings,[2] 56 per cent; Oshogbo, according to Schwab's sample,[3] 80 per cent. In Oshogbo, 7 per cent of the inhabitants described themselves as pagan; in the more sophisticated Ijẹbu Ode and Abẹokuta, on the other hand, Islam and Christianity between them accounted, officially at least, for the whole population (Ijẹbu Ode: 31 per cent Christian according to the 1952 Census; Abẹokuta: 44 per cent Christian in Leighton and Lambo's sample). Leighton and Lambo, however, pressed their questioning further; and found that, in Abẹokuta itself, 12 per cent of their sample (while professing Islam or Christianity) were members of a traditional cult group; while 28 per cent observed some taboo dictated by the old religion, and a further 19 per cent when questioned 'felt that traditional religion should be maintained'.[4] It is clear, then, that Christianity and Islam cannot be thought of as excluding either the practices of traditional Yoruba religion, or the sociological groupings based on such practices. Even where diminished or transformed, such practices and groupings persist: *òrìṣà* festivals are still celebrated, Muslim or Christian *ọbas* continue to perform traditional Yoruba ceremonial on behalf of the town, *egúngún* masqueraders still dance, on certain occasions, along the streets.

There have even been a few cases of new native cult groups established in reaction to the imported religions. One such is Ìjo Ọrúnmìlà, based in Lagos,[5] which in 1949 claimed 5,600 adherents

---

[1] P. C. Lloyd, 1959(a).   [2] Leighton, *et al.*, op. cit.
[3] Schwab, 1954.   [4] Leighton, *et al.*, op. cit.   [5] Comhaire, 1949.

in Lagos and Ijebu; this was 'centred on the cult of the supreme deity vaguely known by all African religions', i.e. Ọlọrun, and is remarkable chiefly as an innovation, since no cult group devoted to that supreme but remote divinity exists in traditional Yoruba religion. On the whole, however, Yoruba have shown no great tendency towards thoroughly 'nativistic' reactive religions such as are described by various authors[1] for other parts of Africa; though many modern cults exist,[2] nearly all of them are clearly recognizable as nearer or more remote offshoots of the Christian churches. Islam, as usual, has been less fissiparous.

Christian missions have a history of over 100 years in Yoruba-land.[3] The first, historically as well as in the order of present-day importance, is the Church of England (CMS) mission, which first established itself in Abẹokuta around 1845. Also important are Roman Catholic, Methodist, Baptist, and Seventh Day Adventist missions.[4] The activities of all these are closely correlated with the spread of literacy and Western education in general, since all the Christian denominations ran schools, which were until recently the only schools in the Yoruba country.

Most towns have at least one large church, the mother church of the area, to which the educated élite of the town go, together with the most important of the Christian 'strangers'; other churches, each within its own denomination, draw their congregations largely from the immediately surrounding quarters of the town.

Anglican churches, together with some others, organize their parishes at two levels. At one, there is a council of baptized but illiterate and probably polygynous church elders; these are given prestige titles such as baba ẹgbẹ́, baba ìsàlẹ̀. Aside from this there is an inner ring of full church members; these are generally literate and have, by undergoing a church marriage ceremony, taken vows of monogamy; they constitute the Parochial Church Council proper. Office within the latter (e.g. churchwarden) carries high prestige in the town; indeed, Lloyd[5] says: 'One of the most important functions of the churches in Yoruba towns would seem to be the provision of opportunities for the literate to achieve status of high prestige.' The rank and file of the faithful are grouped

[1] Balandier, 1955(b); Sundkler, 1948.
[2] Cf. Parrinder, 1953 and Webster, 1964.   [3] Webster, op. cit.
[4] Parrinder, 1953.   [5] P. C. Lloyd, 1959(a).

into smaller associations by sex, age, and marital status; these groups are organizationally modelled on the secular *ẹgbẹ́* or social clubs,[1] and called by the same name. They meet, like secular *ẹgbẹ́*, once a week, mainly for devotional purposes and for the collection of church revenue at Harvest Levies. A large church *ẹgbẹ́* may be subdivided into geographical units. It is an indication of the closure of the traditional Yoruba town against recently arrived 'strangers', and of their own aloofness from the life of a town not their own, that they usually have their own church *ẹgbẹ́*.

There are also, particularly in the larger towns, a great number of smaller religious sects of Christian origin; some of them, such as the Apostolic Church, the 'Church of God', Jehovah's Witnesses, and the Salvation Army, have connections with and support from abroad; others represent more or less autochthonous splits from the larger churches: Parrinder[2] lists for Ibadan the United Native African Church, The African Church (Incorporated), the United African Methodist Church, the Unity African Christ Church, the Christ Apostolic Churches, the Prayer Church, the Sacred Cherubim and Seraphim Society, the Holy Flock of Christ, the Church of the Lord's People, the Church of Christ's People, the Church of the Spirit and the Apostolic Faith—roughly in order of diminishing orthodoxy. All of these sects have at least one church and congregation in Ibadan, and some have several; nearly all have adherents in Lagos, Ijẹbu, Abẹokuta, and other towns as well. On the whole it is true to say that the separatist sects afford greater indulgence to polygyny, and also incorporate a greater proportion of African singing, drumming, and dancing into their ritual; both these may be factors in their popularity. In any case, as Parrinder[3] notes, the Yoruba 'is accustomed to the sight of a variety of cults, to any of which he may go in time of need. The idea of an imposed orthodoxy is foreign to him. Hence the swarming of sects may not be entirely due to the so-called "fissiparous tendency" of Protestantism,' but may reproduce, in the language of Christianity as it were, the Yoruba tradition of the multiplicity of religious groups and possible choice between them.

In towns where Islam is predominant, each quarter has its own

---

[1] Cf. below, Section XI of the present Chapter.   [2] Parrinder, 1953.
[3] Parrinder, op. cit.

mosque,[1] the forecourt of which often acts as a meeting place; an elder among the devout will lead prayers for the quarter, though the town as a whole will have its own *imam*. Organization seems to be simpler than for Christian churches, partly because Islamic tradition calls for no specialized priesthood, and partly because, since polygyny is not frowned upon, there is no need for a two-tier structure such as many churches have adopted as a compromise. Neither is there any central organization, comparable to the hierarchical structure of the churches, uniting the mosques of different towns (except among the Ahmadiya and other small reformist groups): thus Islam, both in permitting polygyny and in confining its religious organization—as distinct from its influence—to the single town unit, appears to be somewhat more easily assimilable to traditional Yoruba values than Christianity; which may account for its greater diffusion, especially among non-literate townsmen.

X

With the coming of colonial government, the political functions fulfilled in certain towns by the old politico-religious associations gradually decayed. Moreover, the spread of Western education called forth new sets of common political interests, clustering around the new statuses based on literacy or on various degrees of further education. Aside from the reforms carried out at various times in the structure of local government itself,[2] and which were brought about partly by the action of the new interest groups described below and partly by the efforts of the political parties and the British Colonial Government, two types of such interest groups emerged: the 'Progressive' or 'Improvement Unions' of the citizens of provincial towns, and the wider, more centralized organization which started as the Ẹgbẹ́ Ọmọ Odùduwà and eventually became the largely Yoruba-based Action Group Party within Nigeria's later party system.

The traditional social system of the Yoruba, including its political structure, laid great emphasis on seniority; nonetheless, there seems to have been channels, through the age-set meetings or, where *ògbóni*-type associations were important, the meetings of the

---

[1] Parrinder (op. cit.) counts 190 mosques of all types in Ibadan.
[2] P. C. Lloyd, 1958.

lower grades of these societies, for the younger men of a town to voice their opinion on its affairs, which was then transmitted further up the hierarchy by the junior chiefs attending such meetings.[1] As *ògbóni* and age-sets—their political importance unrecognized by the colonial officials responsible for mapping out and implementing the details of Indirect Rule[2]—began to decay, this machinery for consultation of the younger elements of the town population decayed with them; while at the same time it was precisely these younger elements who were acquiring a Western education, and with it both access to certain prestige statuses associated with the colonial authorities (teachers, Government clerks) and a number of new ideas as to modern improvements, social services, etc., which might be of benefit to their town.

A fanciful description of what such young men want for their native town is given by A. Tutuola[3] in *My Life in the Bush of Ghosts*. He describes meeting his dead cousin in the '10th Town of Ghosts', and how his kinsman, 'one of the staunch members of the Methodist Church in our earthly town', had introduced modern improvements among the ghosts. The cousin explains how first he established 'THE METHODIST CHURCH OF THE BUSH OF GHOSTS'; then:

After the sixth month that the church was opened, I converted it to both church and school . . . My work after the church services is only to be supervising churches and schools . . . In my leisure hours, I taught many scholars who had been passed out from the schools sanitary work, surveying, building, first aid nursery work, but only this 'first aid' nursery work I could teach them, because I am not a qualified doctor . . . Then new houses were built which made this town to link up as the most beautiful town in the Bush of Ghosts. Though it was only disqualified at that time for the hospital which was not established in the town, although there was provision for it but not a qualified doctor who could carry on the works . . . But as this town is well improved but only disqualified by the hospitals which were not then in it, so as my wife is a qualified doctor before she died, she established hospitals in this town and acted as the Director of Medical Services. Having trained several thousands of nurses and medical officers.

This lively interest in municipal improvement, finding no ready-made institutional channel of expression, resulted in the emergence of town 'Progressive' or 'Improvement Unions', generally

[1] P. C. Lloyd, 1954.   [2] P. C. Lloyd, 1958.   [3] Tutuola, 1954.

composed of the younger, more forward-looking men of a given town, and led by the most educated among them. These Unions seem to be a phenomenon characteristic of a certain phase in a town's life since the beginning of colonial rule: that at which modern amenities such as schools and hospitals have not yet been introduced, but the more progressive elements of the population begin to feel the want of them—a want whose source is a desire for town prestige quite as often as a conviction of the benefits of wider education or medical care. Nowadays, according to Lloyd,[1] such Unions are most active in backward towns like Iwo or else in

small subordinate towns endeavouring to win a share of the amenities which accrue to the metropolitan town. Conversely some associations developed in Ado Ekiti in opposition to the (more widely based) Ekiti Progressive Union since the latter sought to have the new secondary schools and hospitals built in other towns in the Division, whilst the Ado members rather unreasonably demanded that Ado, being centrally located and an administrative headquarter, was the best site for the new amenities, notwithstanding the existence of schools and medical centres in the town.

In such cases, Progressive Unions act, in part, as an expression of a town's cohesion and sentiment of solidarity against all comers— particularly other, neighbouring towns, which are seen as rivals for the new amenities. 'When a subordinate town seeks to secede from a kingdom, supporting its claim with myths and legends of its historical independence, it is usually the progressive union which is most active in the campaign.'[2] In other cases, Progressive Unions serve to 'reflect and accentuate' already existing cleavages: 'Elsewhere, rival associations developed, as in Iwo, from conflict between the literates and illiterate radicals of the town, exacerbated by personal hostilities.'[3] The overt objective of these Progressive Unions is to bring pressure to bear on ọba and chiefs; their policy is not to oppose these traditional authorities, but to help them understand twentieth-century changes. Among their latent functions, as we have seen, is the expression of either town cohesion or internal cleavages, whichever may predominate in any given situation. Aside from that, the Progressive Union, like the Parochial Church Council, gives the young literate a chance to shine: office in these institutions, unlike the secretaryship or treasurership of a craft guild or a purely social ẹgbẹ́ or recreational

[1] P. C. Lloyd, 1959(a).   [2] Ibid.   [3] Ibid.

club, carries considerable prestige in the town, and may, indeed, lead to its holder being considered a promising candidate for election to a Local Government Council. (The Progressive Unions also find jobs, and sometimes scholarships, for school leavers.)[1]

But as more and more of the abler leaders of a Progressive Union are siphoned off into local government or move elsewhere in search of employment opportunities—and as the town, largely owing to their efforts, becomes progressively modernized in its social services—these associations themselves tend to decay, at any rate in their towns of origin. This is what has happened in Ijẹbu Ode, where the local branch was extremely active at the beginning of the century;[2] now, its place has largely been taken by political party offices. But in their new towns of employment— Lagos, Ibadan, and also non-Yoruba towns like Kaduna—the same young men, now clerks or teachers, are 'strangers'. They are not, as we have seen in Chapter IV, absorbed into their towns of employment; they intend one day to return to their town of birth, build a fine house there, and start farming or trading, perhaps using their pension and/or savings as capital. They tend to band together: they are usually young, either unmarried or monogamous, and their distance from the town of birth absolves them from the many wider kinship obligations which would otherwise impinge on their spare time; nor can they easily acquire responsible status within the close-knit structure of their town of employment.

These strangers from the same town form the 'away' branches of their town's Progressive Union; and often, nowadays, these branches of homesick 'strangers' in Ibadan or Lagos keep the home branch alive where it would otherwise have died out. They often contain the home-town's most educated men, who feel it a duty to share their experience, and some of their earnings, with those citizens who have stayed at home.

The sociological functions of these 'away' branches, however, are quite different from those of the 'home' ones, and much more like those performed by similar Ibo associations based on the village or area of origin, or by the tribally based *compins* of Freetown immigrants,[3] or the *amicales* of young men from the same small area described by Balandier[4] for Brazzaville. In an urban environment to which their members do not, as they do in their

---

[1] P. C. Lloyd, 1959(a).   [2] Ibid.
[3] Banton, 1957; Little, 1966.   [4] Balandier, 1955(a).

towns of birth, belong as *ará ìlú*, these 'away' branches of home-town Progressive Unions furnish them with a group with which they can identify, as well as with an easily accessible social life. Such 'away' branches, in fact, also function as *ẹgbẹ́* or social clubs, the members meeting at least weekly and taking it in turns to entertain each other; which the 'home' branches of the same Unions are not described as doing.

The first pan-Yoruba association was started, significantly enough, by such educated 'strangers' in Ibadan in 1948. This was a cultural association, the *Ẹgbẹ́ Ọmọ Odùduwà* (Association of the Children of Odùduwà) which, as its name implies, was aimed at creating ideals of Yoruba unity by appealing to those myths and traditions that were common to all Yoruba and transcended the *ilu* unit. Its first secretary, the then Mr. O. Awolowo, was, character-istically, not a native of Ibadan, but a teacher from Ìjẹbu Rẹ̀mọ.[1] Out of it came the Action Group political party; which, like the *Ẹgbẹ́ Ọmọ Odùduwà* itself, was at that time primarily the expres-sion of the new educated Yoruba élite,[2] and was slow to kindle any great enthusiasm in the older or more remote towns. Later political developments, however, led a greater number of the Yoruba people to identify themselves with what started out as a somewhat alien élite party.[3]

XI

Most traditional Yoruba towns appear to have had a system of age-sets called *ẹgbé*; each of these contained all the men of a town born within a period of three years—which corresponds to the traditionally prescribed period between child-births (allowing for a long suckling period, during which intercourse was for-bidden), so that no two *ọmọ ìyá* brothers would ever be members of the same *ẹgbẹ́*. There is some reason to believe that the traditional age-sets, like other non-kin associations, showed greater vitality where lineage organization was weakest. Lloyd[4] writes:

In Ijebu Ode the last age set ... to be named by an *oba* and thus formally recognized, was created twenty-five years ago. Those formed before this period (and thus including men today above 45 years of age) still continue to exist, however. In the Ijebu villages weekly meetings are

---

[1] Awolowo, 1960.   [2] Cf. Chapter VI, below.
[3] Cf. Sklar, 1963.   [4] P. C. Lloyd, 1959(a).

still held by each age set . . . In Ekiti, age sets and . . . grades . . . have vanished. In Oyo towns it is not certain that such sets or grades existed into the late nineteenth century.

The military functions of these sets and grades disappeared in the nineteenth-century wars, which were largely fought by companies of semi-independent warriors. Age-grades were also responsible for certain public works (roads, town walls) and in some towns seem to have had some police duties; these tasks are now performed by local government bodies. It was within the age-set that the ǎró work-group was recruited.[1] We have seen how the political functions of the age-sets have devolved upon the Progressive Unions.

The purely social functions of the traditional age-sets—providing a circle of friends beyond the kinship circle, a recreative peer-group which might offer solace from family strains and stresses—have been taken over by a new form of association which has grown out of them, and which is still called by the same name, ẹgbẹ́. These are voluntary associations formed by both men and women[2] of about the same age; in a large town, the ẹgbẹ́ may be a neighbourhood group, based upon the quarter, but this is not necessarily so.

The ẹgbẹ́ usually meets weekly, members taking it in turns to provide food and drink; at these meetings, they discuss the personal affairs of members; a troublesome wife, a bad debt. Yoruba often say that they will take such a problem to their ẹgbẹ́ meeting before discussing it with the elders in their own compound.[3] An ẹgbẹ́ may also, as the old age-set did, discuss town affairs, though there is no recognized channel of communication with either the traditional or the modern town authorities.

Once a year, ẹgbẹ́ members display their solidarity more publicly; after a large feast, they dance through the town all dressed alike—the aṣọ ẹgbẹ́, like the aṣọ ẹbí for the kin group at marriages and other family celebrations, acting as a badge of unity. Members also entertain the ẹgbẹ́ with food, drink, and drummers when they get married, participate in a funeral, or celebrate the festival of their own òrìṣà.

Organizationally, the ẹgbẹ́ usually has a president, secretary, treasurer, etc., as well as a patron chosen from among the more prominent citizens of the town. Office within an ẹgbẹ́ carries no formal status:

[1] Cf. Section II, above. [2] Bascom, 1944. [3] P. C. Lloyd, op. cit.

yet the qualities of leadership displayed by office holders do not pass unnoticed, and may often mark out a likely candidate for a chieftancy title or election to the local government council. Well led, an *egbe* will flourish for several years, have a large membership and stage lavish annual dances; conversely, the leaderless *egbe* quickly peters out and its members join rival groups.

Lloyd[1] adds that 'wealth is rarely an important criterion of membership', whereas Bascom[2] claims that some *ẹgbẹ́* have more prestige than others, and that this is correlated with expenses of initiation, entertainment, and gifts. But then, Bascom in general tends to see rank and prestige differentials where Lloyd does not;[3] this may correspond to specific features in Ifẹ.

We have already noted that the modern *ẹgbẹ́* organization appears also in church and craft '*ẹgbẹ́*', and that its recreational and social functions are performed also by market-women's professional associations and the 'away' branches of town Progressive Unions. All in all, the *ẹgbẹ́* seems to be the Yoruba model for a type of urban association that is not uncommon in African cities; it has affinities, for instance, with the recreational aspects of the Freetown *compin*.[4] But unlike the *compin*, which represents immigrant response to unfamiliar urban pressures, the *ẹgbẹ́*, as it were, flourishes on its home ground, its ties criss-crossing with those of a number of other groupings: kin group and compound, craft guild, religious group, Progressive Union; it therefore has a less heavy load to carry. Although it provides an alternative focus of interest to the kin group, the *ẹgbẹ́* does not substitute itself for the latter, as the *compin* to a large extent has to do, in providing some form of social security; nor does it, except their home-town Union for strangers in a strange town, function as an exclusive group for identification.

XII

The above descriptive catalogue of Yoruba urban associations is not, of course, exhaustive. It may, however, show something of their vitality and variety, and indicate how many types of social contacts are open to the *ará ìlú* outside his own kin group and compound.

[1] Op. cit.   [2] Op. cit.
[3] P. C. Lloyd, 1955; cf. Bascom, 1951. Schwab, 1965, agrees with Bascom.
[4] Banton, 1957.

It is true that a number of the Yoruba associations have grown out of groupings recruited by such 'non-urban' criteria as kinship and age; though as Bascom[1] points out in connection with òrìṣà cult groups, instances of ' "pure" associations—that is those where kinship lines do not figure at all' are probably less frequent even in our own culture than is often supposed. In any case, the ethnographic evidence remains: òrìṣà groups are not recruited, or even believed to be recruited, by descent alone; the old craft guilds based on compound specialization have, in a new economic situation, burst their boundaries and become the new guilds of individual masters and apprentices; the ẹgbẹ́ as age-set has not simply died out, but branched out into a number of new, voluntary and alternative ẹgbẹ́ social clubs. The different associations change in form and function, borrow organizational features from each other, shade off into each other; often only the old names remain to show that a rich tradition of associational life has merely changed and adapted itself to new circumstances, without any sharp break in continuity.

Associations are, of course, a prominent feature of social life in the whole West African region. There is probably no single Yoruba association for which some close parallel could not be cited from some other West African people, and not necessarily in an urban context; an outstanding example are the neighbouring Ibo. What appears to be characteristic of the Yoruba, however, is the number and variety of such groupings; or, to put it another way, the number of different interests of the individual which are catered for through associations.

This, it will be remembered, was Wirth's[2] definition of the 'heterogeneity' which he believed was characteristic of the social life of large, dense, and permanent clusters of population: 'No single group has the undivided allegiance of the individual . . . By virtue of his different interests arising out of different aspects of his social life, the individual acquires membership in widely divergent groups, each of which functions only with reference to a single segment of his personality.' The extent to which this heterogeneity of allegiance and membership is valued by the Yoruba themselves can be illustrated by a quotation from Fadipẹ,[3] himself a Yoruba. Describing the 'phase of young man about town' which precedes marriage, he says: 'At this period it is the

[1] Bascom, 1944.　　　[2] Op. cit; cf. above, Chapter I.　　　[3] Op. cit.

aim of the young man to belong to as many associations and clubs as he possibly can, including both religious associations, convivial, social and so on. It is the period of showing off *par excellence*.' After marriage, the cares of a family impinge somewhat on a man's associational social life; yet 'If a lay official of his church or chapel, he continues in the duties of his office. He also, according to his means, endeavours to keep up membership of his clubs and societies.'

This positive value set upon membership of as many associations as possible may well be part of the high estimation in which the Yoruba hold urban life: it is the mark of an *ará ìlú* to belong to many associations; the despised *ará oko* has no such opportunities. It also seems possible that the number and variety of such associations in Yoruba towns is, as Wirth thought, closely connected with the clustered mode of settlement;[1] and that this complex interweaving of associational groupings constitutes an institutional expression of Yoruba urban life.

[1] Cf. also Durkheim, 1964, Book I, Chapters V and VI.

VI

SOCIAL STRATIFICATION

I

1956, the year in which U.N.E.S.C.O. published the proceedings of its Conference on the Social Implications of Industrialization and Urbanization in Africa South of the Sahara,[1] also witnessed the publication of two collections of papers dealing with another, related problem that was beginning to exercise the minds of social scientists at work in Africa. One was put out by the Institute of Differing Civilisations at Brussels, under the title, *Development of a Middle Class in Tropical and Sub-Tropical Countries*;[2] the other, again a U.N.E.S.C.O. publication, was called 'African Elites'.[3] The two terms, 'middle class' and 'élite', have ever since haunted every discussion of possible changes in the pattern of stratification among non-European peoples, particularly among urban Africans; 'middle class' was more fasionable ten years ago that it is now, and even 'élite' is, as E. Ardener[4] points out, showing some signs of having outlived its heuristic usefulness in this context, though nobody seems very certain of what to put in its place. As Lloyd[5] says: 'One feels that both terms were adopted by their users as a means of referring to an important category of persons. A recent writer who referred to the "middle-class élite" seems to have tried to get the maximum of descriptive elements into his terminology !'

It is hardly surprising that social scientists find neither term entirely satisfactory; both are importations—in themselves highly controversial—from two almost totally distinct streams of thought in Western sociology, designed by and for Western industrial

---

[1] Forde (ed.), 1956. Cf. above, Chapter I, Section I.   [2] I.N.C.I.D.I., 1956.
[3] U.N.E.S.C.O., 1956.   [4] E. Ardener, 1967.
[5] P. C. Lloyd, 1966(a). I should like at this point to acknowledge how much my treatment of social stratification in Yoruba towns owes to this writer's recent and abundant publications on Yoruba and other élites.

societies. In describing such societies, the two terminologies are seldom used by the same writer.[1]

Élite, in its common usage in Western sociology, refers essentially to Top People; to the superior persons in any given society.[2] These are contrasted with the undifferentiated rest of society, 'the masses', who try to emulate the behaviour of the élite. The élite must therefore be imitable; but not *too* imitable, or it would lose its exclusiveness, and thus its superiority. It must remain sufficiently above the masses to provide leadership, not only in setting life-styles, but also in creating and transforming the ideas and values of the society. It must, in other words, be able to act as a 'reference-group' for the masses: a reference group, moreover, which is positively valued even by those outside it who do not necessarily seek membership of it.

The term also implies that the élite constitute the top category in an open society;[3] indeed, 'élite' has come to be used preferentially in describing societies with a high degree of vertical mobility, and is in this sense contrasted with such terms as 'caste' and 'hereditary aristocracy' which refer to a well-defined, generally endogamous upper stratum. Pareto's original theory of élites[4] contained the concept of their 'circulation'; this to a large extent is still current, and implies a certain impermanence in élite status.

Other aspects of Pareto's theory are more debated. For him, a society had a number of élites: the word denoted the top persons of each occupation or profession. Nowadays perhaps most social scientists would argue that the superiority of the élite is of a general character, common to all its members; though opinions differ as to the cohesiveness of the group, and as to whether the masses conceive of the élite as a recognizable category, or see simply a collection of enviable individuals.

As for class, this is an even more controversial subject. One school of thought, which traces its descent back to Marx, sees classes as economic or political-interest groups, largely hereditary in character and logically opposed to one another. As against this, the American school typified by L. Warner[5] sees classes essentially as status groups, arranged in a hierarchical continuum. However, most sociologists would probably agree that economic stratification—though not only in the strict Marxist sense of relation to the

[1] P. C. Lloyd, 1966(a).   [2] Nadel, 1956; Bottomore, 1964.
[3] Popper, 1945.   [4] Bottomore, 1964.   [5] Warner, 1942.

means of production—plays an important part in class structure; and those that are not rigid Marxists would probably further agree that differential wealth is not the only criterion of class membership. The other, not strictly economic, criteria are generally loosely grouped under 'prestige'; the difficulty of definition arises out of the fact that they are both manifold and culturally variable. Granted that public opinion, in many societies, accords different degrees of prestige to different categories of people, the grounds on which such prestige differentiations may be based are almost infinite in number. Some of these grounds, such as sex and age, have no place in a class structure; but many others do: 'A special social arithmetic depends upon an intuitive balancing and weighting of the individual's social standing according to several prestige dimensions simultaneously. Only by this method can income be added to occupation, family background to power, and participation to life-style.'[1] The sheer number of different criteria used in this type of 'intuitive social arithmetic' means that many different combinations of them are possible. Some societies, and some sub-societies within them, will attach more weight to income in defining class, others to birth, education, style of life. Even within the same large country, e.g. the U.S.A., we would expect to find class structure to differ from region to region; and this is in fact what happens. Even where its presence is indisputable, class is one of the most culturally variable of social phenomena.

There is, however, another feature of class systems upon which there seems to be fairly wide agreement—this time a formal rather than a semantic one: in a class structure, there is a limited but genuine mobility between the classes. In this sense, an upper class, for instance, lies conceptually somewhere between an élite, which we have seen is associated with a very high degree of vertical mobility in the society within which it occurs, and such rigid upper strata as a hereditary aristocracy or a superior caste.

The characteristic of limited but genuine mobility logically includes two others: first, the generally agreed importance of differentials in wealth; secondly, the statistical predominance of a kinship-residential unit consisting essentially of parents and dependent children.

Wealth, at least in a money economy, can be acquired or lost during a single lifetime; it can also, in certain durable forms, be

[1] Reissman, 1960.

transmitted to the next generation. In this it differs, both from purely ascriptive advantages, which are either non-transmissible (statuses based on sex or age) or transmissible by rigorous rules (statuses based on birth into a given existing stratum); and from purely achieved ones (e.g. personal prestige acquired through noble deeds or wisdom) which cannot be transmitted in the same form at all. Achievable and inheritable wealth is thus almost a paradigm of the curious mixture of ascription and achievement that characterizes a true class structure, and differentiates it, on the one hand, from more rigid modes of social stratification and, on the other, from fluid, non-stratified forms of prestige ranking.

But the criterion of limited but genuine mobility does not merely require the possibility of transmitting to one's children differential social advantages based on achievable wealth; it also implies that children need not, when they grow up, remain in their parents' social stratum. While young and dependent, they will be assigned by outsiders to the class of their parents; in later life, however, they may individually 'rise above' or 'fall below' it—although, if class stratification is to exist at all, a certain degree of inertia will operate to hold them in the class of their birth. (This degree of inertia varies between the class structures of different societies, and within one society may vary over a period of time: it is in this sense that one can speak of a class structure 'emerging', 'solidifying' or 'dissolving'.

Adult sons and daughters, in other words, may belong to a different class from that of their parents; and adult brothers and sisters, similarly, be assigned to different classes. This means that class structure is inimical to the cohesion of the wider kinship group: the type of family structure associated with it is the narrow and shallow 'biological family' of Western urban sociology, consisting of parents and dependent children.

In African sociology, the terms 'middle class' and 'élite' have, as we have seen, been used almost too interchangeably, to talk about the same 'important category of persons'—the category, recognizably similar in most African countries despite national and local variations, from which nationalist political leaders have predominantly emerged.[1] Its characteristics are comparative affluence and a degree of Western education; for the Yoruba, Lloyd[2] uses 'the term élite to denote those men and women who have

---

[1] P. C. Lloyd, 1966(a).   [2] P. C. Lloyd, 1966(b).

received a substantial western education and are (almost in conse-
quence) relatively wealthy.'

During the colonial period, it made a certain amount of sense
to speak of these people as a 'middle class' in that they were placed
between the expatriate colonial officials and the illiterate mass of
the population;[1] nowadays, it is clear that if they can be said to
form a class at all, it is an upper one: these are the people at the
top of the social scale, who hold the reins of power in their hands,
who have prestige as well as wealth. Accordingly, since Independence the term 'middle class' has been more and more replaced by
'élite'.[2] I shall here follow Lloyd's usage of that term, including
its connotation of relatively impermanent status; in the final
Section of this Chapter, the possible hardening of this élite into a
well-defined upper class will be discussed.

II

Classes in the Marxist sense of property-owning and non-own-
ing groups exist in neither traditional nor modern Yoruba society.
Most land is still vested in descent group or community;[3] industry
is overwhelmingly owned and controlled either by the State or by
foreign companies:[4] and even the urban wage-earner generally
has some land-rights elsewhere. Thus, there is only the faintest
indication, even in the modern sector of the economy, of either
bourgeoisie or proletariat.

Differences of income, however, are very sharply defined in
modern Yoruba society; but, very largely, they relate, not to
differences in property ownership, but to varying positions within
a bureaucratically defined occupational structure, access to whose
higher ranks is by educational qualifications:

Thus, in Western Nigeria the national income per head is £30 per
annum; the farmer usually pays tax on an assessed income of £50; the
unskilled labourer earns £75 a year and the most skilled artisan nearly
£300. The holder of a West African School Certificate (gained on
successfully completing five years of secondary schooling) will expect to
start earning £240 as a clerk or teacher. *The university graduate,*

---

[1] P. C. Lloyd, 1966(a).
[2] P. C. Lloyd, *et al.*, 1966; P. C. Lloyd, 1967(b) and (c); Smythe and Smythe,
1960; Morton-Williams, 1956; Tardits, 1956.
[3] But cf. P. C. Lloyd, 1962.   [4] But cf. Callaway, 1967(a).

however, commences at £750, with a ceiling at £3,000: in addition, he is given a loan to buy a car and a monthly allowance to run it; he may, if in the higher ranks, occupy a part-furnished house, paying one-twelfth of his income (rent of a privately owned house would take between a quarter and a fifth of his income).[1] [Italics mine.]

When a Nigerian describes a man as 'senior service', he means, therefore, something quite definite: a bureaucratic post, a well furnished house, and a car.

The possession of a car sharply divides those who are able to live in the suburban residential areas from those who must live in the crowded town [of Ibadan]; it distinguishes those who may visit widely separated friends from those who cannot. In government service one is eligible for a loan to buy a car and a monthly allowance to run it when one reaches a salary of about £600. This is thus the major income divide between the élite and the masses.[2]

Membership of the élite (as defined by Lloyd, which excludes, for instance, wealthy but poorly educated traders)[3] is thus almost coterminous with membership of the higher reaches of the bureaucracy. During the colonial period, the private professions were very attractive to educated Africans, since the successful were not frustrated by being employed in ranks below those of expatriates with similar qualifications, as in the Civil Service; today, though lawyers have largely remained in private practice, most doctors are employed in the public service.[4]

Before the recent official abolition of the Regions, the government of Western Nigeria was by far the largest employer of high-income earners. In late 1963 it had working in Ibadan about 500 persons earning above £1,000 a year, and a similar number earning between £500 and £1,000.[5] The salary scales are basically those of the colonial period, when salaries paid to British officials were generally higher than they would have earned with similar qualifications in Britain, as an inducement to encourage them to work overseas; as Nigerians have occupied their posts, they have claimed the same salaries and other perquisites.[6] Conditions of employment and salary structures are very similar in the public

---

[1] P. C. Lloyd, 1966(a).
[2] P. C. Lloyd, 1967(b). For the importance of the car as an élite status symbol, cf. also Achebe, 1960. The hero of the novel is an Ibo, but the situation would be recognized by any young Yoruba man in the same situation.
[3] P. C. Lloyd, 1966(a).   [4] P. C. Lloyd, 1967(b).   [5] Ibid.   [6] Ibid.

corporations: the University of Ibadan was, in 1963, employing over 400 senior staff, of whom one-third were Nigerian; the proportion is almost certainly higher today and, with the departure of the Ibo, more of them are Yoruba. University salaries range between £1,200 at the bottom of the lecture grade and £3,000 for a professorship.[1]

These bureaucratic corporations have set the style for the major expatriate commercial firms. The incomes of private professional men are more difficult to estimate; income tax figures suggest, however, that in Ibadan the number of self-employed men earning over £1,000 a year is roughly equivalent to the number of bureaucrats with this salary. Among these must be reckoned a few wealthy traders; but these mostly 'live in the heart of Ibadan; few are westernized in the sense of being well educated or maintaining a European style of life'.[2] Though they may be wealthier than the bureaucrats and professionals, their status is by no means comparable.

Access to this *bourgeoisie de la fonction publique*[3] is, as we have noted, almost entirely in terms of educational qualifications. Rank at entry into the structure depends on the school or university qualification previously obtained; in this sense, as Lloyd points out,[4] university graduation, once achieved, becomes 'virtually an ascribed status'. Subsequent promotion is by seniority —a feature which, now that the rates of both Nigerianization and expansion have slowed down appreciably, appears to be producing considerable frustration among highly qualified younger bureaucrats.[5]

Another source of frustration, and one not widely understood, is that the educational level required for entry into the élite is continually rising. Once, a completed primary-school education was enough to ensure entry into the ranks of clerks and teachers— occupations which at that time counted as having élite status.[6] Now, when the prizes have suddenly become so much greater, the pace has become far more difficult to maintain. Primary education has been free in most Yoruba areas[7] since 1955;[8] and even secondary education no longer suffices to get a youth a job,

---

[1] Op. cit.   [2] Ibid.   [3] Dumont, 1962.   [4] P. C. Lloyd, 1966(a).
[5] Ibid.; cf. also P. C. Lloyd, 1967(b).
[6] P. C. Lloyd, 1967(b) and 1958; cf. also Awolowo, 1960.
[7] i.e. in the former Western Region.   [8] Callaway, 1967(b).

let alone a well-paid élite one.[1] It is important today largely as a stepping-stone to post-secondary training, preferably at a University: 'For many a young man his struggle to achieve ends with his entry to a university—the university will ensure that most of its students will graduate.'[2] Post-primary education, however, costs money:

Boarding and tuition fees in secondary grammar schools amount to about £75 per annum irrespective of the quality of the school; the real costs of education in the better schools are two or three times this figure. Thus, although admission to these schools is by competitive examination, it is in fact restricted to those with financial means. Similarly, the fees charged by the Universities in Nigeria (about £150 per annum) amount to one-eighth of the cost of the education provided.[3]

But, it will be remembered, the university graduate will start earning at about £750 per annum, rising by increments to over £2,000, with his average income perhaps £1,500 a year—or £1,000 a year more than the income of secondary-school leavers. Thus, in crude terms, an investment of £500 in a heavily subsidized university education will yield a gross annual return averaging over 200 per cent in the three following decades.[4] It is in this sense, rather than in that of property ownership, that membrs of the élite can—and do—transmit their status to their children. Wealth is inherited in the form of education; the education of one's children is, indeed, almost the only form of investment which is permissible in a society still largely dominated by the values of kinship and conspicuous expenditure. In such a society, the difficulties of accumulating capital are paralleled only by those of evolving a large-scale, transmissible business organization; but the education of children can —even if it is recognized as potentially lucrative—at the same time be seen both as prestige expenditure, and as generosity to one's kin.

III

The Yoruba do not think of themselves as forming a class society.[5] Where access to élite membership is through the gateway of Western education, there is still, in all sectors of society, a feeling of 'plenty of room at the top'; and the élite themselves stress

---

[1] Callaway, 1967(b). [2] P. C. Lloyd, 1966(a). [3] Ibid.
[4] P. C. Lloyd, 1967(c). [5] P. C. Lloyd, 1966(b).

classlessness as an aspect of the 'African personality', pointing perhaps to solidarity within the wider kin group (which normally contains non-élite as well as élite members) and expressing horror at the 'selfish' Western nuclear family.[1] As Lloyd points out, such an ideology, by playing down the possibilities of discontent lower down the social scale, is itself a sort of defence of élite privileges;[2] moreover, 'the degree of verbal emphasis placed on . . . traditional values [of solidarity with more distant, non-élite kin] may well be the result of their continually threatened erosion as societies become more . . . stratified.'[3]

Nonetheless, it must be admitted that *prima facie* there appears to be a good deal of truth in this self-image of Yoruba society. Most authorities agree in dating the rapid growth of the modern Yoruba élite from the early 1950s, a time at which the rise in world cocoa prices and consequent prosperity and business optimism coincided with the approach of Independence and the consequent rapid Nigerianization of the Civil Service, as well as of the management personnel of some of the larger firms; education, too, expanded enormously at this time.[4] As a result, promotion has, for those who graduated at about this period, been extremely quick; and many of these came from very humble homes indeed. For the Ibadan élite, Lloyd[5] calculates that two-fifths of the men with post-secondary education have fathers who never attended school and were most probably farmers or poor craftsmen; only one-quarter have fathers who received post-primary education (these were, of course, the élite of their own generation). Between two-thirds and three-quarters of the mothers of these men are illiterate; only 5 per cent received post-primary education. The élite women tend to come from rather more educated homes: less than 10 per cent have illiterate fathers, and of present-day élite women having post-primary education, two-thirds have literate mothers.

In these circumstances, and where education is the gateway to the 'senior service' post that brings with it a well-furnished house and a car,[6] it is hardly surprising that Yoruba should see their society as an essentially mobile one; that school-leavers from less modernized towns should flock into Ibadan in the hope of some-

---

[1] P. C. Lloyd, 1966(a) and 1967(b). [2] P. C. Lloyd, 1966(b).
[3] P. C. Lloyd, 1966(a). [4] Callaway, 1967(b).
[5] P. C. Lloyd, 1967(b). Cf. also P. C. Lloyd, 1966(b).
[6] P. C. Lloyd, 1967(b).

how, somewhere, obtaining a 'higher qualification',[1] and that most élite households should contain at least one junior relative, who is given assistance with his own schooling, often in exchange for domestic services.[2]

For it is also true that members of the élite continue to feel a very appreciable degree of solidarity with their less fortunate kin; according to Lloyd,[3] all the élite visit their home towns at least once a year, and many go monthly if their parents are still alive and if the distance does not exceed a hundred miles each way. Many men are in fact spending one-fifth of their income on school fees for relatives. The structure of the family facilitates this inter-kin assistance: the educated man earns a high salary as soon as he leaves university, but with free state primary schools it will be some time before he has to pay secondary school fees for his own children. In the intervening years, he can repay his debt to his family by educating his own junior siblings or the children of his elder siblings. In such an arrangement, the youngest stand most to gain: the next most junior sibling has often lost his chance of schooling before his elder brother is in a position to support him.[4] Lloyd[5] cites 'a striking though not a typical example . . . of a poor farmer whose first son gained a doctorate; the next two sons did not complete a primary education; the following three are now in a University, their education largely financed by their elder brother'. Moreover, this pattern is likely to continue for a long period. The present élite may well find it difficult to finance the education of all their children; but by the time they themselves reach retirement age and the youngest child is ready for university, the eldest will already be earning and will be able to assist him.[6]

Nor is the training of junior siblings or more distant relatives the only form of assistance given to the wider kin group. The élite invariably assume financial responsibility for their parents in old age;[7] and, although a preference is often expressed for living away from the family compound, so that one is freed from the persistent demands of all and sundry, money will continue to be spent on what are regarded as deserving causes within the kin group.[8] This is particularly true of élite men, who, partly under the pressure of Progressive Unions and other ethnically or territorially

---

[1] Callaway, 1967(b).   [2] P. C. Lloyd, 1967(b).   [3] Ibid.
[4] P. C. Lloyd, 1966(a).   [5] P. C. Lloyd, 1967(b).   [6] Ibid.   [7] Ibid.
[8] P. C. Lloyd, 1966(a).

based associations,[1] retain close ties with descent group and home town; the élite wife's responsibility tends to be limited to her own siblings.[2]

There can be no doubt that this persistence of the solidarity of the wider kin group associated with the traditional compound militates against the emergence of a class structure. As we have seen, the latter is tied both to the narrow and shallow 'biological family' and to the existence of some form of transmissible wealth; indeed, despite the ideal of a wider solidarity, there is 'undoubtedly a conflict between the desires of the élite, on the one hand to furnish their own homes and to educate their own children, and, on the other, their feelings of obligation toward . . . kin.'[3] Nonetheless, the ideal has so far shown a surprising persistence and vitality; and the large, cohesive, conceptually permanent unit centred around the descent group carried with it its own values— both the cohesion of the group, and its numerical increase[4] are held, at any rate in theory, to be more important than the desire of any particular member to 'rise in the world' above his elders or transmit to his children either more or less than has been handed to him.

Equally persistent is the positive valuation placed on open-handedness and generosity; and indeed, on display, which seems to be seen almost as a form of generosity in itself. In traditional towns, a rich man's motor car or fine house is held to confer prestige upon the whole town. This is appropriate to a society with a strong, pervasively homogeneous culture and a sentiment of theoretical equality among its full members: it is felt to be right and proper that a rich man should live as a poor man would if he had the chance. The typical reproach against a rich man is not that he is unscrupulous, but that he is miserly; and the forms which his expenditure should take are both traditional and agreed upon by the whole town. The chromium-plated motor-car has replaced the horse, the 'Brazilian' house with balconies and cement lions, the large and solid compound; but these substitutions do not alter the basic pattern. A fine house and motor-car, many wives, a magnificent wardrobe, lavish entertainment, expenditure on

---

[1] Cf. above, Chapter V, Section X. [2] P. C. Lloyd, 1967(b).
[3] P. C. Lloyd, 1966(a).
[4] This carried over into monogamous *élite* households where completed families of six children are by no means uncommon (B. B. Lloyd, 1966).

prestige-conferring title contests—these are the proper use of a rich man's money; and they do not make for the permanence of wealth, or for its transmission, with the prestige it confers, to the next generation. Traditional expenditure patterns, the very mode through which prestige rewards wealth, are as inimical to the birth of a class structure as the kinship system itself. Lloyd[1] writes:

> In each Yoruba town stories are told of the wealthy men who lived in the nineteenth century . . . Foremost in keeping these stories circulating are the descendants of these men who are alive today. Yet few of these descendants, and many of them are only the grandsons of the legendary hero, have themselves reached positions of economic or political importance in the town. . . . Two reasons seem responsible for this: in the first place money could, until recently, only buy luxuries and could not be invested in property or education which would yield a return later; in the second place, these trading businesses each existed in the hands of one man and were maintained through his own efforts and personal contacts; when he died there was no administrative machinery for a son to inherit.

The ideal, in fact, remains the *gbajúmọ̀*, the free spender and generous giver, and perhaps even more, the *ọlọlá*, the wealthy man of the highest character (which also implies generosity, not hoarding one's money but spending it to increase one's honour and good name).[2] Neither of these terms, nor other similar ones,[3] refers to a group of persons, let alone a class; those designated by them 'stand, individually, at the apices of groups consisting of kin and followers, with whom is most of their interaction.'[4]

There are, however, other features of the traditional Yoruba social system that are by no means inimical to the appearance of a class structure. Among these must be reckoned the importance everywhere placed both on differential social prestige, and on wealth as a means of achieving it. Lloyd,[5] asking 'a sample' of informants (we are not told how the sample was chosen) the question: 'What occupations make a man a big man in town?' received the following consensus of answers: first, the *ọba*; then, large-scale traders, lawyers, and doctors; then, in order of ranking, senior Government servants; small-scale traders; occupants of minor clerical posts; the wealthier farmers; craftsmen using

---

[1] P. C. Lloyd, 1958.   [2] P. C. Lloyd, 1966(b).   [3] Cf. Bascom, 1951.
[4] P. C. Lloyd, op. cit.   [5] P. C. Lloyd, 1958.

European techniques; traditional craftsmen; chiefs; and poor farmers. Lloyd comments that the differential appears to be, quite simply, one of wealth—the estimated income or potential income from these occupations—allied in the case of the *ọba* with traditional prestige (but the traditional prestige of the chief, now divorced from wealth—chief's salaries are very low where they exist at all—clearly does not suffice to 'make him a big man').

Moreover, the multiplicity of associations described in Chapter V opens the way to prestige differentiation between them;[1] and it is perfectly possible for a man to belong to different associations from those of which his father was a member. We have already noted that wealth, in the form of fee-payments, was the gateway to the most prestigious of all these associations, which in certain towns also held wide political powers: the higher ranks of *ògbóni* or *òṣùgbó*.

In fact, prestige differentiation within the *ìlú* contains, at different levels of the hierarchy, elements both of ascription and of achievement. On the one hand, the highest status of all, that of the *ọba*, can be filled only by a member of the royal lineage; which in this respect, and in this respect only, was traditionally differentiated from commoner lineages. One of the most interesting features of traditional Yoruba political structure was the way in which a royal lineage persisting through time was prevented from ever becoming a princely ruling class. This was achieved by a complete separation between the *ọba*'s person and his office. Once elected by the town chiefs from among the candidates put forward by the royal lineage (or in Ijẹbu Ode by the palace slaves), and duly consecrated in his office, the new *ọba* was, as it were, lifted out of his former social personality, including membership of his descent group for ordinary purposes: the house and farms he might have possessed were taken over by his immediate heirs at his accession. Conversely, no wealth accruing to the *ọba* by virtue of his office, whether at installation or afterwards, ever went to his kinship heirs; even the royal wives being taken over by his successor after death, rather than by a younger brother or eldest son as in non-royal families.[2] In fact, the members of the royal lineage were generally quite poor, as well as devoid of political power; though a tolerated exception was made in some cases for very near kin. Thus Bascom,[3]

---

[1] According to Schwab, 1965, this is an important factor in Oshogbo.
[2] P. C. Lloyd, 1954.　　　　　　　　　　　　　　[3] Bascom, 1951.

in his account of social stratification in Ifẹ, places the royal kin of the compound from which the ọba was chosen in his second-highest category, with the town and palace chiefs and just below the ọba himself, while members of the other twenty-one royal lineage compounds come at the very bottom of the scale, above only Yoruba 'strangers' and (lowest of all) the non-Yoruba inhabitants.

Commoner descent groups established in the town, on the other hand, are described by Lloyd as being at least putatively equal amongst themselves; though he also tells us[1] that prestige differences existed between these lineages, dependent on such factors as numerical size, length of history within the town, famous origin as substantiated by the myths of each group, and the possession of a senior chieftaincy title in the lineage. We have seen, however, that in Ijẹbu and Ondo on the one hand, Abẹokuta and Ibadan on the other, such senior titles were not the apanage of descent groups as a rule, but developed upon the higher ranks of the ògbóni-type associations, access to which was largely by wealth. In these towns, wealth differentials must therefore also have played a part in the prestige ranking of living descent groups; and this factor must, to some extent, have militated against that of numerical size.

Bascom,[2] moreover, describes for Ifẹ a fairly complex system of social stratification, of which the middle reaches are, from our point of view, the most interesting. After the two top strata—that occupied only by the ọba himself and that consisting of chiefs and the immediate royal kin—come the chief priests; then a rather motley group consisting of the ọba's bodyguard and messengers, the members of the ògbóni (even though in Ifẹ it had no strong tradition of political power) and a special category called lọ́dọ̀kọ̀, 'men of leisure'. After this come the commoner clans, but divided into two strata: the Mọ́dẹwá descent groups from whom the palace chiefs are chosen, and below them the Ifẹ̀ descent groups from whom the town chiefs are chosen. These two categories of descent groups between them make up the bulk of the town's population.

The differential ranking of Mọ́dẹwá and Ifẹ̀ descent groups is correlated with the supposedly greater influence of the palace chiefs chosen from among the former. The original Mọ́dẹwá are said to descend from the ọba's allies, whom, in gratitude for their

[1] P. C. Lloyd, 1960.   [2] Op. cit.

assistance, he allowed to live in the palace. They thus seem, originally, to have been a sort of 'king's men' or clients, representative of the ọba's personal power over against the town's descent groups.

The really interesting feature of the situation, though, is that Módẹwá rank can be achieved, and the fruits of the achievement to some extent transmitted to one's descendants. This is done by taking a lódọ̀kọ̀ title, which requires, in the same way as promotion within the ògbóni-type secret societies, large fee-payments devoted to the feasting of existing lódọ̀kọ̀, and of the town and palace chiefs.

These 'men of leisure' have a number of privileges: exemption from all work including free labour for the ọba; entitlement for their sons to posts in the ọba's bodyguard and messenger corps, and to membership of the ògbóni. In other words, the immediate descendants of a man who has taken a lódọ̀kọ̀ title are assured of a place high up in the social scale. These privileges, however, cannot be transmitted to a third generation; what does so pass down is the status of Módẹwá which the original lódọ̀kọ̀ has acquired for all his descendants. If these wish to re-acquire the other rewards of lódọ̀kọ̀ship, they must take the title and pay the fees again; some do so, but there is obviously less incentive when Módẹwá status has been gained once and for all.

We have here a description of something that comes very close, structurally, to a true class system; the only essential difference being that downward mobility is somewhat limited by the fact that Módẹwá status, once gained, can never be lost (indeed, Bascom tells us that members of Módẹwá descent groups now constitute the most numerous sector of the town's population).[1] The lódọ̀kọ̀ title system does not merely, like ògbóni and other titles, lift the wealthy individual out of his descent group, and even out of his own ọmọ ìyá, by conferring upon him a special prestige acquired by his unusual wealth: his children, and (to the extent of Módẹwá status) all his descendants, are lifted up with and by him. A form of prestige expenditure socially expected of the rich has become a form of transmissible investment. The man who takes a lódọ̀kọ̀ title is 'giving his children advantages' just like any Victorian paterfamilias.

An even more interesting feature than the limitation placed on

[1] Bascom, op. cit.

downward mobility is the fact that what we have seen as 'a form of transmissible investment' is still, as it were, disguised as a prestige expenditure. A rich member of a non-*Módęwá* descent group who did not take a *lódòkò* title would be despised as mean, rather than as improvident—just like a rich man today who did not educate his children.

IV

Several other characteristics of the Yoruba élite can be seen as related to its bureaucratic structure and recruitment through educational qualifications. It is, for obvious reasons, centred around Lagos and Ibadan, with their Governmental institutions, universities[1] and large expatriate firms; other towns have no comparable bureaucracies, and only a few professional men, so that no élite networks of friendships can grow up to maintain and transmit the new values. In speaking of the Yoruba élite, then, we are essentially speaking about Ibadan and Lagos.

Culturally, it is homogeneous to a very high degree. House styles, for instance, are to a large extent determined by the housing provided in the Agodi government residential area, the University of Ibadan campus, and the grounds of the University Hospital. The Agodi houses, originally built in the late 1930s for senior British officials whose children were usually away at school in England, have only two large bedrooms—not very adequate provision for Yoruba families, which even among the élite are large. The houses provided by the Western Nigeria Housing Corporation on Bọdija estate also follow substantially the same pattern; to a large extent the same is true on privately developed housing estates.[2] All these are residential suburbs, with no community facilities or shopping centres, so that motor transport is essential; none of the houses can conveniently accommodate more than a family of two parents with dependent children. All in all, it makes for a very different life from that of the big rambling compounds in the older parts of Ibadan itself, or in the home towns of those members of the élite who have come from elsewhere.

---

[1] It is perhaps worth mentioning that until very recently the University of Ifẹ had a large branch at Ibadan, with a campus adjacent to that of the University of Ibadan.

[2] P. C. Lloyd, 1967(b).

The uniformity of the house styles is perpetuated in their interior decoration; in houses built by a public body the hard furnishings are in fact provided with the house, but even elsewhere the hard-wearing and utilitarian designs of the Public Works Department predominate nearly everywhere. Curtains, carpets, and ornaments are circumscribed by the range of styles offered by the Ibadan shops, particularly Kingsway, which the élite patronize by preference.[1]

The families inhabiting these houses likewise exhibit a certain uniformity of structure. Essentially they consist of the husband and father, his one wife, and their young children—the same monogamous educated family which, in provincial towns, may build its own house within or alongside the larger compound, thus expressing the beginnings of its separation out of the larger group.[2] ('Outside wives' are sometimes tacitly tolerated in Lagos[3] and Ibadan;[4] more often, the official wife has no notion of their existence—and in any case they do not share the élite home.) As we have seen, there is sometimes a young relative or two, of either spouse, studying for some qualification and perhaps helping a little with the housework; also one or more servants, sometimes from the home town of one of the spouses; rather more rarely, an old mother. But 'A mother who has always cooked over a wood fire will inevitably feel awkward in, and even frightened by, her élite daughter's all-electric kitchen . . . In general, educated men and women do not approve of having parents living *en famille*—men in particular are aware of the potential tensions between their own mothers and their wives. The houses, too, are not built to accommodate elderly people who need some privacy.'[5]

Another generic likeness in the constitution of these élite families lies in the pattern of marriage: 'None of the élite has been propelled into marriage arranged by their parents; most have met their spouses during student days and their parents have ratified their mutual choice.'[6]

Most educated men, even in the fifties, demanded a degree of education in their wives. Lloyd[7] noted during that period that 'Their constant demand is for a wife who will know how to behave in front of their colleagues and friends, and the demand seems to

[1] P. C. Lloyd, 1967(b); Smythe and Smythe, 1960.   [2] Fadipẹ, op. cit.
[3] Izzett, 1962; cf. also Marris, 1961.   [4] Levine, Klein and Owen, 1967.
[5] P. C. Lloyd, op. cit.   [6] P. C. Lloyd, 1967(b).   [7] P. C. Lloyd, 1958.

have persisted. True, most men seem to prefer wives whose educational qualifications are slightly lower than their own; nonetheless 'above half the men with university degrees find wives with post-secondary education and only a tenth take women with no more than primary schooling'.[1]

As we know,[2] such girls tend themselves to come from educated homes, in a significantly greater proportion than their husbands who have had a comparable, or higher, standard of education: the bride with a secondary or university training almost certainly had a literate father, and is quite likely to have had a literate mother as well.[3] If we take into account the perpetually shifting educational frontier of the élite, it is probably true to say that the wife is more likely to be a second-generation member of it than her husband, and thus to have absorbed certain non-traditional attitudes and values during her own childhood. She is also quite likely to come from a different town: this may be attributed to the search for an educated wife, coupled with the fact that most men meet such women at university, perhaps even overseas. It does seem to be the case that men who practise 'town exogamy' in this way acquire wives with a slightly higher level of education. The exception is Ijẹbu, whose educated sons do seem preferentially to marry their townswomen; but then Ijẹbu has an unusual number of educated women, so that they have plenty of choice.[4]

These very widespread characteristics of the élite wife—a level of education often comparable to her husband's, a possible longer-established membership of the élite, and the likelihood of her coming from a different town—have an important effect on a number of variables in the social relationships of the élite family: on the extent to which the friendship networks of husband and wife overlap, the closeness of the husband's ties with his home town, the pattern of the marital relationship itself and also of the relationship of the élite father with his children, and perhaps most importantly, from our point of view, upon the functioning of the élite home as a socialization agency for those children.

An educated wife, who, moreover, is not a girl from her husband's home town, is more likely to expect a fairly egalitarian relationship with him, in which the emphasis is on shared roles and responsibilities, and in which she will not be expected to

[1] P. C. Lloyd, 1967(b).   [2] Cf. above, Section III of this Chapter.
[3] P. C. Lloyd, op. cit.   [4] Ibid.

show him the traditional subservience of a Yoruba wife. Her mother, if she was literate and Christian, may already have had some expectations of monogamy in a husband; but she was probably still prepared to see him as a dominant figure, to be revered and obeyed, on the Mission-introduced model of the Victorian pater-familias.[1] The daughter, with a more modern education and possibly some travel overseas, is more likely to expect romantic love and a husband willing to change a baby's nappies; at the same time, and together with these increased demands on her spouse's time and attention, she has probably reverted to her grand-mother's pattern of wanting some earned income of her own.

Such expectations may, of course, be doomed to frustration; but many families in the Lagos and Ibadan élite do seem to approach this egalitarian ideal. Where they do, this impinges upon a number of other domains of social life.

Whatever the pattern of the marital relationship, it is generally true to say that both spouses tend to choose their friends pre-dominantly from among fellow-members of the élite—persons of similar age, occupation, education and income. Even the women rarely choose friends who are neither teachers nor nurses, but traders. In Lloyd's Ibadan sample,[2] three-quarters of the persons cited by the élite members as their closest friends lived in Ibadan itself, and over half were from Yoruba towns and kingdoms other than the informants' own; this proportion seems to be rather larger among the more egalitarian couples, who, in extreme cases, go so far as to have non-Yoruba and even non-Nigerian friends.

For both sexes, about two-thirds of the closest friendships were formed before marriage, typically at school or college; and, in most cases the friendship networks of husband and wife remain largely separate in later life—each spouse spending a large pro-portion of available leisure in visiting and entertaining his own friends, in exclusively male or female gatherings. But where husband and wife do share more friends (or make more friends through each other) the correlation appears to be with the mono-gamous marriage of their own parents[3]—again, one may perhaps guess at a literate mother somewhere in the background.

It is usual for both sexes to participate, though not perhaps very actively, in prestige associations of various kinds; typically, Old Boys' Associations or professional bodies for the men, and the Red

[1] Op. cit. [2] P. C. Lloyd, 1967(b). [3] P. C. Lloyd, op. cit.

L

Cross and other élite charities for the women. Such associations rarely have a membership base wider than the élite; like the friend-ship networks, their tendency is to increase social cohesion among members of the élite, and to exclude other categories.

The extent to which a man participates in the affairs of his distant home town—whether through active membership of the 'away' branch of its Progressive Union[1] or by building a substan-tial house that symbolizes his intention to retire there some day—would appear to be inversely correlated to the degree of egali-tarianism which prevails in his relationship to his wife. But here

It is difficult to disentangle the effects of age and family type. It may well be that these younger men [who are also those who tend towards the more egalitarian relationship with their wives] will become drawn further into their home town affairs as they become older, and thus assume seniority in their own descent groups. Again, as the days of retirement draw nearer they may think more of a small business at home, participation in local politics and perhaps the honour of a chieftancy title. (Title taking is growing in popularity among the more prominent members of the Ibadan élite—the senior civil servants, better-known lawyers, etc.)[2]

In many—perhaps most—élite homes, both husband and wife work. If the wife is herself well-educated, she will want to put her training to good use; moreover, the extra income is often welcome, especially if she has obligations of her own to meet in educating younger siblings, or nephews and nieces; she cannot expect her husband to contribute to the expenses of a descent group not his own.[3] This pattern simply repeats, in modern and affluent conditions, that prevailing in traditional Yoruba society, in which wives always expected, and were expected, to earn money in their own right.[4] The situation is, however, somewhat different in that a woman teacher or doctor or nurse cannot, as a market-trader can, take her baby to work with her strapped to her back; children are therefore usually left in the case of nursemaids—young unmarried girls who come to Ibadan in search of such employment after primary schooling.[5] (In élite conditions, there are no co-wives to leave the children with; and very rarely, except in a family crisis, even a grandmother.)

This absorption in work, friends, associations does not mean,

---

[1] Cf. above, Chapter V.   [3] P. C. Lloyd, op. cit.   [3] P. C. Lloyd, 1967(b).
[4] Ibid.   [5] B. B. Lloyd, 1966.

however, that the élite couple neglect the training of their children; quite the contrary. B. B. Lloyd and others[1] have shown the transformation of the distant father of traditional Yoruba kinship values[2] and the quite equally distant mission-oriented 'Victorian' father into a close, affectionate parent, actively involved in the lives of his children and, if anything, rather tending to spoil them: 'The modern educated father is reported to actively seek a warm, friendly relationship with his children; he plays ball with them, reads to them, and if need be, while living abroad, will help to feed and look after them'.[3] B. B. Lloyd also describes the stress placed on training in manners, and on not playing with non-élite children; the latter, though not the former, would be unthinkable in the family life of the traditional compound, where 'All the compound children play together and are expected to get along well with one another. A mother who tried to choose her child's companions would be thought unsociable and rude.'[4]

Also contrasting with traditional Yoruba upbringing is the emphasis on toys, on being able to amuse oneself quietly, on learning skills such as drawing and music. Quite soon, the élite child will be sent to nursery school; a little later, his parents will use their connections to get him into a primary school with a good reputation, or, if they can afford it, even send him to a fee-paying primary school. More perhaps even than the eleven-plus-obsessed middle-class parent in Britain, Nigerian élite parents tend to see their children's future as a long intricate labyrinth of school places to be won, crucial examinations to be passed and qualifications to be gained—a labyrinth, moreover, through which it is their duty to guide the child using every means open to them; for only through his own education will he be able to retain his parents' élite status.

In all this, and despite the change in the father–child relationship, it is probably the young élite mother who has the most important part to play; and she herself, as we have seen, is likely to have had at least a literate mother herself. All in all, these daughters of the first generation of women literates seem to be a dominant influence in determining many of the most important characteristics of the present élite, including that of probable self-perpetuation. The early 1950s are usually given as the date for the emergence of the present élite, and several authors[5] cite

---

[1] Ibid. Cf. also Levine, Klein and Owen, 1967.   [2] Cf. above, Chapter IV.
[3] Op. cit. [4] B. B. Lloyd, op. cit. [5] P. C. Lloyd, 1967(b); Callaway, 1967(b).

relevant economic and political factors. But could it not also have been the time at which the first sizable group of second-generation literate women reached marriageable age?

V

It is difficult to determine how far the Yoruba élite in fact functions as a reference group for the wider masses of the population. The prestige of élite members is undoubtedly high; on the other hand, they are perhaps too distant, both spatially in Ibadan and Lagos, and economically in terms of the difference between their incomes and those of the craftsmen and farmers, to exert any great influence in this respect. Lloyd[1] is probably right in thinking that the 'marginal élites' of educated provincial ọbas and wealthy but often illiterate traders and the 'sub-élite' of teachers and clerks may be more important as reference groups. The sub-élite in particular appears to have considerable potential significance in this respect. This is the group we have met several times before, often consisting of 'strangers' living in the new quarters on the fringes of traditional inland towns like Oshogbo: literate and generally Christian, often monogamous, potentially mobile both geographically and socially, unusually active participants in their home town's Progressive Union, the members of this sub-élite white-collar stratum seem quite as deeply committed to change and modernity as their élite counterparts; and they are in a much better position to transmit their values to the ordinary farmer or craftsman.

The élite itself, on the other hand, seems to show unmistakable signs of hardening into a semi-hereditary social stratum. Against such emergent stratification militate the ties with the home town and the wider kin group; the latter have undoubtedly been weakened by the spatial separation consequent upon the clustering of the élite in Ibadan and Lagos; the former too may be growing more tenuous, though it is still perhaps too early to tell. Upward mobility into the élite would certainly seem to be lessening; if the present élite achieve their aim of training all their children to an educational level equivalent to their own—and, with their sophisticated manipulation of the educational facilities, there is every reason to believe they will—then the size of their families

[1] P. C. Lloyd, 1966(a).

will, in the next generation, effectively preclude any substantial new recruitment from below. Lloyd[1] is in no doubt about it: 'Over a longer period the elite will become a quasi-hereditary group through its control and manipulation of the higher educational system.' Friendship networks and preferential marriage patterns likewise serve to stiffen the emerging stratum.

Since a measure of mobility does, however, still appear to exist, it seems most appropriate to refer to this stratum as an upper class. But a class is normally thought of as part of a system of classes; it is not, like an élite, simply contrasted with an undifferentiated social mass. Is there any evidence of other classes crystallizing out of Yoruba society?

At the broad farming base, it seems unlikely. Yoruba farmers continue to live in their descent-group-based compounds; traditional loyalties to kin and local groupings—including the *ìlú* itself—remain paramount. The same probably applies to traditional craftsmen, many of whom are in any case part-time farmers. Modern craftsmen, on the other hand, seem increasingly to have primary and sometimes post-primary education, as have the clerks and primary-school teachers—Lloyd's 'sub-élite'. Many of these people still have hopes of themselves attaining élite membership through additional educational qualification; the literate *ọba* and the wealthy, perhaps semi-educated trader, on the other hand, are more likely to covet élite membership for their children. Both categories seem, as time goes on, less and less likely to succeed in their aims; they may yet coalesce into a discontented, largely urban stratum with some of the characteristics of a Western lower middle class. But—once again—one cannot be too cautious about importing such alien labels into the study of indigenously African towns.

[1] Op. cit.

VII

CONCLUSIONS

THE existence among the Yoruba, over several centuries, of large, dense, permanent nucleated settlements not developed in response to European contact must, in the present stage of our knowledge, remain an unexplained datum. A number of speculative explanations have been advanced, some stressing the permissiveness of the ecological environment, others the effect of centralized political institutions. None of these attempts at explanation, however, can really account satisfactorily for the opposed instances: the dense Ibo agricultural population living in scattered village groups,[1] the highly centralized, 'bureaucratic' pre-colonial Baganda changing the site of their capital with the accession of each new Kabaka.[2] The most recent concept, advanced by Miner,[3] of the city as a 'power phenomenon', a 'centre of dominance over outlying areas', seems more descriptive than explanatory; it applies, certainly, to Yoruba towns—but it applies equally well, if 'power' and 'dominance' are to be interpreted as widely as Miner proposes, to any other large nucleated centre. The real answer in this particular case is that we do not know why the Yoruba preferred to live in large towns; but they did, and do—a fact that, on evidence from the literature, appears to have been surprisingly difficult for many students of urban social phenomena to swallow.

One reason for the difficulty has been the fact that the economy of the towns is to a large extent still agriculturally based; and can be presumed to have been more so in the past. It is, of course, true that most towns in pre-industrial societies have been closely linked with their immediate agricultural hinterlands, in that it was local excess of food production that made their existence possible at all; if there is one thing on which Plato[4] and Aristotle[5] agree, it is the importance to the city-state of its farming population. But, in discarding Weber's hallmarks of urbanism—the fortification,

---

[1] Cf. Green, 1947.   [2] Cf. Gutkind, 1963.   [3] Miner, 1967.
[4] Jowett transl. 1953, Vol. II.   [5] Sinclair transl. 1962, Book IV

the market, the degree of political and legal autonomy,[1]—we have discarded also his insight that 'the full urbanite of antiquity was a semi-peasant.'[2]

It is true that Yoruba towns are linked to their surrounding countryside by even stronger ties, in that the Yoruba living in the country traditionally looks upon the town as his 'real' home, and owes direct social allegiance to it. But Goddard[3] is surely right in stressing that, for all the rootedness of the traditional Yoruba town in the surrounding farms, for all the political and socio-religious ties between farm hamlet and town compound, there is between the two an economic discontinuity quite as sharp as the physical frontier once marked by the town wall: the excess of food produced on the farms is not taken into town to sustain the urban-dwelling members of the producers' descent group. Farm hamlet and town compound, in other words, do not form part of a single household economy; there is a cleavage between them, mediated first by the rural periodic market, and then by the town market.[4]

But traditional Yoruba towns have not only refused to fit into the theoretical scheme whereby large urban agglomerations arise essentially in response to industrialization or (in sub-Saharan Africa) 'European contact' or a 'colonial situation'; they have at least two other characteristics which urban sociologists, trained in Western industrial cities, find it difficult to conceive of in association with a strongly nucleated settlement pattern: large cohesive descent groups with the associated kinship values, and a conspicuous lack of 'the *anomie* . . . to which Durkheim alludes'.[5] Yoruba towns in fact do not fit the Wirthian conception—from which urban sociology has never really freed itself—of 'urbanism as a way of life': their citizens have mutual social contacts insufficiently 'impersonal, superficial, transitory and segmental' to be recognizable as townsmen in the eyes of Western sociologists.

Durkheim,[6] who never regarded *anomie* as anything but a transitory social dysfunction, would probably had been surprised to see it erected into a necessary and determinant condition of urban social life as such; but is it in fact such a condition? If it is, it is obviously right to call Yoruba towns 'non-urban' or 'scarcely

---

[1] Cf. above, Chapter II, Section III; and Weber, op. cit.   [2] Weber, op. cit.
[3] Op. cit.   [4] Cf. above, Chapter V, Section II.
[5] Wirth, op. cit. Cf. above, Chapter II, Section III.   [6] Durkheim, 1964.

urban', as has been done in the past. But it will be remembered that Miner[1] experienced similar difficulties in Timbuctoo; though he pacified his sociological conscience by reflecting that in the market-place relationships between members of the different ethnic groups that make up the population were as impersonal and transitory as anything Wirth could have imagined. As indeed to some extent they are in a large Yoruba market;[2] the Yoruba themselves seem to give a symbolic recognition to this, by erecting in each market-place the aniconic effigy of Èṣù, god of chance and change, of crossroads, commerce, and thieves.[3]

Can we then regard 'urbanism as a way of life' on the Wirthian model as something that appears either in the absence of, or between, cohesive groupings based on descent or ethnicity, but not within such groupings? To some extent this is certainly so. And yet, as one of the most eminent students of industrialized African towns[4] has recently complained, this still leaves the picture 'curiously lopsided, and leaves out of account many of the more positive features of urban life . . . What is so universally striking about the life of African towns is its ebullience and gusto, its camaraderie, and the casual ease with which social contacts are established.'

But perhaps this gusto, ebullience, and ease are specifically sub-Saharan characteristics, part of an 'African personality', however vaguely conceived. And yet, there is a small but growing body of evidence[5] to show that even in Western industrial slums, life is not quite as impersonal or as anomic as the exponents of 'urbanism as a way of life' would have us believe; that there are many relationships, even commercial ones, that are personal and lasting; that norms, arrived at by a talked-out consensus between door-to-door gossips, are observed and can even be formulated; that personal ties can have strength and permanence, and at the same time some of the easy camaraderie so readily attributed to African towns. It begins to look, in fact, as though it might be wise to return to another of Weber's insights: that concerning the cultural variability of the size of urban agglomeration 'at which "impersonality" tends to appear'.[6]

Weber himself was well aware that 'precisely this impersonality was absent in many historical localities possessing the legal

---

[1] Miner, 1953.   [2] Cf. Bascom, 1955.   [3] Cf. above, Chapter V, Section VI.
[4] Epstein, 1967.   [5] Cf. Young and Willmott, 1962; Townsend, 1957.
[6] Cf. above, Chapter II, Section III; and Weber, op. cit.

character of cities.'[1] It is only since Wirth's unfortunate common-sense description of the mode of social life in cities that sociologists have carried ethnocentricity to the extent of exluding from their definition of urban life Jerusalem and Kyoto, Mecca and Venice and Tenochtitlan, as well as Athens and Rome in their earlier days (though not perhaps the Alexandrian cities, or Rome during the later Empire).

It seems clear enough that impersonality and *anomie* are *not* necessary concomitants of the social life in large, permanent, densely nucleated settlements, but must be regarded as an independent variable; this much should already have been evident from E. Ardener's discussion[2] of the 'urban' problems arising in the plantations of the Southern Cameroons. Another independent variable, on the evidence of Yoruba towns (and also of the classical Graeco-Roman cities in their earlier stages, as well as of certain Renaissance Italian towns) is the presence or absence of large cohesive 'primary groups'[3] recruited on a kinship basis. On the evidence, it is not living in a densely populated settlement as such that is inimical to the persistence of such groups, but a number of other factors, which, though often occurring simultaneously, should as far as possible be held separate for purposes of analysis: industrialization, the emergence of a class structure, and what used to be known as 'Westernization', for which Lerner[4] has recently proposed the less ethnocentric (though perhaps still not entirely satisfactory) term 'modernization'.

In the face of so many factors potentially separable from the settlement pattern as such, it might in the last resort be simpler to revert unambiguously to size, density, and permanence as criteria; i.e. to retain the loose, common-sense meaning of the words 'town', 'city', and 'urban' to refer to all large, permanent, closely nucleated settlements. 'City' and 'town' might have quantitative referents, if these could be agreed upon; if not, they could continue to be used as quasi-synonymous. We could then rely on one or more sets of descriptive categories to indicate the variables that may affect urban social life.

A. L. Epstein,[5] starting out from Southall's 'type A' and 'type B' classification,[6] has recently proposed for African towns three such sets or dimensions of variability. One refers to the economic sub-

---

[1] Op. cit.   [2] E. Ardener, 1961.   [3] Wirth, op. cit.   [4] Lerner, 1967.
[5] Epstein, 1967.   [6] Southall, 1961. Cf. above, Chapter II, Section II.

structure, and would differentiate, for instance, between industrial centres with their 'company town' characteristics, commercial towns, and administrative or governmental towns. Another is in terms of civic structure, with particular regard to the participation of Africans in city government; a third has reference to demographic factors, such as the rate and permanence of migration, and the degree of imbalance in sex and age in the structure of the population.

This—even if the application of Epstein's criteria merely takes us back to the 'A' and 'B' classification by a methodological *détour*—is at any rate a step in the right direction. It seems clear, however, that a certain refinement of concepts must precede any further attempt at classification. The inclusive definition of 'urban' (implicit both in Southall's classification and in much later work including Epstein's article) is a beginning, in that it makes it possible to separate out such characteristics as industrialization, modernization, impersonality, and large kin-based social groups and assign to them their proper status as variables that may or may not accompany the way of life of large, dense, nucleated settlements (or indeed, each other). But these variables must themselves, in some cases, be given a more workable definition; and there are other possible dimensions of sociological variation to be considered.

Take, for instance, industrialization. That this is a variable potentially independent of the urban pattern of settlement has long been recognized, at least in certain quarters; notably by G. Sjoberg[1] in his definition of the 'pre-industrial city'. But neither Yoruba nor other sub-Saharan pre-colonial agglomerations such as Kumasi, Abomey, or Benin (nor for that matter the capital of the Inca empire) would qualify for inclusion into this conceptual category: Sjoberg so defines his pre-industrial city as to make the presence of literacy (at least among a small group of highly placed organizers) a necessary part of his definition. He believes that the existence of a group of this nature is an inevitable concomitant of any technology sufficiently advanced to support major agglomerations of population. On the evidence, he is plainly mistaken in this; J. Gugler[2] is probably right in hinting that 'the academic tends to over-emphasize the importance of the literati and the formal education systems that propagate them'.

[1] Sjoberg, 1960.   [2] Gugler, n.d.

Or take on what is probably the most valuable part of Wirth's original characterization of city life:[1] the social (*not* necessarily ethnic or class) heterogeneity, whereby 'No single group has the undivided allegiance of the individual . . . By virtue of his different interests arising out of different aspects of his social life, the individual acquires membership in widely divergent groups, each of which functions only with reference to a single segment of his personality.' Such social heterogeneity by multi-membership of associations is indeed widely associated with urban life; indeed, as Durkheim[2] long ago saw, a certain degree of social density is probably a prerequisite for the multiplicity of social ties. Nonetheless, the relationship between an urban settlement pattern and the existence of associational forms has been taken for granted; there has never, so far, been a systematic exploration of the interrelation of these two factors.

Such an exploration might yield interesting results. It might show, for instance, that sociological thinking has been too ready to accept a fundamental opposition between kinship and association as principles of social grouping; Yoruba towns offer some indications[3] that the two may coexist in the same social field to a greater extent than has generally been assumed.

But the inclusive definition of urban phenomena would not only permit us to isolate general sociological variables of this kind, that could facilitate inter-cultural comparison. It would also enable us to appreciate, and perhaps attempt to classify, the variety of urban social organization that can exist within a single culture and at a single period. We have seen that some Yoruba towns have a predominantly segmentary political structure: whether in terms of descent groups like Ọyọ and other northern towns, or in terms of actual separate 'townships', each with its ọba and palace, co-existing within the same urban continuum, like Abẹokuta, Shagamu, and Kabba. Others, like the Ijẹbu and Ondo towns, fill political offices through membership of associations; it may be significant that these are much smaller towns, and that they have a different descent reckoning and different systems of inheritance and land tenure and also a higher proportion of their inhabitants engaged in urban occupations. Finally, there are the milling cosmopolitan cities of Lagos and Ibadan—neither, by this time, purely

---

[1] Op. cit; cf. above, Chapter II, Section III.   [2] Durkheim, 1964.
[3] Bascom, 1944; Schwab, 1965.

Yoruba—the homes of the 'new élite' committed by its values to change and modernity.[1] It seems at least possible that a class system is here emerging; not one on the European model, but a distinct type, specific to the situation, with education as the main form of transmissible investment from the very beginning;[2] but, so far, the system is still characterized by a very high degree of mobility. Occupational roles are increasingly diversified, and increasingly replace descent in forming the basis for recruitment to social groups; modern associations, with overlapping membership, multiply and become increasingly varied in character. It is, indeed, a form of urban society so largely determined by the distribution of education and consequent occupation that it is tempting to borrow Durkheimian terminology once again and call it 'organic'.

Although they are not primarily industrial, Ibadan and Lagos have obvious affinities with Southall's 'B' towns, and indeed with the classical 'Western city' as conceived by urban sociology. In the same way, Ọyọ and similar towns may be thought to resemble Miner's Timbuctoo[3] (though there the segments were well defined ethnic groups) or Fustel de Coulanges's 'ancient cities'.[4] Similarly, the 'associational' towns of Ijẹbu and Ondo may have affinities with the late medieval or early Renaissance 'guild town', for instance pre-Medicean Florence. Such affinities might lead to yet another possible dimension in urban classification, and one more unambiguously sociological than, for instance, that based on the type of economic infrastructure.

The fact that I have used the Durkheimian terms 'segmentary' and 'organic' for the first and last categories in my tentative typology of Yoruba towns should not be construed as meaning that I intend the typology as a developmental continuum; as far as we know, the 'associational' kind of town is quite as ancient in Yoruba culture as the variety I have labelled 'segmentary'. If we are to posit developmental trends, however, it seems likely that all the Yoruba styles of urban society are at present tending towards the 'organic' now typified by Lagos and Ibadan. It is, of course, too soon to tell; we cannot know at this time what the sociological future of the

---

[1] Cf. Miner, 1967; Levine, Klein and Owern, 1967.

[2] In our own society, certain trends would seem to show that a similar part is increasingly played by education at the expense of other factors in the intergenerational transmission of class membership.

[3] Miner, 1953.   [4] Fustel de Coulanges, 1956.

'new élite' will be—whether the Civil Servants and lawyers, doctors and University lecturers, so many of whom were not born in Ibadan, will in the end retire to their home towns and spread the new life-styles and values there; whether their children, born for the most part in Ibadan and strenuously groomed there for membership of their parents' social stratum, will feel any ties at all to their fathers' towns of origin.[1] But it seems at least probable that, if the rich sociological diversity offered by Yoruba towns is to be fully exploited, there is not very much time left for research.[2]

Such research, together with further inter-cultural comparison and the necessary refinement of concepts, would undoubtedly result in time in more sophisticated systems of classification than Southall's 'A' and 'B' towns; though even that simple polarity marked, at the time, a major theoretical advance. But all its advantages will have been lost if all those interested in African urban sociology accept Mitchell's recommendation that 'the focus of sociological interest in African urban studies must be on the way in which the behaviour of town-dwellers fits into, and is adjusted to, the social matrix created by the modern commercial, industrial and administrative framework of a modern metropolis.'[3] Certainly such problems are interesting; but it is not easy to see why there must be a single 'focus of sociological interest in African urban studies': if there is more than one kind of urban community, there can surely be more than one kind of urban study, and more than one focus of interest.

But a diversified research programme of this kind must to some extent depend on the laying of the persistent ghost of 'urbanism as a way of life', which has so long bedevilled urban studies in Africa and elsewhere. Epstein, in a recent article,[4] offers a compromise solution. He is dissatisfied with the simple quantitative meaning classically attached to 'urbanization', which 'refers to living in towns as against living in rural settlements' and on the basis of which it is possible to construct simple quantitative indices; for instance, urbanization is sometimes measured by the proportion of a population resident in towns of a given population size at a given moment. But what, he asks, 'is to be made of a measure which is based on the number of cities with a population

---

[1] Ties with their mothers' towns of origin will, for reasons specified in Chapter VI above, be in any case more tenuous.
[2] Cf. Schwab, 1965.   [3] Mitchell, 1966.   [4] Epstein, 1967.

of 100,000 or more and gives Nigeria an index of urbanization of 4·3 whereas Zambia, whose Copperbelt constitutes a large, modern industrial and urban complex, does not even register?' Clearly wishing to make his peace with West Africanist scholars such as Bascom[1] who insist on regarding the Yoruba as an urban people, he suggests a distinction between 'urbanization' and 'urbanism'. Urbanization, he says, cannot be regarded as a merely quantitative phenomenon: it has 'demographic, social structural, and cultural aspects, each of which poses separate problems'; it should be regarded as 'involving a process of movement and change; its essence is that it creates the possibility of discontinuity with some pre-existing set of conditions'. 'Urbanism', on the other hand, is to stand for 'the way of life of the town themselves'. 'In this way it may be possible to speak for example of Yoruba urbanism without necessarily implying Yoruba urbanization, though it is clear that this process too is occurring on an increasing scale.'

Unfortunately, this ingenious terminological distinction just will not work. I entirely agree that 'urbanism' should be disentangled from its unfortunate heritage of cultural preconceptions and used simply for 'the way of life of the towns themselves'—of any large, stable, densely nucleated settlement; but if it is to be so used—if it is no longer to refer to a particular sub-species of urban society, then 'urbanization' cannot have a narrower connotation. If 'urbanization' is to imply 'the possibility of a discontinuity with some pre-existing set of conditions', then the new set of conditions which creates discontinuity must be urbanism in the sense of 'the way of life of the towns themselves'.

Above all, 'urbanization' cannot be used, *either* of the movement of people from one sort of urban centre to another—for which 'inter-urban migration' would be the correct term[2]—*or* of a change in the character of an urban centre such as Oshogbo, which must be described, like other kinds of social change, with such conceptual tools as have so far been elaborated for that purpose, plus such others as may be devised in the future.

Epstein is certainly right, on the other hand, in rejecting 'indices of urbanization' so constructed that the Copperbelt appears as non-urbanized, and in wishing to tie the concept of 'urbanization' to movement and change. All this means, in effect, is that urbanization must be measured over a period of time—i.e. not the num-

---

[1] Bascom, 1955, 1958, 1959, 1962.   [2] Kuper, 1965.

ber of people resident in towns of a specified size *at a given moment*; but, in the first place, the numbers that have moved there from settlements below the specified size over a given period of time; and, in the second, the numbers that have remained there over a second (longer) period. This processual diachronic aspect of urbanization, and the difficulty of 'adapting synchronic methods [of fieldwork] to diachronic problems' have been explicitly discussed by P. Mayer.[1]

The problem is a real one, and the discussion of possible solutions potentially fruitful. What does not seem likely to be so is a sort of terminological 'gentlemen's agreement', a division of the field between 'urbanization' specialists studying 'type B' towns in the Copperbelt or South Africa, and 'urbanism' experts studying 'type A' towns in West Africa. That way lies madness. Unfashionable though it may be to say so, I still think that a more general acceptance of the following propositions would advance the cause of urban sociology:

An urban settlement (town or city) is a large, permanent, densely nucleated centre of population; numerical parameters, which may have to be varied culturally, can be established for all these characteristics. There are different kinds of towns, with different kinds of urban social life; these can be studied, and a typology can be elaborated, corrected, and refined as necessary. Within a given town, urban social life may change over time, whether of its own momentum or in response to various pressures from outside; the different forms such change may take can be explored. Individuals can migrate from one kind of town to another; this inter-urban migration can, like other kinds of migration, be more or less permanent, and its degree of permanence will affect its sociological consequences for both the towns concerned. Individuals can also migrate, more or less permanently, from small non-urban settlements to towns; such migration, if permanent, constitutes urbanization, in that people who did not previously live in urban centres are now doing so.

It is a reasonable working hypothesis that all these demographic movements, including urbanization, will involve social change; the degree of social change will probably depend, among other things, on their amplitude and permanency. Like other aspects of change, these can be measured only over time.

[1] Mayer, 1963.

Acceptance of any such inclusive scheme would, of course, involve the renunciation of what have in practice become vested interests in the words 'urban', 'urbanism', and 'urbanization'. Such an abandonment is always a difficult matter; it does, however, seem to have become necessary if the field of discussion in African urban studies is not to be restricted to those towns that seem best to reproduce Western industrial-urban characteristics.

SELECT BIBLIOGRAPHY

ABRAHAM, R. C. (1958) *Dictionary of Modern Yoruba*. London: University of London Press.

ACHEBE, C. (1960) *No Longer at Ease*. London: William Heinemann.

ACQUAH (née CRABTREE), A. I. (1958) *Accra Survey*. London: University of London Press.

ADAMS, R. McC. (1960) 'The Origin of Cities', *Scientific American*, vol. 203, No. 3, pp. 153–68.

ADAMS, R. McC. (1966) *The Evolution of Urban Society: Early Mesopotamia and Prehistoric Mexico*. London: Weidenfeld & Nicolson.

AJAYI, J. F. A. and SMITH, R. S. (1964) *Yoruba Warfare in the Nineteenth Century*. Cambridge: C.U.P. in association with the Institute of African Studies, University of Ibadan.

AJIṢAFẸ, A. K.: (1924a) *History of Abeokuta*. Bungay, Suffolk: R. Clay.

AJIṢAFẸ, A. K. (1924b) *The Laws and Customs of the Yoruba People*. London: Routledge.

AKINOLA, R. A. (1963) 'The Ibadan Region', *Nigerian Geographical Journal*, No. 6, pp. 102–15.

ARDENER, E. (1959) 'Lineage and Locality among the Mba-Ise Ibo', *Africa*, vol. XXIX, No. 2, pp. 113–33.

ARDENER, E. (1961) 'Social and Demographic Problems of the Southern Cameroons Plantation Area', in A. SOUTHALL (ed.), *Social Change in Modern Africa*, pp. 83–97.

ARDENER, E. (1967) 'The Notion of the Elite: A Review Article', *African Affairs*, vol. XVI, No. 262, pp. 64–6.

ARDENER, S. (1964) 'The Comparative Study of Rotating Credit Associations', *J.R.A.I.*, vol. XCIV, No. 2, pp. 201–29.

AREMO, O. (1963) 'Yoruba Markets', unpublished thesis submitted for the B.A. Honours Degree of the University of London.

ARISTOTLE (1962) *The Politics*. Transl. T. A. SINCLAIR. Harmondsworth, Middlesex: Penguin Books.

AWE, B. (1967) 'Ibadan, Its Early Beginnings', in P. C. LLOYD, A. L. MABOGUNJE and B. AWE (eds.), *The City of Ibadan*, pp. 11–25.

AWOLOWO, O. (1960) *Awo*. Cambridge: C.U.P.

BABALQLA, S. A. (1966) *The Content and Form of Yoruba Ijala*. Oxford: The Clarendon Press: Oxford Library of African Literature.

BAKER, T. and BIRD, M. (1959) 'Urbanization and the Position of Women', *Soc. Rev.*, n.s. vol. VII, No. 1, pp. 99–122.

BALANDIER, G. (1952) 'Approche sociologique des Brazzavilles noires: étude préliminaire', *Africa*, vol. XXII, No. 1, pp. 23–34.

BALANDIER, G. (1955a) *Les Brazzavilles noires*. Paris: A. Colin.

BALANDIER, G. (1955b) *Sociologie actuelle de l'Afrique noire*. Rev. edn., Paris: P.U.F.

BALANDIER, G. (1956) 'Urbanism in West and Central Africa: The Scope and Aims of Research', in D. FORDE (ed.), *Social Implications of Industrialization and Urbanization in Africa South of the Sahara*, pp. 495–510.

BALANDIER, G. (ed.) (1962) *Social Implications of Technological Change*. Paris: International Social Science Council.

BAMGBOŞE, E. A. (1963) 'Industrial Policy and Small Scale Industries in Nigeria', *N.I.S.E.R. Conference Proceedings*, March 1962. Ibadan: N.I.S.E.R.

BANTON, M. (1957) *West African City*. London: O.U.P.

BANTON, M. (1961) 'The Restructuring of Social Relationships', in A. SOUTHALL (ed.), *Social Change in Modern Africa*, pp. 113–25.

BANTON, M. (ed.) (1965) *Political Systems and the Distribution of Power*. A.S.A. Monographs 2. London: Tavistock Publications.

BARBOUR, K. M. and PROTHERO, R. M. (1961) *Essays in African Population*. London: Routledge & Kegan Paul.

BASCOM, W. R. (1939) 'Secret Societies, Religious Cult Groups and Kinship Units among the West African Yoruba', unpublished thesis submitted for the degree of Ph.D. at Northwestern University.

BASCOM, W. R. (1941) 'The Sanctions of Ifa Divination', *J.R.A.I.*, vol. LXXI, pp. 43–53.

BASCOM, W. R. (1942a) 'The principle of Seniority in the Social Structure of the Yoruba', *A.A.*, vol. XLIV, No. 1, pp. 37–46.

BASCOM, W. R. (1942b) 'Ifa Divination', *Man*, vol. XLII, No. 21, pp. 41–3.

BASCOM, W. R. (1944) 'The Sociological Role of the Yoruba Cult Group', *A.A.*, vol. XLVI, No. 1, Part 2, Memoir No. 63, pp. 1–75.

BASCOM, W. R. (1951) 'Social Status, Wealth and Individual Differences among the Yoruba', *A.A.*, vol. LIII, No. 4, Part 1, pp. 490–505.

BASCOM, W. R. (1952) 'The Esusu: A Credit Institution of the Yoruba', *J.R.A.I.*, vol. LXXXII, pp. 63–9.

BASCOM, W. R. (1955) 'Urbanization among the Yoruba', *Am. J. Soc.*, vol. LX, No. 5, pp. 446–54.

BASCOM, W. R. (1958) 'Yoruba Urbanism: A Summary', *Man*, vol. LVIII, No. 253, pp. 190–1.

BASCOM, W. R. (1958–9), 'Les premiers fondements historiques de l'urbanisme yoruba', *Présence Africaine*, n.s., No. 23, pp. 22–40.

BASCOM, W. R. (1959) 'Urbanism as a Traditional African Pattern', *Soc. Rev.*, n.s., vol. VII, No. 1, pp. 29–43.

BASCOM, W. R. (1962) 'Some Aspects of Yoruba Urbanism', *A.A.*, vol. LXIV, No. 4, pp. 699–709.

BASCOM, W. R. (1966) 'Two Studies of Ifa Divination. I. Odu Ifa: The Names of the Signs', *Africa*, vol. XXXVI, No. 4, pp. 408–21.

BASTIDE, R. (1960) *Les religions africaines au Brésil.* Paris: P.U.F.

BEALS, R. L. (1951) 'Urbanism, Urbanization, Acculturation', *A.A.*, vol. LIII, No. 1, pp. 1–10.

BEIER, U. (1958) 'The Changing Face of a Yoruba Town', *Nigeria Magazine*, No. 59, pp. 373–82.

BEIER, U. (1959) *A Year of Sacred Festivals in One Yoruba Town.* Lagos: Nigeria Magazine Special Publications.

BEIER, U. (1960a) 'Sacred Yoruba Architecture: Islam', *Nigeria Magazine*, No. 64, pp. 93–104.

BEIER, U. (1960b) 'Oshogbo: Portrait of a Yoruba Town', *Nigeria Magazine*, Special Independence Issue, pp. 149–56.

BIOBAKU, S. O., DINA, I. O., and LLOYD, P. C. (eds.) (1949). *Ibadan.* Zaria: Gaskiya Corporation.

BIOBAKU, S. O. (1955) *The Origin of the Yoruba.* Lagos: Federal Information Service.

BIOBAKU, S. O. (1957) *The Egba and their Neighbours, 1842–1872.* Oxford: The Clarendon Press.

BOHANNAN, L. (1952) 'A Genealogical Charter', *Africa*, vol. XXII, No. 4, pp. 301–15.

BOHANNAN, P. and DALTON, G. (eds.) (1962) *Markets in Africa.* Northwestern University Press.

BOTTOMORE, T. B. (1955) *Classes in Modern Society.* London: Ampersand.

BOTTOMORE, T. B. (1964) *Elites and Society.* London: C. A. Watts.

BOWEN, T. J. (1857) *Central Africa: Adventures and Missionary Labours in Several Countries in the Interior of Africa from 1849 to 1856.* Charleston: Southern Baptist Publication Society.

BRADBURY, R. E. (1964) *The Benin Kingdom and the Edo-Speaking Peoples of South-Western Nigeria. Ethnographic Survey XIII.* (Reprint, with supplementary bibliography, of 1957 edition.) London: I.A.I.

BRADBURY, R. E. (1967) 'The Kingdom of Benin', in D. FORDE and P. M. KABERRY (eds.), *West African Kingdoms in the Nineteenth Century*, pp. 1–35.

BROWN, P. (1951) 'Patterns of Authority in West Africa', *Africa*, vol. XXI, No. 3, pp. 261–78.

BUCHANAN, K. M. and PUGH, J. C. (1955) *Land and People in Nigeria: The Human Geography of Nigeria and Its Environmental Background.* London: University of London Press.

BURTON, R. F. (1863) *Abeokuta and the Cameroons Mountains*. London: Tinsley Brothers.

BUSIA, K. A. (1950) *Report on a Social Survey of Sekondi-Takoradi*. London: H.M.S.O.

CALLAWAY, A. (1967a) 'From Traditional Crafts to Modern Industries', in P. C. LLOYD, A. L. MABOGUNJE, and B. AWE (eds.), *The City of Ibadan*, pp. 153–71.

CALLAWAY, A. (1967b) 'Education, Expansion and the Rise in Youth Unemployment', in P. C. LLOYD, A. L. MABOGUNJE, and B. AWE (eds.), *The City of Ibadan*, pp. 191–211.

CAPELIE, A. (1947) *La cité indigène de Léopoldville*. Elisabethville.

CLAPPERTON, H. (1829) *Journal of a Second Expedition into the Interior of Africa, from the Bight of Benin to Soccatoo*. Philadelphia: Carey, Lea & Carey.

COHEN, A. (1965) 'The Social Organization of Credit in a West African Cattle Market', *Africa*, vol. XXXV, No. 1, pp. 8–20.

COHEN, A. (1966) 'Politics of the Kola Trade', *Africa*, vol. XXXVI, No. 1, pp. 18–36.

COHEN, A. (1967) 'The Hausa', in P. C. LLOYD, A. L. MABOGUNJE, and B. AWE (eds.), *The City of Ibadan*, pp. 117–27.

COLEMAN, J. S. (1959) *Nigeria: Background to Nationalism*. Berkeley and Los Angeles: University of California Press.

COMHAIRE, J. (1949) 'La vie religieuse à Lagos', *Zaïre*, May, pp. 549–56.

COMHAIRE-SYLVAIN, S. (1949) 'The Status of Women in Lagos, Nigeria', *Pi Lambda Theta Journal*, vol. XXVII, No. 3, pp. 158–63.

COMHAIRE-SYLVAIN, S. (1951) 'Le travail des femmes à Lagos, Nigéria', *Zaïre*, February and May, pp. 169–87.

DENNETT, R. E. (1910) *Nigerian Studies*. London: Macmillan.

DUMONT, R. (1962) *L'Afrique noire est mal partie*. Paris: Editions du Seuil.

DURKHEIM, E. (1964) *The Division of Labour in Society*. Transl. G. Simpson. New York: The Free Press.

EPSTEIN, A. L. (1958) *Politics in an Urban African Community*. Manchester: Manchester University Press.

EPSTEIN, A. L. (1967) 'Urbanization and Social Change in Africa', *Current Anthropology*, vol. VIII, No. 4, pp. 275–95.

FADIPẸ, N. A. (1939) 'The Sociology of the Yoruba', unpublished thesis submitted for the degree of Ph.D. at the University of London.

FAGE, J. D. (1965) *Introduction to the History of West Africa*. Third edition. Cambridge: C.U.P.

FORDE, D. and SCOTT, R. (1946) *The Native Economies of Nigeria*. London: Faber & Faber.

FORDE, D. (1951) *The Yoruba-Speaking Peoples of South-Western Nigeria. Ethnographic Survey IV*. London: I.A.I.

FORDE, D. (ed.) (1956) *Social Implications of Industrialization and Urbanization South of the Sahara*. Paris: U.N.E.S.C.O.: Tensions and Technology Series.

FORDE, D. (1956) 'Social Aspects of Urbanization and Industrialization in Africa: A General Review', in D. FORDE (ed.), *Social Implications of Industrialization and Urbanization South of the Sahara*, pp. 11–34.

FORDE, D. (1964) *Yakö Studies*. London: O.U.P./I.A.I.

FORDE, D. and KABERRY, P. M. (eds.) (1967) *West African Kingdoms in the Nineteenth Century*. London: O.U.P./I.A.I.

FORTES, M. (1945) *The Dynamics of Clanship among the Tallensi*. London: O.U.P.

FORTES, M. (1949) *The Web of Kinship among the Tallensi*. London: O.U.P.

FORTES, M. (1953) 'The Structure of Unilineal Descent Groups', *A.A.*, vol. LV, No. 1, pp. 17–41.

FOX, R. (1967) *Kinship and Marriage*. Harmondsworth, Middlesex: Penguin Anthropology Library.

FRAENKEL, M. (1964) *Tribe and Class in Monrovia*. London: O.U.P./I.A.I.

FROBENIUS, L. (1913) *The Voice of Africa*. London: Hutchinson.

FROBENIUS, L. (1926) 'Die Atlantische Gotterlehre', *Atlantis*, vol. X. Jena: Eugen Diederichs Verlag.

FUSTEL DE COULANGES, N. D. (1956) *The Ancient City*. Transl. W. Small. Garden City, N.Y.: Anchor Books.

GALLETTI, R., BALDWIN, K. D. S., and DINA, I. O. (1956) *Nigerian Cocoa Farmers*. London: O.U.P.

GLEAVE, M. B. (1963) 'Hill Settlements and their Abandonment in Western Yorubaland', *Africa*, vol. XXXIII, No. 4, pp. 343–52.

GLUCKMAN, M. (1961) 'Anthropological Problems arising from the African Industrial Revolution', in A. SOUTHALL (ed.), *Social Change in Modern Africa*, pp. 67–82.

GLUCKMAN, M. and EGGAN, F. (eds.) (1965) *Political Systems and the Distribution of Power*. A.S.A. Monograph 2. London: Tavistock Publications.

GLUCKMAN, M. and EGGAN, F. (eds.) (1966) *The Social Anthropology of Complex Societies*. A.S.A. Monograph 4. London: Tavistock Publications.

GODDARD, S. (1965) 'Town–Farm Relationships in Yorubaland: A Case Study from Ọyọ', *Africa*, vol. XXXV, No. 1, pp. 21–9.

GODWIN, J. (1966) 'Architecture in Nigeria', *Nigeria Magazine*, No. 91, pp. 247–54.

GOODENOUGH, W. H. (1961) Review of G. P. MURDOCK (ed.), *Social Structure in South-East Asia. A.A.*, vol. LXII, No. 6, pp. 1341–7.

GOODWIN, A. J. H. (1958) 'Walls, Paving, Water-Paths and Land-marks', *Odù*, No. 6, pp. 45–53.

GORDON, T. and LANCASTER, M. (1961) 'Orisha Houses in Ibadan', *Ibadan*, No. 11, pp. 22–3.

GREEN, M. M. (1947) *Ibo Village Affairs*. London: Sidgwick & Jackson.

GUGLER, J. (n.d.) 'The Interrelation of Urbanization and Industrialization', Sociology Working Paper No. 60, Department of Sociology, University of Makerere.

GUILBOT, J. (1947) *Petite Etude sur la main d'œuvre à Douala*. Dakar: I.F.A.N.

GUTKIND, P. C. W. (1963) *The Royal Capital of Buganda: A Study of Internal Conflict and External Ambiguity*. The Hague: Mouton.

HARRISON CHURCH, R. J. (1959) 'West African Urbanization: A Geographical Review', *Soc. Rev.*, n.s. vol. VII, No. 1.

HAUSER, P. M. and SCHNORE, L. F. (eds.) (1965) *The Study of Urbanization*. New York: John Wiley.

HAUSER, P. M. (1965) 'Urbanization: An Overview', in HAUSER, P. M. and SCHNORE, L. F. (eds.), *The Study of Urbanization*.

HEADS, J. (1958) 'Urbanization and Economic Progress', *N.I.S.E.R. Conference Proceedings, December 1958*. Ibadan: N.I.S.E.R.

HERSKOVITS, M. J. and F. S. (1947) *Trinidad Village*. New York: Alfred A. Knopf.

HODDER, B. W. (1962) 'The Yoruba Rural Market', in P. BOHANNAN and G. DALTON (eds.), *Markets in Africa*, pp. 103–17.

HODDER, B. W. (1967) 'The Markets of Ibadan', in P. C. LLOYD, A. L. MABOGUNJE, and B. AWE (eds.), *The City of Ibadan*, pp. 173–90.

IDOWU, E. B. (1962) *Olódùmarè: God in Yoruba Belief*. London: Green.

IDOWU, E. B. (1967) 'Traditional Religion and Christianity', in P. C. LLOYD, A. L. MABOGUNJE, and B. AWE (eds.), *The City of Ibadan*, pp. 235–47.

IGUN, A. A. (1956), 'The Demographic Consequences of Social Change in West Africa', *Proceedings of the Fourth Annual Conference of W.A.I.S.E.R.* Ibadan: U.C.I.

I.N.C.I.D.I. (1956) *The Development of a Middle Class in Tropical and Sub-Tropical Africa: Record of the 29th Session. London, 13–16, IX, 1955*. Brussels, I.N.C.I.D.I.

ISONG, C. N. (1959) 'Modernization of the Esusu Credit Society', *N.I.S.E.R. Conference Proceedings, December 1958*. Ibadan: N.I.S.E.R.

IZZETT, A. (1955) 'The Fears and Anxieties of Delinquent Yoruba Children', *Odù*, No. 1, pp. 26–33.

IZZETT, A. (1961) 'Family Life among the Yoruba in Lagos, Nigeria', in A. SOUTHALL (ed.), *Social Change in Modern Africa*, pp. 305–15.

JOHNSON, S. (1921) *A History of the Yoruba*. Lagos: C.M.S. Bookshop.

KRAPF-ASKARI, E. (1966) 'Time and Classifications', *Odù*, n.s., vol. II, No. 2, pp. 3–18.

KROEBER, A. L. (1948) *Anthropology*. Rev. edn. London: George G. Harrap.

KUPER, H. (ed.) (1965) *Urbanization and Migration in West Africa*. Berkeley, Los Angeles, and London: University of California Press and C.U.P.

KUPER, H. (1965) Introduction to H. KUPER (ed.) *Urbanization and Migration in West Africa*, pp. 1–22.

LEIGHTON, A. H., LAMBO, T. A. *et al.* (1963) *Psychiatric Disorder among the Yoruba*. Ithaca: Cornell University Press.

LERNER, D. (1967) 'Comparative Analysis of Processes of Modernization', in H. MINER (ed.), *The City in Modern Africa*, pp. 21–38.

LEVINE, R. A., KLEIN, H. H., and OWEN, C. R. (1967) 'Father–Child Relationships and Changing Life-Styles in Ibadan, Nigeria', in H. MINER (ed.), *The City in Modern Africa*, pp. 215–55.

LEWIS, I. M. (1965) 'Problems in the Comparative Study of Unilineal Descent', in M. BANTON (ed.), *A.S.A. 1: The Relevance of Models for Social Anthropology*, pp. 87–112.

LITTLE, K. L. (1953) 'The Study of Social Change in British West Africa', *Africa*, vol. XXII, No. 4, pp. 274–84.

LITTLE, K. L. (1957) 'The Role of Voluntary Associations in West African Urbanization', *A.A.*, vol. LIX, No. 4, pp. 579–96.

LITTLE, K. L. (1959) 'Some Urban Patterns of Marriage and Domesticity in West Africa'. *Soc. Rev.*, n.s., vol. VII, No. 1, pp. 65–82.

LITTLE, K. L. (1962) 'Some Traditionally Based Forms of Mutual Aid in West African Urbanization', *Ethnology*, vol. I, No. 1, pp. 196–211.

LITTLE, K. L. (1965) *West African Urbanization*. Cambridge: C.U.P.

LLOYD, B. B. (1966) 'Education and Family Life in the Development of Class Identification', in P. C. LLOYD (ed.), *The New Elites of Tropical Africa*, pp. 163–81.

LLOYD, B. B. (1967) 'Indigenous Ibadan', in P. C. LLOYD, A. L. MABOGUNJE, and B. AWE (eds.), *The City of Ibadan*, pp. 59–93.

LLOYD, P. C. (1952) 'The Integration of New Economic Classes into Local Government in West Africa', *African Affairs*, vol. LII, No. 209, pp. 327–34.

LLOYD, P. C. (1953a) 'Craft Organization in Yoruba Towns', *Africa*, vol. XXIII, No. 1, pp. 30–44.

LLOYD, P. C. (1953b) 'Some Modern Changes in the Government of Yoruba Towns', *W.A.I.S.E.R. Annual Conference, Sociology Section, March 1953*. Ibadan: U.C.I.

LLOYD, P. C. (1954) 'The Traditional Political System of the Yoruba', *Southwestern Journal of Anthropology*, vol. X, No. 4, pp. 366–84.

LLOYD, P. C. (1955) 'The Yoruba Lineage', *Africa*, vol. XXV, No. 3, pp. 235–51.

LLOYD, P. C. (1956) 'The Changing Role of the Yoruba Traditional Rulers'. *Proceedings of the Fourth Annual Conference of W.A.I.S.E.R., Sociology Section*. Ibadan: U.C.I.

LLOYD, P. C. (1958) 'Local Government in Yoruba Towns'. Unpublished thesis submitted for the degree of D.Phil. at the University of Oxford.

LLOYD, P. C. (1959a). 'The Yoruba Town Today', *Soc. Rev.*, n.s., vol. VII, No. 1, pp. 45–63.

LLOYD, P. C. (1959b) 'Sungbo's Ẹrẹdo.', *Odù*, No. 7, pp. 15–22.

LLOYD, P. C. (1960) 'Sacred Kingship and Government among the Yoruba', *Africa*, vol. XXX, No. 3, pp. 221–37.

LLOYD, P. C. (1962) *Yoruba Land Law*. London: O.U.P./N.I.S.E.R.

LLOYD, P. C. (1965) 'The Political Structure of African Kingdoms: An Exploratory Model', in M. GLUCKMAN and F. EGGAN (eds.), *A.S.A. 2: Political Systems and the Distribution of Power*, pp. 63–112.

LLOYD, P. C. (ed.) (1966) *The New Elites of Tropical Africa*. London: O.U.P./I.A.I.

LLOYD, P. C. (1966a) 'Introduction: The Study of the Elite', in P. C. LLOYD (ed.), *The New Elites of Tropical Africa*, pp. 1–65.

LLOYD, P. C. (1966b) 'Class Consciousness among the Yoruba', in P. C. LLOYD (ed.), *The New Elites of Tropical Africa*, pp. 328–40.

LLOYD, P. C. (1966c) 'Agnatic and Cognatic Descent among the Yoruba', *Man*, n.s., vol. I, No. 4, pp. 484–500.

LLOYD, P. C., MABOGUNJE, A. L., and AWE, B. (eds.) (1967) *The City of Ibadan*. Cambridge: C.U.P. in association with the Institute of African Studies, University of Ibadan.

LLOYD, P. C. (1967a) Introduction to P. C. LLOYD, A. L. MABOGUNJE, and B. AWE (eds.), *The City of Ibadan*, pp. 3–10.

LLOYD, P. C. (1967b) 'The Elite', in P. C. LLOYD, A. L. MABOGUNJE, and B. AWE (eds.), *The City of Ibadan*, pp. 129–50.

LLOYD, P. C. (1967c) *Africa in Social Change*. London: Penguin Books.

LUCAS, J. L. (1948) *The Religion of the Yoruba*. Lagos: C.M.S. Press.

MABOGUNJE, A. L. (1961) 'Some Comments on Land Tenure in Egba Division, Western Nigeria', *Africa*, vol. XXXI, No. 3, pp. 258–69.

MABOGUNJE, A. L. (1962) *Yoruba Towns*. Ibadan: Ibadan University Press.

MABOGUNJE, A. L. (1967a) 'The Morphology of Ibadan', in P. C. LLOYD, A. L. MABOGUNJE, and B. AWE (eds.), *The City of Ibadan*, pp. 35–56.

MABOGUNJE, A. L. (1967b) 'The Ijebu', in P. C. LLOYD, A. L. MABOGUNJE, and B. AWE, (eds.), *The City of Ibadan*, pp. 85–95.

MABOGUNJE, A. L. (1967c) 'The Problems of a Metropolis', in P. C. LLOYD, A. L. MABOGUNJE, and B. AWE (eds.), *The City of Ibadan*, pp. 261–71.

MACIVER, R. M. and PAGE, C. H. (1949) *Society, Its Structure and Changes*. Rev. edn. London: Macmillan.

MARRIS, P. (1961) *Family and Social Change in an African City*. London: Routledge & Kegan Paul.

MARRIS, P. (1967) 'Motives and Methods: Reflections on a Study in Lagos', in H. MINER (ed.), *The City in Modern Africa*, pp. 39–54.

MAYER, P. (1963) *Townsmen or Tribesmen: Conservatism and the Process of Urbanization in a South African City*. Capetown: O.U.P. for the Institute of Social and Economic Research of Rhodes University.

McLELLAND, E. M. (1966) 'Two studies of Ifa Divination. II: The Significance of Numer in the Odu of Ifa', *Africa*, vol. XXXVI, No. 4, pp. 421–31.

MINER, H. (1953) *The Primitive City of Timbuctoo*. Princeton: Princeton University Press.

MINER, H. (1965) 'Urban Influences on the Rural Hausa', in H. KUPER (ed.), *Urbanization and Migration in West Africa*, pp. 110–30.

MINER, H. (ed.) (1967) *The City in Modern Africa*. London: Pall Mall Press.

MINER, H. (1967) 'The City and Modernization: An Introduction', in H. MINER (ed.), *The City in Modern Africa*, pp. 1–20.

MITCHEL, N. C. (1961) 'Yoruba Towns', in K. M. BARBOUR, and R. M. PROTHERO, (eds.), *Essays in African Population*, pp. 279–301.

MITCHELL, J. C. (1966) 'Theoretical Orientations in African Urban Studies', in M. GLUCKMAN and F. EGGAN (eds.), *A.S.A. 4: The Social Anthropology of Complex Societies*, pp. 37–68.

MOLONEY, A. (1890) 'Notes on Yoruba and the Colony and Protectorate of Lagos', *Proceedings of the Royal Geographical Society*, n.s., vol. XII, No. 10, pp. 596–614.

MORTON-WILLIAMS, P. (1953) 'The Social Consequences of Industrialism among the South-Western Yoruba', *W.A.I.S.E.R. Annual Conference, Sociology Section, March, 1953*. Ibadan: U.C.I.

MORTON-WILLIAMS, P. (1956) 'A Discussion of the Theory of Elites in a West African Context', *Proceedings of the Fourth Annual Conference of W.A.I.S.E.R., Sociology Section*. Ibadan: U.C.I.

MORTON-WILLIAMS, P. (1960) 'The Yoruba Ogboni Cult in Ọyọ', *Africa*, vol. XXX, No. 4, pp. 362–74.

MORTON-WILLIAMS, P. (1964) 'An Outline of the Cosmology and Cult Organization of the Ọyọ Yoruba', *Africa*, vol. XXXIV, No. 3, pp. 243–61.

MORTON-WILLIAMS, P. (1966) 'Two studies of Ifa Divination. Introduction: The Mode of Divination', *Africa*, vol. XXXVI, No. 4, pp. 406–8.

MORTON-WILLIAMS, P. (1967) 'The Yoruba Kingdom of Ọyọ', in D. FORDE and P. M. KABERRY, (eds.), *West African Kingdoms in the Nineteenth Century*, pp. 36–69.

MUMFORD, L. (1961) *The City in History*. London: Secker and Warburg.

NADEL, S. F. (1942) *A Black Byzantium*. London: O.U.P.

NADEL, S. F. (1956) 'The Concept of Social Elites', U.N.E.S.C.O., *International Social Science Bulletin*, vol. VIII, pp. 413–24.

NEWBURY, C. (1961) *The Western Slave Coast and Its Rulers*. London: O.U.P.

OJO, G. J. A. (1966a) *Yoruba Culture*. London: University of Ife and University of London Press.

OJO, G. J. A. (1966b) *Yoruba Palaces*. London: University of London Press.

OKONJO, C. (1967) 'The Western Ibo', in P. C. LLOYD, A. L. MABO-GUNJE, and B. AWE (eds.), *The City of Ibadan*, pp. 97–116.

OREWA, G. (1959) 'Property Rating in Western Nigeria', *N.I.S.E.R. Conference Proceedings, December 1958*. Ibadan: N.I.S.E.R.

PACHECO PEREIRA, D. (1937) *Esmeraldo de Situ Orbis*. Transl. and ed. G. H. KIMBLE. London: Hakluyt Society.

PARRINDER, E. G. (1947) 'Yoruba-Speaking Peoples in Dahomey', *Africa*, vol. XVII, No. 1.

PARRINDER, E. G. (1953) *Religion in an African City*. London: O.U.P.

PARRINDER, E. G. (1961) *West African Religion*. 2nd edn., revised and enlarged. London: The Epworth Press.

PARSONS, T. (1952) *The Social System*. London: Tavistock Publications with Routledge & Kegan Paul.

PERHAM, M. (1937) *Native Administration in Nigeria*. London: O.U.P.

PIRENNE, H. (1925) *Medieval Cities*. Transl. F. D. HALSEY. Princeton: Princeton University Press.

POPPER, K. R. (1965) *The Open Society and Its Enemies*. 5th edn., revised. London: Routledge & Kegan Paul.

Population Census of the Western Region of Nigeria 1952. (1953) Bulletins 1–8. Prepared in the Regional Census Office, Ibadan, and published by the Census Superintendent (The Government Statistician), Lagos.

REDFIELD, R. (1953) *The Primitive World and Its Transformations*. Ithaca: Cornell University Press.

REISSMAN, M. L. (1960) *Class in American Society*. London: Routledge & Kegan Paul.

ROYAL ANTHROPOLOGICAL INSTITUTE (1951) *Notes and Queries on Anthropology*. 6th edn., revised and rewritten by a Committee of the Royal Anthropological Institute of Great Britain and Ireland. London: Routledge & Kegan Paul.

SCHWAB, W. (1952) 'Growth and Conflicts of Religion in a Modern Yoruba Community', *Zaïre*, October, pp. 829–35.

SCHWAB, W. B. (1954) 'An Experiment in Methodology in a West African Urban Community', *Human Organization*, vol. XIII, No. 1, pp. 13–19.

SCHWAB, W. B. (1955) 'Kinship and Lineage among the Yoruba', *Africa*, vol. XXV, No. 4, pp. 352–74.

SCHWAB, W. B. (1958) 'The Terminology of Kinship and Marriage among the Yoruba', *Africa*, vol. XXVIII, No. 4, pp. 301–13.

SCHWAB, W. B. (1962) 'Continuity and Change in the Yoruba Lineage System', *Annals of the New York Academy of Sciences*, XCVI.

SCHWAB, W. B. (1965) 'Oshogbo—an Urban Community?', in H. KUPER (ed.), *Urbanization and Migration in West Africa*, pp. 85–109.

SJOBERG, G. (1960) *The Pre-Industrial City: Past and Present.* Glencoe: The Free Press.

SJOBERG, G. (1965) 'Theory and Research in Urban Sociology', in HAUSER, P. M. and SCHNORE, L. F. (eds.), *The Study of Urbanization*, pp. 157–89.

SKINNER, E. P. (1963) 'Strangers in West African Societies', *Africa*, vol. XXXIII, No. 4, pp. 307–430.

SKLAR, R. L. (1963) *Nigerian Political Parties.* Princeton: Princeton University Press.

SMITH, M. G. (1956) 'On Segmentary Lineage Systems', *J.R.A.I.*, vol. LXXXVI, Part II, pp. 39–80.

SMYTHE, H. H. and M. M. (1960) *The New Nigerian Elite.* Stanford: Stanford University Press.

SOUTHALL, A. W. and GUTKIND, P. C. (1957) *Townsmen in the Making.* Kampala: East African Studies No. 9.

SOUTHALL, A. W. (ed.) (1961) *Social Change in Modern Africa.* London: O.U.P./I.A.I.

SOUTHALL, A. W. (1961) Introductory Summary, in A. W. SOUTHALL (ed.), *Social Change in Modern Africa*, pp. 1–66.

SOUTHALL, A. W. (1966) 'The Concept of Elites and their Formation in Uganda', in P. C. LLOYD (ed.), *The New Elites of Tropical Africa*, pp. 342–63.

STAPLETON, G. B. (1959) 'Nigerians in Ghana, with Special Reference to the Yoruba', *N.I.S.E.R. Conference Proceedings, December 1958.* Ibadan: N.I.S.E.R.

TARDITS, C. (1956) 'The Notion of the Elite and the Urban Social Survey in Africa', U.N.E.S.C.O., *International Social Science Bulletin*, vol. VIII, pp. 492–5.

TARDITS, C. (1958) *Porto-Novo: Les nouvelles générations africaines entre leurs traditions et l'occident*. The Hague: Mouton.

THOMAS, B. J. (1965) 'The Location and Nature of West African Cities', in H. KUPER, (ed.), *Urbanization and Migration in West Africa*, pp. 23–38.

TIGER, L. (1967) 'Bureaucracy and Urban Symbol Systems', in H. MINER, (ed.), *The City in Modern Africa*, pp. 185–214.

TOWNSEND, P. (1957) *The Family Life of Old People*. London: Routledge & Kegan Paul.

TUTUOLA, A. (1954). *My Life in the Bush of Ghosts*. London: Faber & Faber.

VERGER, P. (1953) *Les Afro-Américains*. Dakar: I.F.A.N.

VERGER, P. (1957) *Notes sur le culte des Orisa et Vodun*. Dakar: I.F.A.N.

VERGER, P. (1964) *Bahia and the West Coast Trade (1549–1851)*. Ibadan: Ibadan University Press for the Institute of African Studies of the University of Ibadan.

WEBER, M. (1958) *The City*. Transl. and ed. D. MARTINDALE and G. NEUWIRTH. Glencoe: The Free Press.

WEBSTER, J. B. (1964) *The African Churches among the Yoruba, 1881–1922*. Oxford: The Clarendon Press.

WELLDON, R. M. C. (1957) 'The Human Geography of a Yoruba Township in South-Western Nigeria', unpublished thesis submitted for the degree of B.Litt. at the University of Oxford.

WELLS, F. A. and WARMINGTON, W. A. (1962) *Studies in Industrialization in Nigeria and the Cameroons*. London, O.U.P./N.I.S.E.R.

WESCOTT, J. (1962) 'The Sculpture and Myths of Eshu-Elegba, the Yoruba Trickster: Definition and Interpretation in Yoruba Iconography', *Africa*, vol. XXXII, No. 4, pp. 336–54.

WESCOTT, J. and MORTON-WILLIAMS, P. (1962) 'The Symbolism and Ritual Context of the Yoruba *Laba Shango*', *J.R.A.I.*, vol. XCII, Part I, pp. 23–37.

WILLIAMS, D. (1964) The Iconology of the Yoruba *Edan Ogboni*', *Africa*, vol. XXXIV, No. 2, pp. 139–66.

WILSON, G. and M. (1945) *The Analysis of Social Change*. Cambridge: C.U.P.

WIRTH, L. (1938) 'Urbanism as a Way of Life', *Am. J. Soc.*, vol. XLIV, No. 1, pp. 1–24.

WIRTH, L. (1940) 'The Urban Society and Civilization', *Am. J. Soc.*, vol. XLV, No. 5.

YOUNG, M. and WILLMOTT, P. (1962). *Family and Kinship in East London*. Rev. edn. London: Penguin Books.

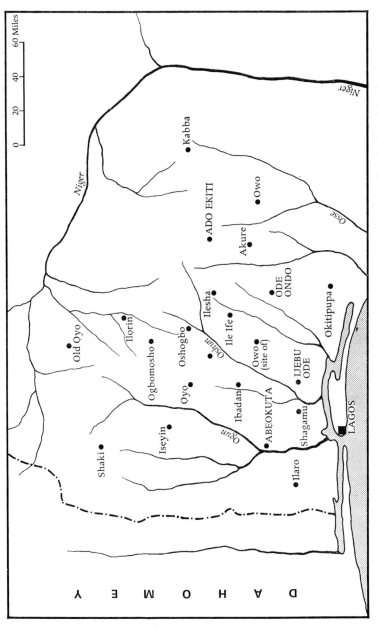

MAP 1. Location of Main Yoruba Towns and Cities (from LLOYD: *Yoruba Land Law*)

177

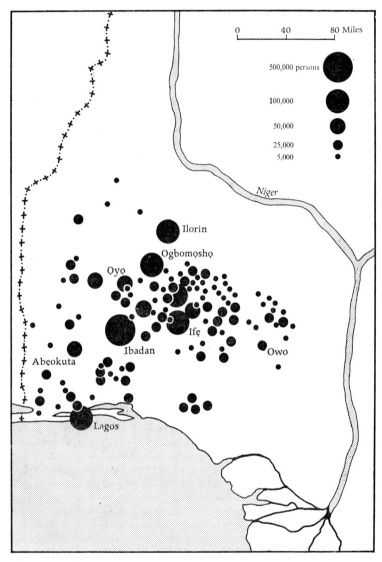

MAP 2. Yoruba Towns and Cities by population size (from OJO: *Yoruba Culture*)

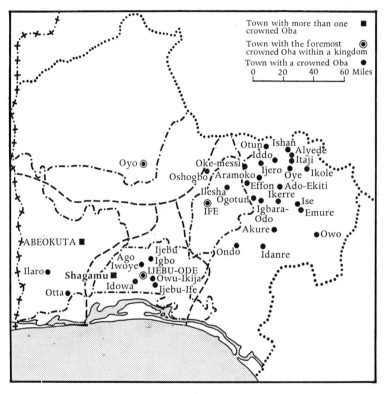

MAP 3. Distribution of *ÌLÚ ALÁDÉ* (from OJO: *Yoruba Culture*)

The following labels appear on the map:

Legend:
- Town with more than one crowned Oba ■
- Town with the foremost crowned Oba within a kingdom ◉
- Town with a crowned Oba ●

0   20   40   60 Miles

Otun, Ishan, Iddo, Alyede, Itaji, Oke-messi, Ijero, Oye, Ikole, Oshogbo, Aramoko, Oyo ◉, Effon, Ado-Ekiti, Ilesha, Ikerre, Ogotun, Ise, IFE ◉, Igbara-Odo, Emure, Akure, Owo, ABEOKUTA ■, Ijebu, Ondo, Idanre, Ago, Igbo, Iwoye, IJEBU-ODE ◉, Ilaro, Shagamu ■, Owu-Ikija, Idowa, Otta, Ijebu-Ife

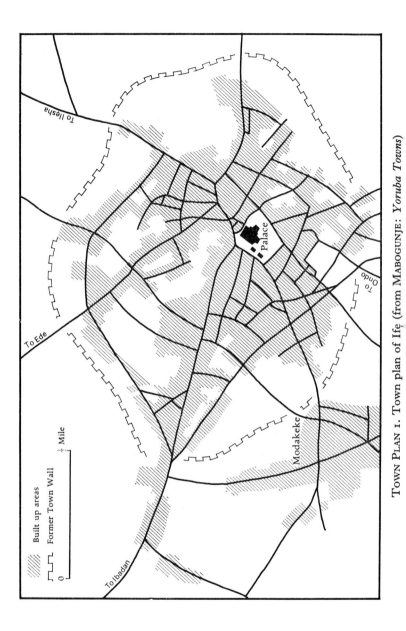

To Ilesha

To Ede

To Ibadan

Palace

Modakeke

To Ondo

Built up areas
Former Town Wall

0   ½   Mile

TOWN PLAN 1. Town plan of Ife (from MABOGUNJE: *Yoruba Towns*)

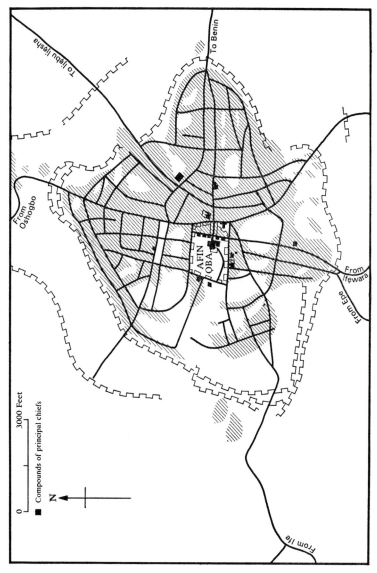

TOWN PLAN 2. Town plan of Ilẹsha (from Ojo: *Yoruba Culture*)

TOWN PLAN 3. Arrangement of quarters and compounds in relation to the palace in Ado Ekiti (from Oyo Yoruba Palaces)

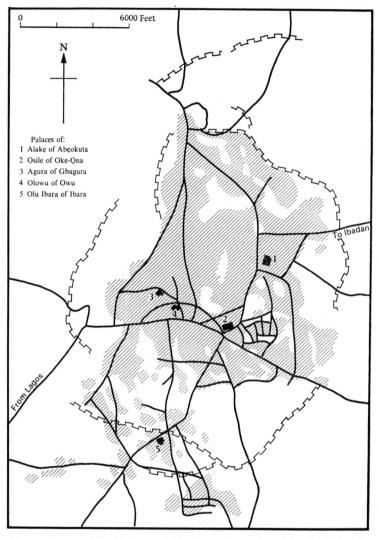

TOWN PLAN 4. The Palaces of Abẹokuta (from OJO: *Yoruba Palaces*)

Palaces of:
1 Alakẹ of Abẹokuta
2 Ọsile of Oke-Ọna
3 Agura of Gbagura
4 Olowu of Owu
5 Olu Ibara of Ibara

To Ibadan

From Lagos

183

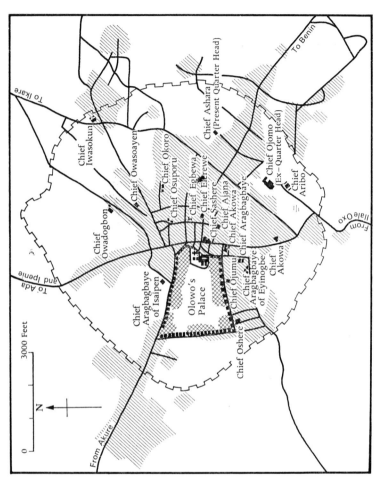

TOWN PLAN 5. Location of the Palace in Ọwọ in relation to the town and compounds of the Inner Council Chiefs (from Ọjọ: *Yoruba Palaces*)

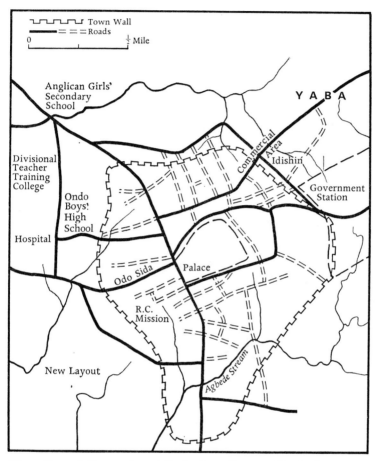

Town Plan 6. Town plan of Ondo (from Lloyd: *Yoruba Land Law*)

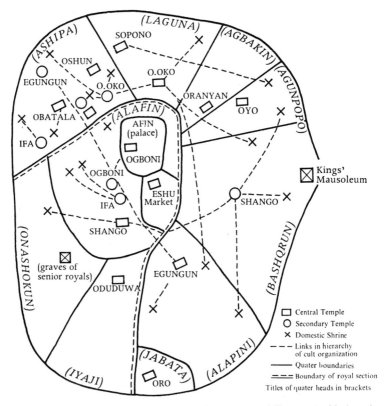

SCHEMA I. Pattern of distribution of Temples and Domestic Shrines in
Ọyọ (from MORTON-WILLIAMS: *An Outline of the Cosmology and Cult
Organization of the Oyo Yoruba*)

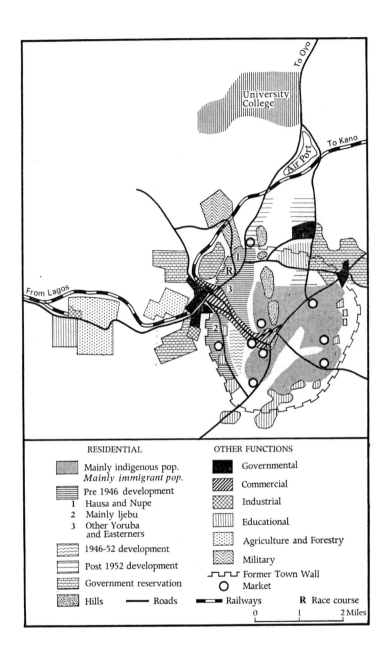

RESIDENTIAL

- Mainly indigenous pop.
- *Mainly immigrant pop.*
- Pre 1946 development
- 1 Hausa and Nupe
- 2 Mainly Ijebu
- 3 Other Yoruba and Easterners
- 1946-52 development
- Post 1952 development
- Government reservation
- Hills

OTHER FUNCTIONS

- Governmental
- Commercial
- Industrial
- Educational
- Agriculture and Forestry
- Military
- Former Town Wall
- O Market
- —— Roads
- Railways
- R Race course

0   1   2 Miles

University College

To Oyo

To Kano

Air Port

From Lagos

SCHEMA 2. Functional areas of Ibadan (from MABOGUNJE: *Yoruba Towns*)

187

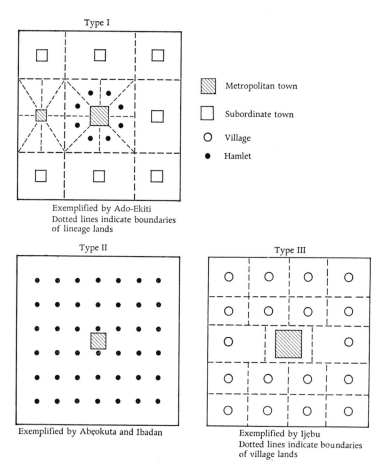

DIAGRAM 1. Types of settlement pattern (schematic representation)
(from LLOYD: *Yoruba Land Law*)

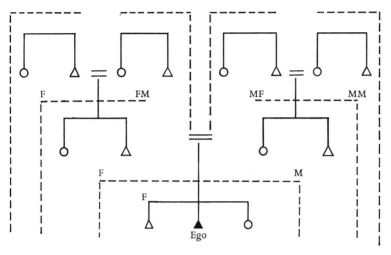

DIAGRAM 2.

Ego's view backwards over time of the various ǫmǫ iyá of which he is a member in a cognatic descent system. The dotted lines mark the backward and outward boundaries of each group. The groups overlap at each generation, but none totally includes any of the others.

△	man	F	father
○	woman	M	mother
▲	ego	FF	father's father
=	marriage	FM	father's mother
		MF	mother's father
		MM	mother's mother

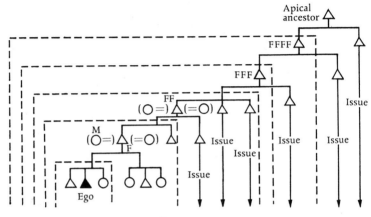

DIAGRAM 3.

Ego's view backwards over time of the various ọmọ iyá of which he is a member in an agnatic descent system.

Dotted lines mark the backward and outward boundaries. Each unit is wholly included, together with other ọmọ iyá within the ọbakàn, in the one immediately above it.

Above the level of FF, ọmọ iyá are seen as single ancestors. The line goes back for five generations to an apical ancestor. Affinal relatives, who are not members of the ìdí'lé, are indicated between brackets.

FFF = father's father's father
FFFF = father's father's father's father

INDEX

Abẹokuta, Abẹokuta Province, 3, 5–7, 26, 29, 32, 35, 36, 41, 44, 45, 49, 50, 53, 54, 59, 73, 80, 84, 97, 101, 103, 104, 117, 119, 120, 144, 159 (*cf. also* Ẹgba).
Abraham, R. C., 104, 118.
achievement, 70, 116, 134, 145 (*cf. also* ascription).
Ado Ekiti, 7, 29, 34, 44, 58, 124 (*cf. also* Ekiti).
àfins, *cf.* palaces.
age-sets, 122–3, 126–7, 129.
agnatic grouping, 53, 54, 56, 63, 65–67, 69–70, 72, 74–75, 79–80, 108, 113, 116, 159 (*cf. also* descent groups; cognatic grouping).
Aiyede, 30.
Ajayi, J. F. A., 6.
Ajiṣafẹ, A. K., 108.
Akitoye, ọba of Lagos, 104.
Alafin of Ọyọ, 7, 26, 39, 40, 44, 49, 100, 115, 117.
Alakẹ of Abẹokuta, 6, 26, 41, 80 (*cf. also* Abẹokuta; Ẹgba).
allegiant population, 31, 52, 63–64.
anomie, 22, 155.
apprenticeship, 86, 87–88, 90, 92–93, 94–96, 98.
ará ìlú, *cf. ìlú*.
ará oko, *cf. ìlú*.
Ardener, E., 17, 130, 157.
Aristotle, 154.
Arriens, C., 47.
artisans, *cf.* crafts.
ascription, 66, 70, 94, 116, 134 (*cf. also* achievement).
associations, 12–13, 16, 18, 20–21, 33, 69, 75–76, 79–83, 88–90, 93–98, 103–9, 112–30, 159–60 (*cf. also* church associations; convivial associations; èsúsú; guilds; prestige associations).
Awe, B., 5.
Awolowo, O., 126.
Awujalẹ of Ijẹbu Ode, 8, 26.

Balandier, G., 9, 11–13, 16, 36, 108–9, 125.

bálé:
of compound, 56, 60, 73–74, 77, 88, 92.
of craft guild, 88–89, 92, 93, 94, 96.
bálẹ̀:
of town or village, 26, 41, 45.
Bascom, W. B., 24–25, 35, 64, 82, 105, 108, 110, 112, 114, 128, 129, 143, 144, 145, 162.
Beier, U., 59.
Benin, 52, 109, 158.
biological family, *cf.* nuclear family.
Bowen, T. J., 4, 35, 36.
'Brazilian' influence, 1, 44, 56, 59–60, 62, 79, 90–91, 97, 141.
Brazzaville, 9, 11, 12, 108–9, 125.
Burton, R. F., 45.
Busia, K. A., 10–12, 14.

Callaway, A., 84, 85, 94.
Capelle, A., 10, 12.
capital accumulation, 71, 92, 94, 95, 102, 105, 106–8, 138.
capital towns; *cf.* metropolitan towns.
Census figures, *cf. Population Census.*
chiefs, chieftaincy titles, 25, 37, 39–40, 50, 51, 66–69, 73, 75–80, 82, 89, 113, 142–4, 150 (*cf. also* Council of State).
Christianity, 60, 62, 73, 83, 111, 117, 119–22, 149, 152 (*cf. also* Missions; churches; education; monogamy).
church associations, 120–2, 128, 130.
churches, 58–59, 83, 120–1.
Clapperton, H., 4, 36, 54, 85, 100.
class(es), 11–13, 16, 21, 131–5, 138, 141–5, 153 (*cf. also* élite(s)).
clerks, 18, 34, 62, 123, 125, 137, 142, 152–3.
clubs, *cf.* convivial associations.
C.M.S., *cf.* Missions.
cocoa, 3, 31, 59–60, 76, 92, 98–99, 101–2, 106, 139.
cognatic grouping, 53, 54–55, 56–58, 67–70, 72, 74–75, 87, 98, 110, 159

(*cf. also* agnatic grouping; descent groups).

Comhaire-Sylvain, S., 71, 103.

compound, *cf.* unit of residence.

commuting, 26, 30–31, 84.

convivial associations, 83, 93, 97, 124–5, 126, 127–9, 130.

Council of State, 26–27, 37, 40, 63, 115–7, 124 (*cf. also* chiefs).

crafts, craftsmen, 4, 71, 75, 83–102, 108, 113, 139, 142–3, 153 (*cf. also* guilds).

credit, *cf.* debt; capital accumulation.

debt, 31, 71, 86–87, 95, 106–8, 117, 127.

descent groups, 30–31, 34, 36–37, 41, 44, 47–48, 53–54, 56–57, 65–70, 72–81, 87–90, 106, 108, 110–3, 115, 126, 135, 141, 143–5, 153, 155, 157, 159 (*cf. also* agnatic grouping; cognatic grouping).

division of labour, 84–86, 102–3 (*cf. also* specialization).

Durkheim, E., 22, 85, 86, 155, 159, 160.

Ẹdẹ, 29, 35, 101.

education, 32, 34, 58–60, 62, 71, 77–78, 81, 117, 120, 122–6, 134 *et seq.*, 146–52, 158, 160.

Ẹgba, 5, 6, 41, 49, 84, 104, 115 (*cf. also* Abẹokuta).

Ẹgbado, 7.

ẹgbẹ́, cf. age-sets; guilds; convivial associations; church associations.

Ẹgbẹ́ Ọmọ Odùduwà, 122, 126.

Ekiti, 30, 34, 52, 56, 57, 75, 85, 87, 93, 124, 127 (*cf. also* Ado Ekiti).

Ẹlẹ́gba, *cf.* Èṣu.

elementary family, *cf.* nuclear family.

élite(s), 120, 126, 131–8, 140–52, 160 (*cf. also* class(es))
  marginal élite, 152
  sub-élite, 152–3.

Epstein, A. L., 11, 16, 157–8, 161–3.

Èṣù, 40, 47, 106, 109, 113–14, 156.

èsúsú rotating-credit associations, 97, 106–8.

European influences, 4, 7, 56, 58–59, 90, 137, 146–7, 155.

Ewi of Ado Ekiti, 7, 44.

Ẹyọ, *cf.* Ọyọ.

Fadipẹ, N. A., 27, 56, 57, 64, 65, 72, 73, 74, 78, 80, 84, 85, 104, 115, 118, 129.

Forde, D., 17, 80.

Freetown, 19, 125, 128.

Frobenius, L., 39–40, 43, 44, 45, 47–49, 51, 110, 112.

Fulani, 5, 119.

Fustel de Coulanges, 160.

Goddard, S., 31, 52, 63, 84, 155.

Greek city-state, 28, 154, 157, 160.

Gugler, J., 158.

Guilbot, J., 10, 12.

guilds:
  European medieval craft guilds, 93, 96, 160.
  male traders' guilds, 103, 104.
  market-women's guilds, 103–4, 128.
  modern craft guilds, 83, 93–98, 103, 113, 124, 128–9.
  traditional craft guilds, 83, 88–90, 93, 108, 109, 113, 129.

Gutkind, P. C., 16–17.

hamlets, 26, 27, 31, 33, 52, 53, 63, 84, 155.

Hausa, 3, 34, 43, 62, 101, 119.

Hellman, E., 108.

heterogeneity, 20–21, 25, 128–30, 159.

home town, 31, 33, 62, 78, 123–6, 139, 140–1, 146, 148, 150, 152, 155.

Ibadan, Ibadan Division, 3, 5–7, 19, 27, 28, 29, 30, 32, 33, 34, 35, 36, 41, 45–46, 47–49, 53, 54, 55, 59, 61, 62, 72, 73, 75, 80, 83, 89, 90, 91, 97–102, 121, 125–6, 137, 139, 144, 146–7, 149–50, 159–61.

Ibo, 3, 4, 37, 62, 104, 125, 129, 137, 154.

ifá, 111–12, 114.

Ifaki, 30.

Ifẹ (Ilé-Ifẹ̀), 1, 2, 3, 4, 5, 8, 26, 29, 35, 36, 39, 40, 42, 43, 45, 49, 51, 52, 54, 64, 82, 103, 109, 114, 115, 128, 144.

Igbirra, 62.

Ijẹbu, Ijẹbu Ode, 3, 5, 8, 26, 29, 34, 41, 50, 52, 54, 55, 57, 58, 61, 62, 67–70, 75, 76, 79, 87, 91, 97, 98, 103, 105, 115–7, 119–21, 125, 126, 143, 144, 148, 159, 160.

Ijẹbu Remo, 126.

Ijo Òrúnmìla, 119.

Ikẹrrẹ, 29.

Ikoro, 30.

Ilaro, 100.

Ilé-Ifẹ̀, cf. Ifẹ.

Ilẹsha, 3, 29, 35, 39, 42, 51, 52, 54.

Ilọra, 100

Ilọrin, 29, 35, 47, 101, 119.

ìlú, 25–28, 31, 37, 41, 80, 97, 98, 126, 143.
  ará ìlú, 25–26, 30–34, 36, 63, 75, 116, 126, 128, 130.
  ará oko, 25, 31, 84, 130.

ìlú aládé, cf. metropolitan towns.

ìlú eréko, cf. subordinate towns.

industrialization, 4, 10, 11, 14, 18, 36, 135, 155, 158.

Ipoti, 30.

Isẹhin, cf. Isẹyin.

Isẹyin, 29, 35, 47, 57, 99, 101.

Islam, 83, 98, 111, 117, 118, 119, 120, 121–2.

Iwo, 29, 33, 34, 35, 36, 61, 88, 89, 92, 93, 95, 96, 97, 98, 119, 124.

Johnson, S., 4, 5, 7, 39, 106, 107.

job opportunities, 32, 62, 75, 136–8, 139–40, 150.

Kabba, 62, 159.

Katunga, cf. Old Ọyọ.

kings (ọbas), 1, 2, 4, 6, 7, 8, 25–27, 28, 34, 37, 39, 41–45, 47, 50, 51, 59, 61, 62, 63, 68–69, 73, 76, 79–80, 82, 85, 88–89, 93, 96, 104, 115–7, 126, 142–5, 152, 159.

Kroeber, A. L., 22–23, 36.

Lagos, 7, 19, 27, 29, 31, 33, 34, 35, 36, 41, 44, 59, 60, 61, 71, 72, 75, 76, 77, 78, 79, 97, 101, 103, 104, 105, 119–20, 121, 125, 146, 147, 149, 152, 159, 160.

land rights, 52–53, 54–55, 65–69, 76, 87, 106, 113, 135.

Lander, J. and R., 4, 36, 100.

Leighton, A. H. and Lambo, T. A., 84, 119.

Lerner, D., 11, 157.

lineages, cf. descent-groups; agnatic grouping.

literacy, cf. education.

Lloyd, B. B., 151.

Lloyd, P. C., 24, 31, 33, 37, 52, 53, 54, 55, 56, 61, 63, 64, 65, 67, 69, 70, 78, 89, 93, 98, 103, 113, 121, 124, 126, 128, 131, 134, 136, 139, 140, 143, 144, 147, 152, 153.

MacIver, R. M. and Page, C. H., 37, 82.

Madam Tinubu, 104.

markets, 5, 20, 45–47, 50–51, 53, 55, 58, 72, 84, 90, 99–104, 156 (cf. also guilds; trade).
  king's markets, 46, 51.
  periodic rural markets, 46, 84, 99, 155.
  urban day markets, 46–47, 84, 99, 100, 102.
  urban night markets, 46–47, 99–100.

Marris, P., 31, 60, 61, 71, 77, 79.

Marx, K., 132, 133, 135.

Mayer, P., 163.

McCulloch, M., 13.

metropolitan towns, 26–28, 30, 37, 42, 45, 51, 52, 53.

migration, 4–6, 32, 34, 61–62, 73, 75, 139–40, 150, 162–3.

Miner, H., 19–20, 24, 154, 156.

Missions, 6, 35, 58–59, 62, 120, 149.

Mitchel, N. C., 4, 34.

Mitchell, J. C., 11, 17, 161.

modern public buildings, 5, 41, 43–44, 46, 50, 55, 58–60, 123–4.

Moloney, C. A., 35.

monogamy, 60, 71, 120, 125, 147–52 (cf. also Christianity; education; nuclear family).

Morton-Williams, P., 114, 115.
mosques, 58, 59, 83, 121–2.

Nadel, S. F., 93.
nineteenth-century tribal wars, 4–7, 30, 53, 73–75, 80, 100–1, 104, 126.
northern Yoruba, 53, 54, 56–57, 63, 65–67, 69–70, 74–76, 79–80, 86–87, 92, 100, 116, 159.
nuclear family, 60, 64, 80, 133–4, 139, 141, 146–52.
Nupe, 62, 84, 88.

ọbà kan, 64 (cf. also ọmọ iyá).
ọbas, cf. kings.
Ọbàtálá, 40.
Odùduwà, 1, 2, 48, 109, 115, 122, 126.
Ogbomọshọ, 28, 29, 30, 35, 36, 57, 61, 73, 101.
ògbóni, 5, 79, 114–8, 119, 122–3, 143, 144, 145.
Ọgọtun, 30.
Ògún, 40, 89, 109, 113.
Ogunbiyi, T. A. J., 117.
Ojo, G. J. A., 4, 26, 30, 39, 42, 44, 58.
Olódùmaré, cf. Ọlọ́run.
Ọlọ́run, 39, 109, 120.
Olubadan of Ibadan, 41, 46.
ọmọ iyá, 64–66, 70–71, 74, 76, 77, 126, 145 (cf. also ọbà kan).
Ondo, Ondo Province, 3, 8, 29, 32, 50, 52, 54–55, 57–58, 61, 67–70, 75–76, 78–79, 87, 98, 110, 115–7, 144, 159–60.
Oni of Ifẹ, 4, 8, 26, 40, 43, 45, 143–5.
Ọ̀rányàn, 109.
òrìṣà, 26, 39–40, 47–49, 66, 75, 77, 82, 89, 106, 109–14, 119, 127, 129.
Oshogbo, 14–18, 19, 24, 29, 35, 36, 54, 62, 64, 80–81, 99, 101, 109, 119, 152, 162.
Ọ̀sun, 109.
òṣùgbó, cf. ògbóni.
Ọwọ, 29, 54.
Ọyọ, 3, 5, 7, 26, 29, 31, 32, 35, 36, 44, 47, 50, 52, 54, 56, 57, 63, 73–76, 85, 87, 89, 93, 99–101, 106, 109, 113–7, 127, 159, 160.
   Old Ọyọ (Ẹyọ, Katunga), 2, 5, 7, 8, 36, 39, 44, 54, 87, 100.
Ọyọ Ekiti, 30.

Pacheco Pereira, D., 8.
palaces, 4, 39–45, 50–51, 58–59, 62, 159.
Pareto, V., 132.
Parrinder, G., 48, 59, 114, 121.
Plato, 154.
Population Census of the Western Region of Nigeria, 1952, 8, 28–35, 68, 98, 119.
prestige, 33, 106, 120, 123–5, 128, 141–6, 149.
   prestige associations, 117, 149–50
Progressive Unions, 122–6, 127, 128, 140, 150, 152.

quarters (wards), 12, 39–40, 44, 49, 51–52, 53, 58, 61–62, 68–69, 74, 79–81, 89, 120–2, 127, 152 (cf. also townships).

recreational associations, cf. convivial associations.
roads, 39, 41, 50–51, 53, 55, 73, 76, 127.
Rousseau, J. J., 22.

sacred groves, 49–50, 58–60, 110.
Ṣàngó, 40, 47, 49, 109.
schools, cf. education.
Schwab, W. B., 14–17, 19, 24, 62, 64, 80, 81, 119.
settlement pattern, 3–4, 7–8, 20–21, 23, 25, 26, 51 et seq., 57–58, 63, 67, 74–75, 113, 130, 154–9.
Shagamu, 29, 41, 159.
Shaki, 29, 61, 85.
shrines, 42, 47–49, 110.
Sjoberg, G., 158.
slaves, 1, 42, 73, 84, 87, 100–1, 117, 143.
Smith, R. S., 5.
sociological population, 31.
Ṣọpọná, 109.
Southall, A., 11, 16–19, 36, 157, 158, 160, 161.
southern Yoruba, 53, 54–55, 57–58, 65, 67–70, 74–76, 87, 116.
specialization, 83–87, 91, 99–100, 102–103 (cf. also division of labour).

by compound, 86–89, 92, 129.
'storey-houses', 44, 55, 58–62, 90–91, 141.
'strangers', 33–34, 61–62, 72–73, 80–81, 93–94, 120–1, 125–6, 128, 144, 152.
subordinate towns, 26–27, 30, 45, 51, 124.

taxes, 96, 136 (*cf. also* tribute).
teachers, 62, 123, 125, 137, 150, 152–3 (*cf. also* education).
Timbuctoo, 156, 160.
Tönnics, F., 23.
town of employment, 31, 32, 33, 62, 72, 80–81, 125–6, 128, 139–40.
townships, 6–7, 53, 80, 159.
trade, 4, 18, 45–46, 62, 71, 73, 82, 86, 99–106, 136, 142, 150, 152.
traders, *cf.* traders' guilds.
tribute, 50–51, 89, 95 (*cf. also* tax).
Tutuola, A., 123.
typology of urban centres, 15, 17–19, 33, 36, 157–63.

U.N.E.S.C.O., 11, 13, 14, 15, 131.
units of consumption, 64–65, 70–72, 77.
units of production, 72, 86–88, 91 *et seq.*
units of residence (compounds), 6, 26, 30–31, 36, 51, 52, 55–58, 63–75, 84, 108, 128, 140, 146–7.

urban culture, 12, 20, 21, 22–26, 114, 117, 128–30, 155 *et seq.*
urban occupations, 72, 84–85, 87, 93, 98, 142, 159, 160.
urban residence, 20–21, 26, 28, 30–32, 63–64, 84.
'urbanism as a way of life', *cf.* urban culture.
Urhobo, 3.
Uyin, 30.

villages, 27, 28, 30, 67, 68, 87, 117, 126.

wards, *cf.* quarters.
Warner, L., 132.
wealth, 3, 18, 59–61, 70, 78, 81, 91–92, 98–100, 105–8, 116, 117, 118, 128, 133–45, 152.
Weber, M., 19–21, 24–25, 28, 154, 156–7.
Western sociology, 13–14, 19–24, 64, 131–4, 153, 155–7, 160, 164.
Wirth, L., 20–25, 98, 114, 129–30, 155–9.
women, status and activities of, 18, 70–72, 77–78, 84–87, 91, 100–105, 108, 118, 139–41, 147–52.

Yakö, 80.